The Dance of Politics

In the series ***African Soundscapes,***
edited by Gregory Barz

Patricia Tang, *Masters of the Sabar: Wolof Griot Percussionists of Senegal*

Lisa Gilman

The Dance of Politics

Gender, Performance, and Democratization in Malawi

TEMPLE UNIVERSITY PRESS
Philadelphia

Temple University Press
Philadelphia, Pennsylvania 19122
www.temple.edu/tempress

Published 2009
Printed in the United States of America

Text design by Westchester Book Group

♾ The paper used in this publication meets the requirements of the American National Standard for Information Sciences—Permanence of Paper for Printed Library Materials, ANSI Z39.48-1992

Library of Congress Cataloging-in-Publication Data

Gilman, Lisa, 1969–
The dance of politics : gender, performance, and democratization in Malawi / Lisa Gilman.
p. cm.—(African soundscapes)
Includes bibliographical references and index.
ISBN 978-1-59213-985-9 (hardcover : alk. paper)
ISBN 978-1-59213-986-6 (paperback : alk. paper)
1. Malawi—Politics and government. 2. Dance—Political aspects—Malawi.
3. Women—Malawi—Social conditions I. Title.

JQ2941.A91G55 2009
320.96897—dc22 2008039544

101811-P

In Memory of M. W. Kanyama Chiume
and to my parents
Charles Gilman and Ruth Kornfield

Contents

Acknowledgments

As with all ethnographic projects, this book owes many debts and is the product of years of research that involved the collaboration and contributions of countless individuals in Malawi. I am deeply grateful to all who at various times hosted me, instructed me in local etiquette, explained cultural intricacies, patiently taught me Chichewa and Chitonga, fed me, gave me directions, looked out for my personal well-being, accompanied me on research ventures, welcomed me to performances and rehearsals, agreed to participate in interviews, directed me to archival sources, transcribed and translated research materials, and introduced me to people whose personal experiences and insights constitute the core of this project. In naming those who were especially helpful, I leave out too many whose assistance was invaluable and to whom I also owe a great debt.

I am especially grateful to the Namate, Ngwira, Tembo, Phumisa, Alide, and Gomonda families, who welcomed me, my husband, and our daughter into their homes at various times, always making us feel that we were part of their families while also helping me with research needs. This extension of my family network gives me a sense of home in Malawi that I will always cherish. I am especially thankful for the friendship of Victoria Mwale, who hosted us during our stay with the Ngwira family. Her humor and patience guided my awkward attempts to learn Chitonga and to settle into life in a rural community. Through her friendship, I was able to share in the celebrations as well as difficult times in the day-to-day lives of the women in her family, all of which greatly informs my understanding of the role of dancing in Malawian women's lives.

I am indebted to all the women who generously allowed me to attend, observe, and videotape their performances and rehearsals and to interview them. I especially thank those dance teams in Nkhata Bay whose rehearsals and performances I regularly attended, especially the chilimika teams from Msani, Nkhwali, Malemba, and Nsanje. To the numerous women from Nkhata Bay, Mzuzu, and Blantyre who dance politically and who agreed to be interviewed and allowed me to hang around at meetings, rehearsals, and rallies, I thank you for your talent, generosity, and openness.

It is with great respect that I acknowledge the politicians and party leaders who exercised their dedication to the new democratic system by allowing me to participate in meetings, rehearsals, and political rallies as well as to interview individuals involved at all levels of the political process. It was a great honor to sit with such important historical figures as Rose Chibambo and the late M.W.K. Chiume, who inspired me with their recollections of the country's movement for independence and their passionate desire for a more socially just Malawi. It was with great sadness that I recently read of the death of M.W.K. Chiume, whom I had always assumed I would meet again. I am grateful for having had the opportunity to sit with his sister Mary Chiume, watching her goat nibble at weeds while we discussed Malawian politics. Later, I sadly sat by her side as she slowly left this world surrounded by her loving family.

I thank my research assistants, the late Simeon Nyirenda, Praise Gondwe, Lillian Moyo, Lovemore Gondwe, and Benson Gomonda, for helping me identify research opportunities and for help with transcriptions and translations. I couldn't have done it without you!

My colleagues in the United States and Malawi have played an invaluable role in shaping and critiquing this research over the years. Drs. Beverly Stoeltje, Richard Bauman, Ruth Stone, Sue Tuohy, and Phyllis Martin greatly influenced my thinking during and after my graduate career. Drs. Enoch Timpunza Mvula and Wiseman Chijere Chirwa at the University of Malawi provided much needed intellectual support. Dr. Linda Semu and Loveness Schafer taught me Chichewa and then provided ongoing support with my often last-minute questions about translations and cultural issues. Clara Henderson has always been quick to reply to my questions about linguistic or musical questions. I am grateful to members of the Gender in Africa/African Diaspora Research Interest Group supported by the Center for the Study of Women in Society at the University of Oregon for their reading of drafts of the introduction and their ongoing support. Thank you especially to Yvonne Braun for our many discussions and whose reading of several chapters greatly sharpened my analyses. Most recently, the manuscript has greatly improved under the care of and with suggestions by Janet Francendese, Gregory Barz, and Daniel Reed.

Funding from the U.S. Department of Education, Indiana University's Graduate School and Folklore Institute, and Texas A&M's Office of the Vice President of Research and Women's Studies Program allowed me to travel to Malawi on multiple occasions so that I could follow transformations in political dancing over a ten-year period. Institutional affiliation with the University of Malawi's Centre for Social Research authorized me to conduct this research and provided research support.

Thanks to my husband, John Fenn, for taking the leap to accompany me to Malawi. I am delighted to have you as my best friend and companion as well as a colleague with whom I can discuss and share research and writing processes and whose comments on drafts of this book helped smooth out many bumps. Our young daughters, Anika and Nora, have indulged me by accompanying me on research trips, and most important, they keep me sane and laughing, even when the pressures of academic life are at their worst. Finally, it is my parents, Ruth Kornfield and Charles Gilman, who first brought me to Malawi and to whom I owe both my love of living in African contexts and my fascination with social, cultural, and political issues.

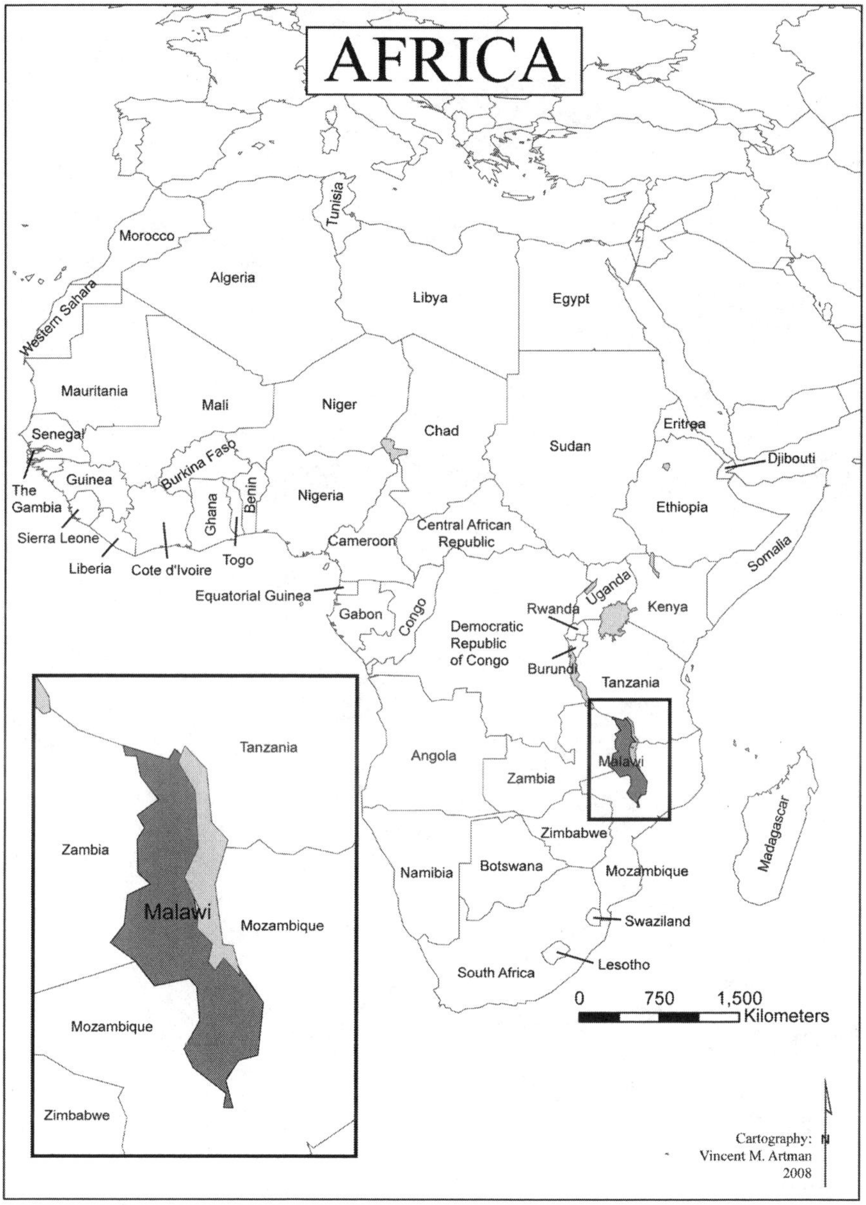

Data Source: U.S. Geological Survey (USGS).

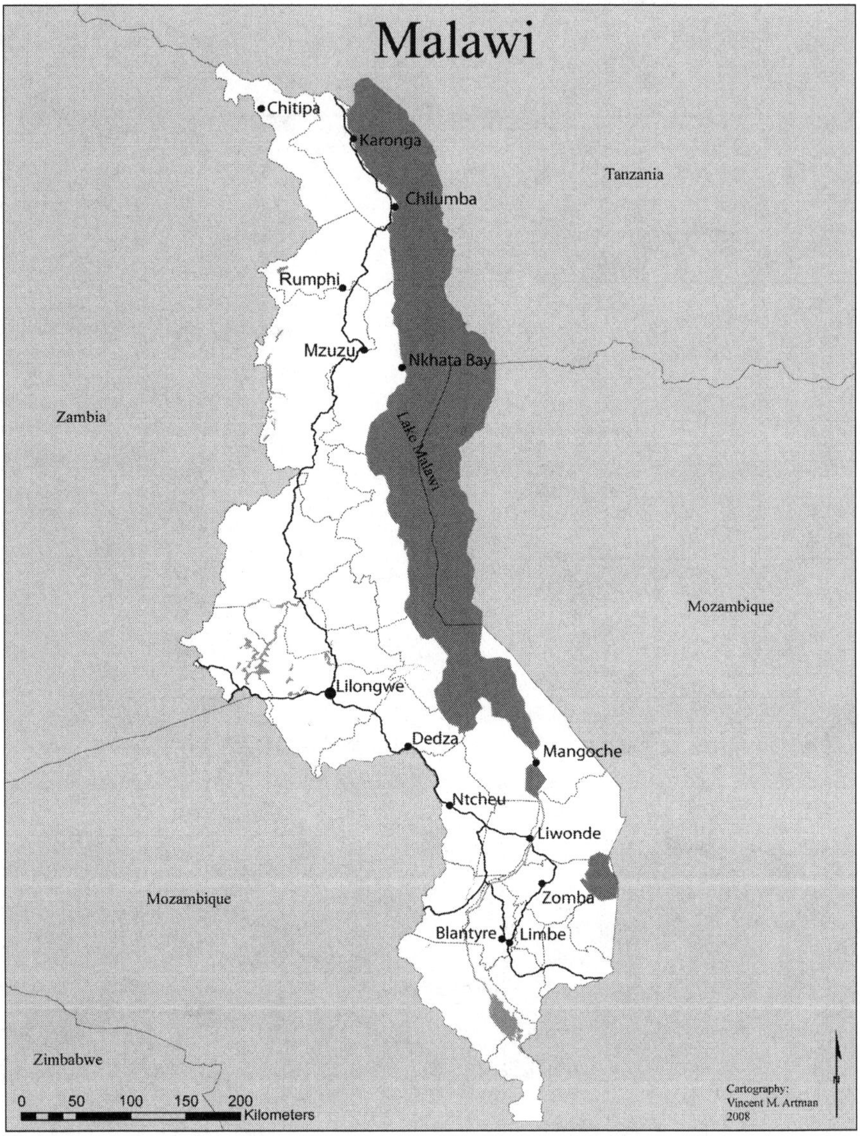

Data Sources: Environmental Systems Research Institute (ESRI); Southern Africa Humanitarian & Disaster Management GIS Library (SAHIMS GIS Library).

1

Introduction

Gender, Power, and Performance

In April 1999, I was in Malawi researching women's political dancing during the campaigns leading to the country's second multiparty elections. I had already spent several months attending political rallies in the country's northern region when Kaliyoma Phumisa—at the time a high-ranking member of the ruling United Democratic Front (UDF) party, a member of Parliament, and a cabinet minister—and his wife, Jane Phumisa, generously invited me to join them as they rigorously campaigned in Phumisa's constituency in the Ntcheu District in central Malawi. On April 23, the Phumisas, several UDF party officials from the Ntcheu District, and I made our way in a four-wheel-drive Toyota covered pickup from the town of Ntcheu to Phumisa's home village of Mphepo Zinai. Bumping along on narrow rocky roads for several hours, we knew we were finally nearing the village when we encountered women lining both sides of the roadway. Many wore clothing made from bright yellow fabric decorated with the turquoise letters *UDF* and the party's symbol of clasped hands. We opened our windows as more women appeared and swarmed around us. As the car slowed and gradually moved forward, the women's singing flooded our vehicle:

Tikuthokoza
Ife tikuthokoza
Oh! Ife tikuthokoza
Tikuthokoza kubwera
Kwa anduna athu
Oh amatikonda tonse
Tikuthokoza kwa anduna athu

We thank you
We, we thank you
Oh! We, we thank you
We, we thank you
For our minister's presence
Oh, he likes all of us
We are thankful for our minister

Phumisa grinned as he held a megaphone to the open window and cued a high-pitched siren. The swarms around the vehicle grew even larger, as did the fevered pitch of the siren combined with the women's singing voices. The car gradually stopped as we arrived in the center of the village. We emerged and followed Phumisa, who was wearing a dark suit over a pale yellow shirt, as he descended into the singing and dancing throng. The women, still singing and moving rhythmically, escorted us to a special seating area consisting of two rows of chairs borrowed from local residents. The women then joined the rest of the audience, who sat around a large open space, and positioned themselves on the ground closest to us.

After local leaders greeted us, the master of ceremonies, a middle-aged man wearing black pants and a bright yellow T-shirt, also decorated with the image of clasped hands and the letters *UDF*, announced the beginning of the rally by yelling out slogans. The audience, led by the women, responded enthusiastically:

MC: U!
AUDIENCE: DF!
MC: UDF
AUDIENCE: *Boma lenileni*
MC: *Pulezidenti wathu ndani?*
AUDIENCE: *Dr. Bakili, Bakili Muluzi, pulezidenti wopanda nkhanza, wosapha, wachitukuko, woyenda m'maliro, kuntunda, wowinawina, komanso ali wosawumira eee!*

MC: U!
AUDIENCE: DF!
MC: UDF
AUDIENCE: The real, authentic government
MC: Who is our president?
AUDIENCE: Dr. Bakili, Bakili Muluzi, a president without cruelty, one who does not kill, who promotes development, who attends funerals, who is highly regarded, who is victorious, yet he is also very generous!

Throughout the speeches made by local leaders, the women occasionally burst into songs praising Phumisa and Bakili Muluzi; the latter was both the state president and chairman of the UDF. Occasionally, the women rose to sing praises or move into the center of the performance space; their undulating bodies interrupted, yet propelled, the event while they sang songs, including the following:

Anduna athu
Anduna athu atukula dziko
Atukula dziko la Malawi
Pa kanthawi kuchepa
Atimangira choyamba
Chipatala

Our minister
Our minister, he has developed the country
He has developed the country of Malawi
Within a short time
He first built us
A hospital

The MC allowed their performance to continue for a moment, and then asked them to return to their positions seated on the ground.

During the entertainment component of this rally, men and women sang while they performed varieties of local dance forms as members of single-sex and coed dance teams, and groups of women party members performed variants of circle dance genres. At one point, about one hundred women crowded into tight concentric rings in front of the politician's entourage. Their bodies, a few with babies tied to their backs, squeezed together, their hips swayed in accented rhythmic patterns, and their arms swung back and forth as they stepped to the drums pounded by two men seated in the center of the circle. Their cheers and ululating punctuated song texts that thanked Phumisa for both his visit and his leadership. During each group's performance, the MP and members of his entourage took turns entering the entertainment arena to give dancers small gifts. At the conclusion of the event, Phumisa and his entourage slowly moved toward the vehicles, again surrounded by singing and dancing women whose songs thanked us for coming and wished us a safe journey back to the town of Ntcheu. Our vehicle slowly accelerated; the dancing women gradually faded into the background.

This political rally resembled many others I attended during the 1999 election campaigns as well as in subsequent years. Political party leaders in contemporary Malawi regularly organize national and local events, salient features of the country's political culture and key components of political strategizing. Women dressed in party colors and dancing and singing songs that extol a party and its politicians almost always feature prominently, whether the event is a large-scale rally held in an urban center that brings together people from all parts of the country, a small localized rally in a single village or urban neighborhood, or a gathering that falls somewhere in between. During election campaigns, rallies are numerous as parliamentary and presidential candidates try to increase their support bases. During noncampaign periods, parliamentarians and other party leaders hold rallies to meet with their constituents, increase party membership, mobilize support for causes, point to the failings of their opponents, and welcome or see off party dignitaries at airports. Other public functions are not explicitly political; yet, because the president of the country or other leading figures in a party attend, they exhibit many of the same characteristics as those organized by political parties. Examples include national celebrations, such as Independence Day, and special days designated by government ministries, such as National Education Day. All such events are usually called *msonkhano* in Chichewa, which translates as "meeting" or "gathering." I use the English term *rally* to refer to all such public political functions to distinguish these events from business meetings, which usually do not include explicit entertainment components.

As with this rally for Phumisa, women almost always participate in these events while clad in party paraphernalia—fabric, T-shirts, buttons, hats—in the sponsoring party's colors decorated with its emblem and acronym. They contribute by attracting crowds, many of whom are enticed by the promise of performances. They welcome guests with their singing and dancing, and they often interrupt speeches with their singing and ululating. They participate more formally by performing circle dances during scheduled entertainment segments. Their song texts always fill the air with praise for the sponsoring party and its politicians and disdain for its opponents. Speakers frequently address themselves directly to the party women, and when they initiate slogans, they count on these women to be the quickest and loudest respondents. Besides being seen and heard at rallies, party women are visible when they walk down streets wearing party symbols; newspapers depict their images; recordings of their singing and dancing are broadcast on local radio and television; and their rehearsals are regularly seen and heard in urban neighborhoods and rural communities. Women praise performers make substantial contributions to political parties in their capacities as symbols, advertisers, voters, morale boosters, and mobilizers of support.

This book examines this institution of women's political performing to detail how the practice emerged and continues to transform in relationship to shifts in the political environment; what roles women's performances have in the political arena; and how women's participation as political performers relates to women's status in politics more broadly.

The practice of women's political dancing in contemporary Malawi, which is rooted in the movement against British colonial rule, has long been fraught with controversy. During the independence movement, women activists in what was then the British colony of Nyasaland capitalized on local performance practices and incorporated singing and dancing in their political activities as a means to draw support, convey messages, and covertly criticize the British. Nationalist leaders also brought together people from across Nyasaland to perform similar dances together and share culturally distinct dances as part of a strategy to invoke feelings of solidarity and construct a national identity based in cultural difference.

After independence in 1964, the country's first president, Dr. Hastings Kamuzu Banda, established an authoritarian single-party government, which he ruled until 1994. Banda was internationally famous for the frequent large-scale events organized by his Malawi Congress Party (MCP). At these events, hundreds of women covered head to toe in fabric decorated with life-size images of the president's face danced complicated variants of local circle-dance forms while singing songs that deified him and vilified those deemed to be political dissidents. Through the pyramid structure of the MCP, party officials required that all women in the country—regardless of their age, health, occupation, or political leanings—regularly rehearse for and participate in these frequently orchestrated political events. They also required all men and boys to regularly participate in these events, sometimes as performers, more often as audience members. The Banda government appropriated and transformed what was the liberatory practice of political activists in the independence movement into a widespread mechanism for controlling the population. By requiring all Malawians to participate in these ubiquitous events, the party ensured that the whole population contributed to projecting images of Banda's legitimacy and performing national identity. This identity was expressed especially powerfully in the togetherness of hundreds of identically clad women dancing in one throbbing mass. The climate of fear generated by the Banda government—known for jailing and sometimes killing dissidents and their family members—largely silenced public debate about Banda's use of women as his embodied cheerleaders (Mkamanga 2000; Chirwa 2001; Lwanda 1993).

Changes in the global political climate and internal ferment in the early 1990s led to a referendum on June 14, 1993, in which the population voted to change Malawi's system of government from single party to multiparty. For the first time since independence, political activists emerged, formed parties, and vied for legitimacy and leadership opportunities. One focal point of opposition politicians' campaigns leading up to the referendum and then in the first parliamentary and presidential elections, held on May 17, 1994, was the issue of women's political dancing. In their rallies, the opposition promised that if the population voted first for multipartyism and then for them as elected officials, women would no longer be forced to dance. They also pledged that they would not devote money intended to develop the country to orchestrating large rallies to promote themselves (Dzimbiri 1998: 92).

Bakili Muluzi of the UDF was the first democratically elected president of Malawi. During the first two years of his presidency, the practice of women's political dancing greatly subsided, and the president confirmed his pledge on two points: not to spend large amounts of government money on elaborate events and not to use women as his personal or party's symbols. I first visited Malawi in the summer of 1995, one year after Muluzi was elected. My intention was to identify a research site where I could explore how women use music and dance forms to negotiate power relations in their day-to-day lives, what I consider to be "informal politics." In my conversations with Malawians, many explained that I had come too late: I had missed the elaborate and ubiquitous political ceremonies staged by the previous government. Some referred to this past under Banda nostalgically, while others credited the opposition politicians who had campaigned for the referendum with freeing women from the ongoing rehearsing and performing.

In a second visit in the summer of 1996, I was visiting friends in Malawi's largest city, Blantyre, on July 6, National Independence Day, a holiday especially associated with the elaborate events of Banda's rule. Controversy erupted in the newspapers when the government decided to hold a celebration in Blantyre's stadium to commemorate this holiday, something it had promised not to do when it first took power in 1994. I made my way to the stadium, video camera tucked into my backpack, walking several miles alongside hundreds of others on the busy four-lane highway that runs through the city. Given the amount of criticism I had heard about the ways in which the Banda government had organized women to dance at its functions, I was struck when I saw at this purportedly nonpartisan event not only dance performances by the Malawi National Dance Cultural Troupe, an ensemble of professional dancers sponsored by the government, as promised in the newspapers, but also the participation of women members of the ruling UDF. The women came clad in bright yellow UDF political fabric in styles similar to those worn by women during Banda's rule. They welcomed Muluzi by surrounding his vehicle upon its arrival while singing praise songs for him, and then they sat together to create a visually prominent presence in the VIP stand. Their participation signaled the resurgence of women's political dancing.

In the days following, Malawians battled over the appropriateness of both this event and the participation of women party members in letters-to-the editor and articles in local ewspapers. Human rights activists complained of the wasted money and claimed that the event echoed the past oppression under Banda. President Muluzi and the event's organizers defended themselves against criticism on the grounds that they did not force anyone to dance, and that this was a national event, not a party function.

I returned to Malawi in 1998 with my husband, ethnomusicologist John Fenn, to the Nkhata Bay District in the northern region. During my visit to the district two years before, I had met the late Simeon Nyirenda, an avid *malipenga* dancer who was actively involved in trying to maintain the liveliness of dance practices in his community. He and I had corresponded in the interim and had arranged that he would help me initiate my research project. Unfortunately, I found him seriously ill and hospitalized when we arrived. We therefore arranged to stay with the Ngwira family, who lived in a rural community near Nyirenda's home. As he gained strength, I hired Nyirenda to be my research assistant. He frequently joined me as we traveled to dance performances across the district, and he was my translator during a number of interviews.

When we settled with the Ngwira family, I was still intent on studying women's performance practices in their day-to-day lives. The Nkhata Bay District attracted me because of the fame of some of its dance practices, especially the all-male malipenga, which I had read about in a number of scholarly articles (Kamlongera 1986; Kerr and Nambote 1983). Their authors mentioned in passing the existence of women's dance forms, but little other published information existed, stimulating my desire to help fill this void in the scholarly literature.

Malawi is divided into three administrative regions: north, central, and south. The southern region is the most developed; the central is the second. Each region is broken down into districts. In each district is a town or city that serves as the government center, or *boma*, for that district. Nkhata Bay District, consisting of hundreds of villages and a number of towns, is located in the northern region along the shore of Lake Malawi. The town of Nkhata Bay is the government center for the district. In my efforts to observe dance performances and spend time with dancers, I frequently traveled to villages and towns throughout the district. As I present material from my research, I therefore distinguish between Nkhata Bay District and the town of Nkhata Bay.

A benefit of settling in this district was that it had been a source of political activism and controversy throughout Malawi's recent history. A number of the most prominent activists during the independence movement came from the district, and because many of these individuals fell out of favor after independence, Banda was especially suspicious of people from Nkhata Bay District during his rule. In the transition to multipartyism, people from this district were once again among the most active. Admittedly, I also fell in love with the district's breathtaking beauty. Hillsides covered in tropical foliage descend into the turquoise blue lake, with occasional beaches tucked within. Canoes dot the lake, appearing especially mysterious at night when fishermen light lanterns; dancing lights flicker across the vast darkness, a strategy for catching fish.

Many living directly on the lakeshore rely on fishing for part of their livelihoods. Almost all in the district, as in much of rural Malawi, engage in small-scale subsistence agriculture, growing crops mostly to meet their family's needs, though many also sell anything left over or grow extra for added income. Women are in charge of most of the day-to-day agricultural and household duties, while men are largely responsible for earning money needed for such things as school fees, clothing, oil, sugar, meat, medical needs, and so on.

My plan when we settled with the Ngwira family was to research *chilimika*, a secular dance form unique to the Nkhata Bay District, performed mostly by young women and girls, though a few boys and men sometimes are also members of dance teams. As my research on chilimika picked up in December 1998, so too did the campaigning for the second multiparty elections, scheduled for June 1999. More and more, members of dance groups informed me that if I wanted to see them perform, I should go to rallies. I eventually changed my research focus to the political arena. We then moved into the town of Nkhata Bay so that I could have greater access to information about rallies and be closer to party headquarters and transportation. In addition to attending and videotaping rallies, I spent time with party members discussing politics, attended dance rehearsals, and conducted formal interviews with dancers, party organizers, and politicians in the Nkhata Bay District and the nearby city of Mzuzu. I also continued my research on chilimika and attended many different types of events that featured dancing, which proved useful for situating political dancing within the larger context of performance practices in the district. In April 1999, we said our good-byes in Nkhata Bay, packed up, and traveled south to Ntcheu District, where we stayed with the family of Kaliyoma Phumisa. We appeared at the height of his reelection campaign, and he and his wife graciously invited us to join them as they tirelessly traveled from village to village, holding sometimes three or four rallies a day, including the one described earlier.

Both the rallies and women's dancing in the current dispensation follow the formulaic structures so well established during Banda's regime. However, contemporary politicians differentiate themselves from the previous government by emphasizing that women now choose whether or not to dance and which party to support. Politicians also frequently assert that they incorporate dancing into their events not as a political strategy, but as a celebration of traditional or local cultural practices. In the name of tradition, politicians have also started giving small material gifts to performers as tokens of their appreciation.

In the year following the 1999 elections, I lived in Blantyre, and I followed women's political dancing as it occurred outside of campaign periods; there, I also had greater access to urban women who participated as dancers in addition to journalists and high-ranking politicians. During this stay, in February 2000, a heated debate broke out in the newspapers between human rights activists and politicians over the practice of using women's dancing at rallies and more specifically over the practice of gifting dancers. Human rights activists challenged politicians' continued use of women's dancing, pointing to the similarities between the current practice and that of the Banda regime. They argued that politicians exploit women's poverty by enticing poor women to dance at their rallies through the possibility of remuneration. Politicians defended themselves, touting the freedoms of association and expression enjoyed by all Malawians and the traditionality of both dancing and the gifting of performers.

I returned to the United States in the fall of 2000. Because of my work obligations, I followed from afar the controversy rampant in the period leading up to the 2004 elections, relying heavily on Web sources. We returned to Malawi five days before the elections were scheduled on May 15, 2004, only to hear that they had been rescheduled for May 18. Allegations of party defections, corruption, violence, and campaign fraud filled the air. When the elections were finally held, on May 20, we sat with our friends in the city of Blantyre, clustered around the radio, as did Malawians across the country, waiting for the outcome. Inaccurate information was announced on some radio stations, causing outbreaks of violence. Official results were not made public until the evening of May 23. Bingu Mutharika, who had been handpicked by Muluzi to run on the UDF ticket, won the presidential bid.

One issue that became especially prominent in the 2004 campaigns was the importance of improving gender parity within political party and state structures and within the society more generally. At the vanguard was then state president Bakili Muluzi, who, along with other southern African heads of state, signed the Declaration on Gender and Development at the Southern African Development Community (SADC) Summit in Blantyre, Malawi, in September 1997, committing Malawi to achieving at least 30 percent female representation in political and decision-making structures by 2005. The 2004 elections were pivotal for achieving this goal. Parties made efforts to endorse female candidates, and a number of Malawian human rights nongovernmental organizations (NGOs) established programs to identify qualified women and provide them with the necessary training and resources (see Geisler 2004). I was curious during these elections to discover how attempts to improve women's political status impacted those women who dance, who for the most part participate at the lowest ranks of the political hierarchies. I sought out human rights activists who had worked hard to promote women candidates, along with some of the women who had run successful campaigns, to discuss their strategies, experiences, and perspectives on women's political dancing. I also met with women who danced during these elections to trace how the practice continued to emerge and to examine how their roles were or were not impacted by politicians' emphasis on improving gender parity.

This book is about women's political dancing in Malawi. It focuses on the contemporary political culture that has emerged since the transition to multipartyism and that continues to develop into the future. In order to understand the present, it is also necessary to understand the process through which the practice has unfolded over time and in relationship to transitions in the political environment. I examine women's political dancing in the present and the past within the webs of social, economic, political, historical, and cultural frameworks that surround the practice and all the actors involved. This project emphasizes the important contributions that women make as political dancers in addition to examining ways in which their performing operates in negotiations of power. Exploring women's participation as performers yields insight into intersections between gender and economics within Malawi's political sphere, highlighting inequities built into the political structures that are affirmed and perpetuated through discourse valuing a local cultural identity exemplified in women's performances. This study also elucidates how this cultural practice continues to emerge in relationship to ongoing political change, and, consequently, how the political use of dancing impacts dance forms, affecting how they manifest outside the political arena.

In my analysis, I consider both women's dancing and the rallies of which they are a part from a performance studies perspective, understanding that performances are often simultaneously reflective and constitutive of political and social realities and that people use performances to establish and sustain relationships, making them crucial sites for social action.[1] Performances do not exist in a vacuum but rather operate as genres: a single political performance in Malawi is modeled on previous ones and influences those that come after (Bakhtin 1986: 61–67; Briggs and Bauman 1992). Unraveling the significance of a performance in the present therefore requires information about how the form first emerged and continues to develop. The steps involved in organizing and rehearsing for an event, and all the discourse that surrounds the performance, are equally important for untangling relationships between any given performance and the social environment in which it takes place. In my examination, I therefore follow Beverly Stoeltje's framework for studying performance and attend to the ways in which the practice developed in the past and continues to transform into the future; the stages of production; details that manifest in situated performances; and the competing discourses that surround it (Stoeltje 1993).

My focus on artistic expression in the political realm necessitates an interdisciplinary approach that draws from scholarly perspectives in the humanities and social sciences. Examining the practice through these multiple lenses yields a nuanced and in-depth explication of the phenomenon. I take into account the perspectives of actors involved in many different capacities, including the women who dance, party organizers, elected officials, journalists, and human rights activists, all of whom have variously been involved in either producing the performances or the discourse that surrounds them.

Women's political dancing is not unique to Malawi; the performative presence of women wearing fabric decorated with party or state symbols who liven up political occasions by dancing and singing songs that promote politicians and political bodies is common across the African continent. The case in Malawi is unusual to the extent that all women during Banda's rule were required to perform, thus contributing to an especially strong linkage between women's dancing and the national political culture. The institution of women's praise performing during Banda's presidency has been the subject of a number of publications, though little has been written about the practice in the post-Banda years.[2] Similarly, though they are widespread, these phenomena in other African contexts have received limited scholarly attention, usually only referred to in passing and or as illustrative of the limited political roles available to women.[3] Yet, in Malawi as in some other African countries, praise performing has become one of the only ways that poor women, who constitute the majority of women in the country, can and do participate in the political process. These women's political performances therefore provide an important entry point for exploring the political status of one of the most underrepresented and marginalized segments of Malawi's population. This study contributes one piece in a large and complicated puzzle that could explain the significance of the widespread use of women's performative bodies across the continent. Those engaged with political realities in other African countries will recognize similarities in patterns of usage and emergence, and probably notice differences as well. My hope is that this book will invite more dedicated and critical attention to these phenomena, eventually crystallizing in a more coherent understanding of the role of women as political performers across the continent.

My descriptions and analyses of women's political dancing are the product of my synthesis of conversations (some informal and others formal tape-recorded interviews) with numerous people involved with political dancing; scholarly literature relevant to performance, gender, and politics in Africa; and my own experiences and reflections. As with any cultural phenomenon so ideologically laden and so controversial, I encountered numerous contradictory opinions about how performance contributes to the political arena and about the political, economic, and cultural ramifications of the continuing participation of women as political praise performers. I attempt to provide a wide range of viewpoints on the topic, but the tone of my analysis and many of my conclusions are my own and do not represent the perspectives of any one constituency involved. My intention is not to provide a definitive statement about the practice, but rather to initiate a conversation about a phenomenon that has serious implications for those marginalized politically because of gender and class, but that has up until now received scant scholarly attention.

Dance in Malawi

As is the case in many African contexts, music making and dancing intertwine with the sociocultural fabric and permeate much public life in Malawi. People sing and move informally while engaging in all sorts of occasions from work to play to worship: weddings, collective farming sites, athletic events, installations of leaders, political rallies, parties, tourist venues, dance clubs, religious and healing rituals, and places of worship (Kamlongera et al. 1992).[4] Each ethnic group in Malawi participates in a repertoire of dance genres associated with that cultural group.[5] Each genre is usually performed by a particular category of people—based on age, gender, and social role—and most are associated with particular secular or sacred functions. To illustrate the varieties of dance forms associated with specific ethnic groups and geographic regions, here I briefly outline the types of dances that were performed during my stay in the Nkhata Bay District in 1998–1999. The majority population in Nkhata Bay District identify as belonging to the Tonga ethnic group, though many Tumbuka families have lived there for multiple generations, as do people from other ethnic groups. Many of those from other ethnic groups participate in Tonga dance genres while living in the district.

Teams of young men and boys danced the all-male malipenga militaristic secular dance at intervillage competitions, political rallies, and tourist venues (Kamlongera 1986; Kerr and Nambote 1983; Gilman 2000a). The mostly women chilimika dance teams, also secular, performed at intervillage competitions, an event at a Catholic church, tourist venues, the installation of a village headman, and political rallies. The sounds associated with *vimbuza/masiawe*, a dance usually performed by a single healer to drumming and women's singing, echoed faintly in the distance almost every night of my Nkhata Bay stay. My hosts explained that vimbuza/masiawe healing rituals often take place at night (Friedson 1996; Chilivumbo 1972). I observed some of these same healers performing in the secular contexts of tourist venues and political rallies. *Honara*, a dance developed when many Tonga men traveled regularly to South Africa to work in mines, is a secular dance performed by men and women in elegant clothing to the melodic turns of live accordion music. I was told that honara was the dance of weddings, though during my stay, recorded Congolese rhumba (*kwasakwasa* and *domboro*) was the music of choice for most wedding organizers. The Phaka Town Band, one of the few remaining honara dance groups, generated great enthusiasm when it entertained at the rallies of several politicians in the district. *Chiwoda*, an all-women circle dance, used to be one of the most popular dances in the district. Whenever large groups of people gather, women join in a rotating circle and move rhythmically to the beating of drums and call-and-response singing. Chiwoda used to be associated with intervillage dance competitions, weddings, and other community events (Chilivumbo 1971). By 1998, women danced chiwoda almost exclusively at political rallies, a change I explain in the final chapter of this book. I did witness a chiwoda performance with only a handful of women at a tourist venue, and a larger number of women gathered to dance at the installation of a village headman. I have been told that the island of Likoma in Lake Malawi is the one place where Tonga women still dance chiwoda in intervillage competitions. *Visekese*, a dance performed by women to the shaking of reed rattles, is rarely performed outside of Usisya in the northernmost reaches of the district. *Kamchoma*, a secular dance once performed by Tonga men, women, boys, and girls for entertainment in the evening hours, is no longer performed and exists only in the memories of elders.[6]

Other ethnic groups in Malawi participate in a similarly diverse range of dance practices. Although the histories of the dances vary, people in Malawi generally refer to all such dance genres in Chichewa as *magule wa makolo athu*, "the dances of our parents/ancestors" or "traditional dances." Similar phrases are used in other Malawian languages. These dances are fluid and flexible forms that can easily be adapted to meet new expressive needs and can be made appropriate for new contexts, as is clear from the example of masiawe performers dancing both in healing rituals and to entertain foreign tourists. Though, *magule* or *zovina*, which I translate as "dances," is the generic label for these forms in Chichewa.

Although I follow local conventions in my use of the word *dance*, as do most Malawians when speaking English, these genres are as much about singing, instrumentation, and costume as they are about movement. As explained by Ruth Stone, "African performance is a tightly wrapped bundle of arts that are sometimes difficult to separate, even for analysis. Singing, playing instruments, dancing, masquerading, and dramatizing are part of a conceptual package that many Africans think of as one and the same" (1998: 7). Though I use the term *dance*, my description and analysis necessarily engages the movement, singing, costuming, and musical components of the performances.

In addition to these emically categorized local genres, Malawians also engage in other types of dance and musical practices. For example, during our 1998–1999 stay, people danced at clubs and parties to popular music by Malawian artists, by musicians from neighboring countries, especially the Democratic Republic of the Congo, Zimbabwe, and Tanzania, and by some artists from the United States. Many youths, mostly male, were committed aficionados of rap and raga (Jamaican dance hall music), and many of these performers moved rhythmically as they pounded out their original lyrics (Fenn 2004; Gilman and Fenn 2006). Many churchgoers moved and sang hymns to local melodies in their churches (Henderson forthcoming; Henderson and Gilman 2004), and sports fans sometimes sang and danced to encourage team members and celebrate victories.

A selection of my video recordings along with my detailed annotations that further describe and analyze dance performances inside and outside of Malawi's political arena, mostly performances in the Nkhata Bay District in 1998-1999, is accessible through the Ethnomusicological Video for Instruction and Analysis Digital Archive Project (EVIADA) in two collections: "Dances of the Nkhata Bay District of Malawi" [http://purl.dlib.indiana.edu/iudl/eviada/5-C5818] and "Music and dance in Malawi's presidential elections 1999" [http://purl.dlib.indiana.edu/iudl/eviada/5-C5833]. Citations to specific events within these collections are provided throughout the book (see Appendix D).

Villages, Towns, and Cities

The distinctions between urban and rural settings in Malawi are complex and must be explained to clarify the circumstances of the women who dance. So much about women's social and economic identities in Malawi, in addition to their distance and relationship to political party centers, is tied to where they live. The definitions of villages, towns, and cities in Malawi, as in other African countries, are fuzzy, making these distinctions somewhat problematic. In the Nkhata Bay District, for example, Tonga people call varieties of settlements *muzi*, or "villages," and "it depends on the context whether this word refers to a hamlet of one hut or to a large village of one hundred huts, or for that matter Johannesburg, London or Chicago" (Van Velsen 1964: 28–29). The Ngwira family, for example, lived in a small cluster of houses on top of a hillside. The residents of this hamlet comprised only one extended family: eight houses for ten to twelve adults and their offspring. The land and by extension the people were under the jurisdiction of a village leadership structure, though the hamlet was physically and socially isolated from others belonging to this loosely defined village. This hamlet and the larger entity to which it belonged were also multicultural, comprising some people who identified as Tumbuka and others who identified as Tonga.[7] By contrast, Msani Village (also in the Nkhata Bay District), where I spent much time with the American State chilimika team, comprised numerous families living in proximity within a well-constituted community under the leadership of Group Village Headman Chilelawana. Within Msani were an elementary school and a church. Nkhwali where I spent time with the Mweluzi chilimika team and Zabweka Tembo, a famed performer who was also the father of a number of Mweluzi's most committed dancers, was even bigger, comprising two villages, each with its own leadership. Because of its proximity to the Vizarra and Chombe rubber estates and the Kawalazi tea estate, Nkhwali attracted people from across the country seeking employment. Many came for work and later settled, making the locale more multicultural than most communities in the district. Nkhwali included several churches, a school, two small restaurants, and several small stores.

Agriculture is the economic mainstay of most people living in rural settings in Malawi, though fishing, small businesses, and wage labor frequently supplement or replace agricultural efforts. A majority of houses within rural communities or villages are constructed using local materials and methods, usually mud-brick walls and floors with thatched roofs. The houses range from very small one- to two-room houses to fairly large dwellings with four or more rooms. Towns and cities comprise political entities distinct from villages, have well-established roads, and include such institutions as municipal governments, hospitals or clinics, banks, markets, stores, post offices, and schools. Housing ranges in size, quality, and access to amenities, though far more large, Western-style houses are found in cities and towns than in villages. Tucked within and often adjacent to cities and towns are clusters of houses and sometimes small businesses in which people live similarly to those in more rural areas. Some of these are institutionally structured as villages with a local leadership framework. Others are less formal; people at lower economic strata build houses near one another using similar materials and methods, as do those in rural areas. Residents in high-density neighborhoods—urban settlements in which houses are often small and close together—belong to a range of economic strata from the very poor, to those subsisting on steady, but small incomes, to up-and-coming professionals. These neighborhoods are often bustling business districts with active nightlifes and lively youth cultures.

To further complicate distinctions between *urban* and *rural*, and *city* and *village*, many people in Malawi have relatives living in a variety of situations, providing opportunities for travel and experience in a range of settings. Many travel between rural and urban areas for work, business, performance opportunities, and so on. Many live in cities or villages at different times in their lives. Regardless of where a Malawian lives, she or he usually refers to either a mother's or father's (or sometimes both) natal village as "*ku muzi*" (Chitonga) or "*ku mudzi*" (Chichewa), translated literally as "at the village," but more accurately as "home." When Malawians ask me where my *mudzi* is, they are not asking me whether I am from "a village" but, rather, where my home is. I could answer with the United States, the state or city where I currently reside, or where I lived as a child. Even when a family has resided in a city for generations, they maintain the connection with their home villages, visiting on occasion, and providing needed resources to individuals and communities; at death, most are buried in their home villages.[8]

Distinguishing individuals as belonging to rural or urban communities is therefore problematic. All Malawians, whether living in a village, town, or city, are cosmopolitan in that they "partake in a social life characterized by flux, uncertainty, encounters with difference, and the experience of processes of transculturation" (Piot 1999: 23; see also Hannerz 1987; Turino 2000). Despite obvious problems, I follow widespread local usage and make these distinctions, only because it provides an orienting framework for discussing the social contexts and class structures in which women dancers live and operate. Though people in all Malawian socioeconomic strata live in villages, towns, and cities, people at the lowest economic strata of the population, including most of the women who dance politically, tend to live in villages in rural or urban areas and in high-density urban neighborhoods. Some do live within more expensive sectors of cities, for example, in house-worker quarters located in the yards of many urban homes. Most people belonging to the country's elite own houses in the most expensive city neighborhoods, and sometimes also own large houses in towns and villages. Distinctions among village, town, and city life are significant to this project for at least two additional reasons. First, the dancing included in political rallies is most commonly performed in village contexts rather than cities in non-political events. Second, because party headquarters and the most active party activities occur in towns and cities, women living in or near towns and cities have more opportunities to participate politically than do those more isolated from political centers.

Performance and Power

Jane Cowan (1990) effectively illustrated ways in which dance events can be sites for both reinforcing and contesting dominant ideologies, especially those having to do with gender (cf. Hanna 1988). In Malawi, as in many countries across the globe, the preponderance of patriarchal social systems—both local leadership structures and imposed or adopted European ones—produces gendering of power structures in which men fill a majority of leadership positions in local and foreign-based institutions, relegating most women to subordinate roles. In some, such as political parties, the majority of women play roles of supporting and legitimating, at least symbolically, those in leadership positions.[9] Malawian political performances are the product of and interact with these gendered power differentials.

The songs women political performers sing can be categorized generally as belonging to a corpus of panegyric or praise singing and poetry genres widespread across the African continent. Ruth Finnegan detailed some common features of these genres, many of which are characteristic of political songs in Malawi. These forms can express self-praise and praise for other humans, supernatural entities, inanimate objects, political organizations, or countries (Finnegan 1970: 112).[10] Composers frequently exploit metaphors and other poetic devices to embellish their elaborate homage, which highlights the often exaggerated qualities, achievements, or abilities of the individual(s) being extolled.[11] The relationships between praise performers and the people they praise are frequently asymmetrical: those uplifted through songs frequently enjoy higher economic, social, cultural, religious, or political status than do those who exalt them. By singing songs of praise, performers symbolically legitimate and accept a leader's authority and can reinforce social hierarchies (Timpunza Mvula 1990; Hale 1998).

However, relationships of power between the praised and the praisee are often much more complicated than those overtly displayed through performance: the possibility of expressing multiple contradictory messages combined with the sometimes liminal status of the performer can obfuscate and complicate locations of power (see, e.g., Hoffman 1995). Here, it is important to recognize that manifestations of power rarely occur only in top-down dualistic relations, but rather within multidirectional webs. All those engaged in relationships have varying access to power, some more overtly articulated than others (Foucault 1990 [1978]: 92–94). In situations where binaries of authority are explicitly delineated, such as in political relationships of leader and led, those in subordinate positions often creatively manipulate resources at their disposals to increase their opportunities for self-expression or to improve their social or material well-being. In *Weapons of the Weak: Everyday Forms of Peasant Resistance,* James C. Scott explained that most subordinate classes do not have the luxury of carrying out open organized political action against those who dominate them. Rather, they frequently pursue more subtle forms of everyday resistance that either go unnoticed or occur indirectly and may not be recognized by those in authoritative positions (1985: xvi). In situations across the world, subordinated women have often capitalized on performance forms as avenues through which to resist domination.[12]

In many African contexts, song texts are one of the more widely recognized channels through which women have historically been able to express discontent or criticize those who have authority over them, such as their husbands or community leaders.[13] Leroy Vail and Landeg White elaborated that in much of southern Africa, there is "the convention that criticism expressed in song is licensed criticism." Through songs, singers define "pungently and accurately the terms of their exploitation" (Vail and White 1991: 41; White 1989; cf. Gunner 1995: 193; Abu-Lughod 1986). Similarly, the *oriki* as described by Karin Barber do not always flatter their subjects, but sometimes point to their most salient trait even if it is negative (1991: 13; 1999). Because song lyrics can be metaphorical or can otherwise express ambiguous messages, it is possible for people to compose songs that outwardly appear to be saying one thing, such as praising an individual or institution, while in fact they are criticizing or making fun of it, through what Joan Radner and Susan Lanser call "coded messages" (1993: 3).

These two patterns—praise and social commentary—in performance practices often occur simultaneously in that people who sing songs praising a leader sometimes use veiled messages or metaphors to criticize the leader within the same song texts.[14] The individual who is being criticized can hear his or her subordinates' complaints while saving face, and he or she is expected to change his or her behavior (cf. Yankah 1995: 11). If the criticism continues without any change, then community leaders may intervene and confront the leader more directly. For example, Enoch Timpunza Mvula (1987) described how Maseko-Ngoni women in Malawi sing songs that criticize their husbands and other people who have authority over them while they pound maize collectively, well within earshot of others in the community. Though these song texts include overt articulations that are considered inappropriate for a woman to express in other public forums, this criticism is socially acceptable within the context of women's collective singing. People who hear these songs usually do not respond directly to the comments made; however, the person criticized is expected by the community to hear the song and to subsequently change. Through their singing, these women are able not only to express themselves, but also to resist domination when it goes too far.[15]

This combination of using singing for expressing praise and for social commentary provides a means through which subordinates can have a voice and to some extent resist domination while at the same time confirming and even reinforcing asymmetrical power structures. Hale provided an example from a female Songhay griotte in Niger, in which she uses the format of a "typical praise-song for a canton chief":

> Father of the poor people
> Husband of beautiful ladies
> At whose absence the city is not interesting
> At whose absence people are not happy . . .
> Be our mother
> Be our father
> Provide us with clothing
> Be the salt we need for our gravy
> Be the oil we need for our porridge. . . .
> You are our eyes
> You are our mirror
> You are our hands and legs
> That we use to walk

Hale explained that this song glorifies a chief while simultaneously reminding him of his responsibilities to the community. "A prince who does not serve as the 'hands' and 'legs' of a people simply does not measure up to the ideal as articulated by the griottes and is therefore, by implication, less of a prince" (Hale 1998: 29). Kelly Askew similarly provided an example of *taraab* musicians who took advantage of the poetic license afforded song texts to overtly criticize Tanzania's president Ali Hassan Mwinyi during an official visit to Zanzibar in 1991 (2002: 228–30).[16]

Women's singing within Malawi's political arena integrates the potential for using performance to bolster leadership structures with the potential for using performance to resist, with both processes often occurring simultaneously despite obvious contradictory goals. Women, at the lowest rungs of the economic and political hierarchies, are often the ones who sing songs that glorify the higher status and mostly male political leaders. Their performances thus affirm gender and power hierarchies. Yet, their performances can also serve as channels for socially sanctioned commentary and activism. At times women have capitalized on their own performativity to achieve social or individual change, for example, in their strategic use of singing and dancing during the movement for independence and during the transition to multipartyism. At other times, those in power-wielding positions have organized women to dance to further their own goals or as strategies for suppression, exemplified by the Banda government. In all situations, performance and power have intersected in ways much more complicated than was immediately apparent. In situations in which performance has been used as a tool for liberation, it has also contributed to social asymmetries, and when it has been exploited as a tool for oppression, dancers have found creative means of using it for personal or collective gain.

Song lyrics comprise only a small part of the possible webs of meanings that can be expressed or interpreted through women's dancing and over the course of the larger events of which they are only one part. Drawing from Bakhtin, I consider a rally to be a complex genre, a communicative style that is at once emically defined as an individual genre at the same time that it is composed of constituent styles, each of which is also emically defined as a genre. This multigenerity of rallies—that they comprise numerous genres, such as speeches, singing, slogan shouting, visual symbols, and dancing—creates multiple channels of communication, producing complementary and contradictory signifiers that radiate during the course of a single event. The multigenerity of a political rally complicates the task of analysis because of this exponential potential for making meanings and accomplishing social goals created by each genre in conjunction with how they interact as the complex event unfolds (Bakhtin 1986: 62; Briggs and Bauman 1992). An individual at a rally, for example, could sing a song supporting a party while wearing a visual symbol for another party, creating a cacophony of confusing messages. A more subtle example would be a woman who sang about how happy she was with the government while moving lethargically to a dance generally expected to be fast paced and cheerful. Her dancing might belie the message in her song. That different actors exert control over the manifestation of different genres during the course of the event further complicates issues of power, intentionality, and meaning—a point I return to throughout this study as I interrogate relationships between performance and power.

Some Issues

Language has been a consistent issue in this research. Because Malawi was formerly a British colony, English is the country's official language, greatly facilitating my research endeavor. However, because of the unequal distributions of educational opportunities, many of the people whose perspectives most interested me did not speak English. This was especially true of most adult women at lower socioeconomic levels, many of whom had had limited opportunities for schooling. When I arrived in 1998 to settle in Nkhata Bay District for the year, I had studied Chichewa in the United States and had achieved conversational proficiency. Chichewa is the second official language of Malawi (after English) and the lingua franca in the central and southern regions. After moving to Nkhata Bay District, I transferred this knowledge to the closely related language Chitonga, widely spoken in the district, and I was able to learn enough to get by in day-to-day living and socializing.[17] To supplement this basic knowledge, I hired assistants to help me conduct tape-recorded interviews with non-English speakers. Most of the time, an assistant translated a question that I asked in English into the language of the interviewee. She or he responded in her or his language. Depending on how well I understood, I either followed with another question or asked for a verbal translation. I later hired people to transcribe and translate the interview tapes. I conducted interviews with English speakers in English alone, though sometimes other people were present depending on the situation (see Appendix B). I videotaped all political rallies I attended. During the events, I understood some of the speeches, slogans, and songs that were performed in local languages. Later, I hired people to transcribe and translate the audio tracks of selected recordings (see Appendix C).

The transcriptions of song texts were difficult given that the recordings occurred in loud settings with lots of overlapping noise. Because of technology limitations, I gave people I hired audiotapes rather than videotapes to transcribe, which often made it difficult for them to follow and to tease out the performance from other distractions or to identify exactly who was performing at any given moment. A further complicating factor was that the songs themselves were often heterophonic in that multiple melodic and sometimes textual lines were sung simultaneously, making it difficult to hear and also to transcribe linearly. Furthermore, call lines usually overlapped with response lines, making it difficult to hear and also difficult to differentiate voices. Because of these problems, my inclusion of song lyrics is intended more for the textual content than as representative of how they were performed. Distinctions between call lines and response lines are often omitted, as is much repetition. When feasible and applicable, I do provide some of this detail, and at times I describe the musical aspects of the performances in more detail.

As a foreigner, and a *mzungu* (white/European/American person)—often perceived to be wealthy and powerful—I was often accorded privileged status. I was usually escorted to the VIP section of rallies, where I was almost always given comfortable seating and a prime view of dance performances, which allowed me to obtain quality video recordings, and I was usually introduced to the leading politicians and sometimes mentioned in their speeches. My position was problematic. Some politicians used me as a symbol to promote themselves, pointing out that only the most powerful and capable politician could attract an American to come to their rallies. Though this made me uncomfortable, the politicians knew that I was also attending the rallies of their opponents. I am hopeful that most in the audience were familiar enough with political propaganda to evaluate the attention given to my presence as only one of many boasts made by speakers. As I elaborate later, the same dancers often performed the praises of opposing politicians on different days, making my presence less marked, as it fell within well-established patterns.

Because of the sensitive nature of this research, the question of how to refer to people has confounded me. Most people whom I interviewed gave me permission to use their full names in publications. However, I am acutely aware that what might be safe in one political climate might suddenly become problematic, even dangerous, at a later date. Further, people interviewed, especially those at the grassroots level—the term used in Malawi to refer to the country's poor majority—did not necessarily always understand my intentions. Though I explained that I was a researcher from the United States intending to write articles and books, for many—most women I interviewed at the grassroots level cannot read or write—the categories of researcher and even journals and books were something with which most had little familiarity. I have therefore chosen to refer to people at the grassroots levels in such a way as to obfuscate their identities. I use the prefix *Mayi* followed by a family name when referring to women dancers. *Mayi* is the Chichewa word for *mother* and is used as a term of respect for adult women.[18] The family names are common, and most people in Malawi have several names that they use in different contexts, assuring me that it would be difficult for readers to trace the women's identities from the information provided. Those familiar with naming practices in Malawi will undoubtedly recognize inconsistencies in the way I refer to people. My intention is not to provide accurate names or to follow the numerous naming practices in the country, but rather to provide enough information to allow a reader to differentiate among individuals.

Others interviewed participated in their capacities as public figures—politicians, human rights activists, and journalists. These individuals were familiar with various types of publications and expected to be quoted in different venues. I attribute names to their quotes most of the time. For those who requested anonymity, I provide only as much information as they specified.

In a few cases, I have made the subjective decision not to include individuals' names when I have felt that a quote is especially sensitive or when I have not wanted to come across as unduly critical.

I recognize that by using a different system for those at the grassroots and those in more powerful positions, I enact the same gender, economic, and political gulfs that I critique. Though uncomfortable and dissatisfied with my decision, I feel that ascribing greater anonymity to highly public and visible figures might lead some to question the validity of some of my accounts, and providing more identification to those at lower levels could increase possible risks. I therefore choose a compromise.

Another problem has been identifying people's political positions and affiliations. Many are no longer in the same positions that they were at the time of research, and many have since changed political affiliations and continue to do so. At the time of writing, some people's allegiances were shifting literally on a day-to-day basis, making it largely impossible to update everyone's current status. My attributions of affiliation are therefore those pertinent to the moment of research. When relevant, I do provide clarifying information about changes either in the text or in endnotes.

Finally, I am saddened by the frequency with which I have had to insert *late* before the name of a friend or acquaintance appearing in this book. The causes of death vary and point to the general lack of adequate medical care available to most Malawians. However, one also cannot ignore the catastrophe wrought by the HIV/AIDs epidemic, which has hit Malawi especially hard and which continues to be a stigma for those personally affected by it. As I insert each *late* into this text, I sadly hope that the government will attend productively to the HIV/AIDS crisis (and lack of adequate medial care more broadly), so that treatments will be made more widely available, people will change their behaviors, and the epidemic will subside.

Chapter Breakdown

The book continues in Chapter 2 by detailing the processes through which the political use of performance developed during Malawi's movement for independence. In their rebellion against British colonial rule, activists capitalized on dance and praise-singing traditions to construct a national identity, disseminate information, and rally support for their cause. The organizational and symbolic structures through which women's participation was organized created a framework that linked gender, performance, economics, and political power, which became the basis for the oppressive use of women's political dancing during the authoritarian rule of Banda. Chapter 3 describes how Banda's government appropriated women's political dancing, transforming it into a mechanism for social control and for disseminating images of its legitimacy. The institutionalization of women's political dancing through the

MCP party structure further entrenched the intersections among gender, economics, and power.

Chapter 4 begins with an examination of the early 1990s, when women's political dancing was a central issue during the campaign for the referendum vote and again during the campaign for the first multiparty elections, held in 1994. I then trace how the practice has evolved since the transition to multipartyism by describing women's participation in rehearsals, in travels to and from events, and in the rallies themselves, in addition to providing information about other types of performances that commonly occur at rallies since the transition. In the post-Banda political context, intersections among gender, economics, and power manifest as patronage relationships, exemplified in rallies in the interactions between politicians, the patrons who provide for the general population, and the women who dance, representatives of the clients who receive from politicians and express their gratitude through performance.

In Chapter 5, I analyze one political rally, the 1999 launch of incumbent president Muluzi's presidential campaign in the northern region. This analysis demonstrates how a rally serves the purposes of political power wielders in its capacity to attract people, disseminate messages, display symbols, and reinforce hierarchies. Women political dancers are especially important because of their multiple roles as wearers of symbols, shouters of slogans, dancers, praise singers, and receivers of material gifts. The potential for dialogism and intertextuality in this complex performance results in the simultaneous diffusion of contradictory messages, some of which directly conflict with those intended by rally organizers.

Chapter 6 answers the question, "Why do women dance?" by first outlining many of the reasons why women participate as praise performers. Many participants are critical of their positioning within the political realm, and human rights activists have at different times contested the practice. I therefore consider complicated issues of agency and resistance by exploring ways in which women dancers manipulate the system to maximize their benefits. Although many such examples exist, I argue that many participants for the most part go along with the practice, and that it is therefore just as important to explore why women choose not to resist as it is to consider their acts of defiance.

Chapter 7 situates the practice within the context of women in Malawian politics more broadly. Discourse about improving gender parity in Malawi's economic and political spheres abounds in contemporary politics, and human rights NGOs are engaged in numerous projects aimed at improving the social, economic, and political status of poor Malawian women. My examination of this discourse in relationship to the activities of male political power wielders, women politicians, and NGOs suggests that few are challenging the cycle that positions women dancers at the lowest levels of political structures, from which they have few opportunities for political and economic mobility.

The concluding chapter highlights how people variously involved—including women who dance, politicians, human rights activists, and journalists—often use discourse of its traditionality to explain why political dancing persists. I contend that women's political dancing is an effective and culturally empowering avenue for political participation at the same time that it perpetuates the political marginalization of poor women. I then consider this discourse about traditionality from a different angle in my examination of how the political use of dance has impacted dance practices outside of the formal political sphere.

Notes

1. See Drewal 1992; Barber 1997; Fabian 1997; Cowan 1990; Bauman 1989, 1992; Stoeltje 1992, 1996; Stone 1988; Turner 1988 [1987], 1969; Askew 1999; Del Negro and Berger 2004.

2. See Lwanda 1993; Mkamanga 2000; Chirwa 2001; Semu 2002.

3. Similar practices occur in Uganda (Tripp 2000: 93), Tanzania (Geiger 1997: 67; Geisler 2004: 24–25), Zimbabwe (Hove 1997: 35; Geisler 2004: 24–25), Mozambique (Geisler 2004: 24–25), Niger (Alidou 2005: 102–3), and Zambia (Crehan 1994: 260; Geisler 2004: 24–25).

4. See Gunderson and Barz, ed. 2000 for a collection of essays on music and dance practices in the region.

5. The term *ethnic group* is problematic in Malawi as in many other African contexts because of complicated relationships among cultural groupings in the region. Contemporary ethnic categories are partly the result of politically motivated groupings and divisions of people in various phases of Malawi's history that sometimes have little to do with people's own cultural identification (Kaspin 1995: 598–602). My use of ethnic names and groupings corresponds to those used by Malawians during my research.

6. These genres are associated with Tonga people, as the numerically dominant population in the district, and by extension with the Nkhata Bay District. However, those identifying as belonging to other ethnic groups living in the district are often just as involved as their Tonga neighbors in these dance forms. Many of the most active chilimika performers I knew, for example, identify as Tumbuka—complicating whether it is more appropriate to identify these genres with an ethnic group or geographic demarcation. People from other ethnic groups living in the district also sometimes perform dance forms associated with their own cultural identities both among themselves and for wider multicultural audiences, and their dances are also featured at the rallies in the district.

7. The Ngwira family was not originally from the Nkhata Bay District. They are Tumbuka from Rumphi District who settled into this location in the early 1990s. A number of the women married to the men in this family are Tonga. The residence pattern for this family is patrilocal. The adult men living in the hamlet are related to one another; the adult women are wives and daughters of Ngwira men. The numbers of adults fluctuate. During our short stay, the two wives of one son each left him on various occasions to return to their home villages. Some of the sons in the family worked and lived outside the district and occasionally returned to their father's home to live.

8. Some ethnic groups in Malawi are matrilineal, others are patrilineal, and still others are bilineal. Additionally, many Malawians have parents from different ethnic groups,

further complicating whether a person considers her or his mother's, father's, or both parents' villages as the home village.

9. That a number of Malawian ethnic groups are matrilineal complicates my statement about the centralization of authority within males in local power structures. Women do enjoy important positions of power within matrilineal systems, and in both matrilineal and patrilineal contexts in Malawi, women do hold chieftaincy positions. Even within matrilineal systems, however, power is often vested among males within kinship structures, such as maternal brothers and uncles, rather than fathers and husbands, as is more common in patrilineal systems (De Aguilar and De Aguilar 1999).

10. For example, see Barber 1989, 1991; Coplan 1994; Hale 1998. Praise-singing traditions have also been incorporated into Christian and Muslim religious practices (see, e.g., Mack 2004: 61). Clara Henderson and I, for example, noted similarities between the songs sung by Presbyterians in Malawi that praise Jesus and those sung at political rallies that praise politicians (Henderson and Gilman 2004).

11. See Cope 1968: 26; Opland 1983; Schapera 1965.

12. See, for example, Raheja and Gold 1994; Koskoff 1989; Danielson 1997; Heath 1994.

13. See Timpunza Mvula 1985, 1986a, 1986b, 1987; Vail and White 1991: 231–77; Hale 1998; Hoffman 1995; Gunner 1999: 51.

14. David Coplan objected to the label *praise* for these genres because "these texts so often include characterizations that are contradictory, inconvenient, and even sharply critical" (1994: 14). The imposition of etic generic categories is necessarily problematic. The peoples engaged in these cultural practices across the continent have their own systems of categorizing and labeling their expressive forms, categories necessarily associated with sets of ideological and formal conventions that are fluid and dynamic (Ben-Amos 1976; Shuman 1993: 72–74; Flueckiger 1991: 182–83). Though it is problematic, I nevertheless use the term *praise singing* because of its wide usage and recognizability. Agreeing with Coplan and following many scholars, I highlight the ways these genres are used to simultaneously praise and resist.

15. For another Malawian example, see Van Alstyne 1993.

16. Using song texts to criticize those in authoritative positions is not always accepted by authorities, and the offending musician can suffer repercussions, as in the examples given by Askew (2002: 224–67).

17. As a child living in the Democratic Republic of the Congo (then Zaire) (1969–1978), I spoke the Bantu language Kiswahili fluently. As a result, I easily acquire linguistic proficiency in closely related Bantu languages when immersed in a new linguistic setting.

18. Though many of the women interviewed are not Chewa, I use *Mayi* for everybody so as not to confuse the reader and because the term is familiar across the country.

2

Dance and Nationalism in the Independence Movement

Mayi Mphase remembered first dancing politically during Malawi's movement for independence in her home district of Nkhata Bay. She later became one of the most prominent dance leaders in the district during Banda's rule and was still an avid MCP supporter when I met her in 1999. I first encountered Mayi Mphase on a video documenting political dancing during Banda's rule that I had purchased in the nearby city of Mzuzu. As my research assistant Simeon Nyirenda and I watched footage from a rally held during the referendum in the town of Nkhata Bay, he pointed out two of the song leaders, Mayi Mphase and Mayi Kondowe, and told me they lived nearby. Several days later we made our way through the pouring rain to Mayi Mphase's house, located in a hamlet near town. Around seventy years old—she was not sure of the exact year of her birth—she sat in her small living room on March 26, 1999, and responded to my requests to recollect the past. She explained, "It's been a long time and I may forget some things. I am growing old, and my tongue is not as active." She recalled that in the 1950s, leaders of the independence movement walked from house to house in the Nkhata Bay District, encouraging women to go dance for the political cause. She joined, optimistic about promises that the colony would soon be freed from colonial rule. She described the oppression under British colonialism, the violence that erupted in the town of Nkhata Bay, and the subsequent arrests of leaders of the independence movement that occurred on March 3, 1958. She generously sang some of the songs that she remembered singing at rallies of that time. Unfortunately, due to technical difficulties, I do not have the Chitonga version; the English translation is nevertheless illustrative:

You, you are whites
Whites have destroyed the country
We, the owners, refuse, what for?
What for? You do that for yourselves
We don't want, what for?
We don't want, what for?
One two, three, let's go
See now, there in Ghana
What the whites did?
They sold the land as if we were together
Like how they bought Malawi
The time, we will rule ourselves
Whites are rude

She explained, "That is how we used to sing, using cowbells. We used to hide behind the elders during those times [of colonial rule]. But little by little we managed to go through until now we are independent. Now we are free without someone asking for a card wherever we go. Kamuzu [Banda] came, went to prison, and then was released. This is when we really started to be free."

As is evident from Mayi Mphase's memories, women's political singing and dancing in contemporary Malawi emerged from the ways in which local performance customs undergirded the movement for independence. Performance has long been inextricably tied to power structures within the geographic area now called Malawi. Local customs of using performance both to sustain hierarchical power structures and as tools for resistance were the foundation for how performance genres catalyzed the struggle for liberation from the British.

Dance, Nationalism, and the Struggle for Liberation

In 1891, The British imposed a protectorate in the territory that is now Malawi. Africans in Nyasaland established political bodies in the early 1900s called native associations, many of which joined together much later, in 1944, to form a national party called Nyasaland African Congress (NAC), the principal organization of the independence movement.[1] Competing political organizations and actors were also involved in the movement. For the purposes of tracing the development of political dancing, my focus is on the activities of the NAC, because it was the most prominent and well-organized political association and because it transformed into the Malawi Congress Party (MCP) in 1961, which became the ruling party after independence (McCracken 2002: 80).

In the late 1940s, the British government and colonial administrators began negotiations for a proposal that would bring together Nyasaland, Northern Rhodesia, and Southern Rhodesia into the Central African Federation (also called the Federation of Nyasaland and Rhodesia), instigating much opposition from the African populations in each colony (Welensky 1964). The Central African Federation was imposed in October 1953. During this period, a group of young men—including M. W. Kanyama Chiume, Orton Chirwa, Henry Blasius Chipembere, Augustine Bwanausi, Yatuta Chisiza, and Dunduzu Chisiza—most with university degrees from African universities (e.g., Fort Hare in South Africa and Makerere University College in Uganda)—returned to Nyasaland from their studies and to a great extent took over the NAC leadership (Short 1974: 80; Williams 1978: 168).

After gaining momentum during the struggle against the federation, the NAC weakened in the 1950s due to conflicts within its leadership and members' disillusionment with the NAC's failure to stop the federation. In an attempt to bolster the movement, the party leadership invited Dr. Hastings Kamuzu Banda, a medical doctor who had been living abroad for more than thirty years in the United States, Britain, Scotland, and Ghana, to be the figurehead of the movement. Banda returned on July 6, 1958 and took over the NAC leadership (Short 1974: 79–89; Virmani 1992).

I was fortunate to spend a good deal of time with the late M. W. Kanyama Chiume, one of the leaders of the independence movement, along with several members of his family during 1998–2000. I had heard rumors that Chiume owned land in the town of Nkhata Bay. Hearing that he was in town, on January 14, 1999, I ventured about an eighth of a mile down the road from where we lived onto what I was told was his property. He had purchased a small piece of land on the lakeshore that had had been an overgrown mess and was previously associated with illicit activities. He was slowly transforming it into a charming rest house, the Banana Grove, shaded within luscious green banana leaves. I found him, a dignified man in his early seventies, relaxing on a beach chair in the sand several feet from the water, looking out over Lake Malawi while jotting in a notebook. His memories of the independence movement were vivid, as he had devoted much of his life to revisiting the activists' optimistic struggles during the movement and contemplating what had transpired shortly after independence, when the Banda government forced him and many of the other activists into exile. In my many long conversations with him about Malawi's political history, he always emphasized the important roles played by women and encouraged me to seek out Rose Chibambo, the most prominent woman activist in the movement, who, like him, had also returned from exile following the opening up of the political arena in the early 1990s.

Rose Chibambo graciously welcomed me into her home in the city of Mzuzu on several occasions in 2000. Her compelling stories about her involvement in the movement shed light on women's roles, information largely omitted in the scholarship I have read. As is the case in the histories of countries throughout the world, historians and Malawian politicians have greatly emphasized the roles played by male leaders in the movement, especially the young college-educated male elite (e.g., Short 1974; Rotberg 1965; Pachai 1973), largely overlooking that women were involved and that a few women held high-level leadership positions.[2] At around the same time that the young men dominated the leadership of the NAC, Chibambo explained that she took the lead in formalizing women's involvement, and that she and other women activists formed the women's wing of the NAC around 1957 (Chibambo, personal communication, February 4, 2000). Like Bibi Titi Mohamed in Tanganyika (Geiger 1997), Chibambo subsequently became a prominent political leader and served on the national executive board of the party.[3]

Using what I learned from my interviews with Mayi Mphase, Chiume, Chibambo, and other elders in the Nkhata Bay District, and my readings of numerous Malawian histories, I outline here a plausible version of the emergence of women's political dancing within the independence movement. As with all histories, my narrative is necessarily selective and subject to the memories and interpretations of the people I interviewed, the historians whose books I read, and my own perspective. It nevertheless provides a useful framework from which to understand how women's political dancing in contemporary Malawi emerged into what it is today, and it elucidates how the practice continues to emerge into the future as people in Malawi navigate ever-shifting social, economic, and political environments. Unfortunately, I was not able to obtain any visual documentation of the dancing at rallies during the movement, nor do historians of the movement describe the dancing in much detail. I therefore am able to provide only limited information about the performances themselves, aside from what I gleaned from the memories of interviewees asked to recollect the distant past.

The integration of performance into politics during the movement occurred along at least two trajectories. In the first, women activists continued local cultural practices by contributing their performative bodies to the movement. Drawing from praise-song traditions, women sang songs at political rallies as a strategy to attract support for the movement and its leaders. In Susan Geiger's *TANU Women: Gender and Culture in the Making of Tanganyikan Nationalism, 1955–1965*, Bibi Titi Mohamed explained that she and other activists used existing women's dance associations, ngoma, to mobilize women in the Tanganyikan movement for independence against British rule. They attended ngoma meetings, which brought women together, to sell the idea of independence to their members (Geiger 1997: 58). Titi Mohamed explained how her position as a song leader of one of these dance associations helped propel her to leadership heights in Tanganyika's movement (Geiger 1997: 50; Geiger 1987: 15; Strobel 1979). Chibambo explained that the Malawian experience was different from that of Tanzania, in that women activists in Nyasaland did not explicitly use dance associations as a strategy for mobilizing women in this way. She and other activists did not plan to use their singing and dancing bodies in the movement. Once gathered at public meetings, they introduced songs as appropriate in the same ways that they were used to doing for other settings in which groups of people assembled. They sang songs already in their repertoires, changing words as necessary to make them relevant to the situation:

> In most cases, our singing, like in the women's league, we would take some of the songs sung in the villages, then we put in political words to suit the occasion. . . . There wasn't any particular person at that time, that this was the one who composed these songs for us to sing. No. It was just general singing. Just as we are here. You could start a song, and our songs in most cases, our African songs, they are traditional. They are not difficult to sing. We could easily pick it up, and then we all would sing. (Chibambo, personal communication, February 4, 1999)

It is likely, given the preponderance of women's dance associations in the region, that these established organizations of women in Malawi might have facilitated the mobilization of women in rural areas in a way similar to the process described by Titi Mohamed for Tanzania; however, little evidence of how this occurred is available. Most women I interviewed who had lived through the movement remembered pre-independence political dancing only vaguely, if at all.

According to Chiume, songs performed at rallies articulated the dream of freedom from colonial rule, praised the party as the organization that would facilitate this goal, glorified the party leadership to make their names known throughout the colony, and repeated the party's symbols to familiarize and reify the party in people's minds. Activists also took advantage of the traditions of using song texts to criticize those with authority and sang songs castigating the colonialists for taking control of their lands, mistreating them, and forcing upon them the federation with the Rhodesias, such as in the following example, also sung for me by Mayi Mphase, translated from the original Chitonga into English:

> You whites
> We, the owners [of the land] do not want to combine with Rhodesia, no
> Why do it for your own sake?
> We don't want it
> The whites have destroyed the land
> We don't want it
>
> (Mayi Mphase, personal communication, March 12, 1999)

In Malawi, as was the case across the continent, activists recognized that using songs for resistance was an especially effective communicative tool because it provided a coded means for raising popular consciousness. Furthermore, most colonialists did not understand the local languages and so did not try to suppress them.[4]

Women also used their music making as action. Chibambo recounted how women protested at the high court after two NAC leaders, James Sangala and T.D.T. Banda, were arrested in 1953:

> When the women's league heard, I organized all the women. We hired a bus on the day the case was being heard and went to Zomba. And there, we caused a real fracas. We were singing and shouting around the high court, all outside. That intimidated the government. They said, "We have the women now. And if we lock up these people, I think there will be a crisis." Just lucky enough, they only charged them with fines. We contributed the money then and there, and paid off the fines, and they were released. (Chibambo, personal communication, February 4, 2000)

Dancing was often as important as the textual content of songs, and especially effective for raising levels of emotion. As with other contexts in which women sang praise songs, a woman sometimes initiated a song, and then others took up the response line. This singing could continue with women exhibiting little movement, or, as energy levels rose, singers often stood and moved in place, or they proceeded into a circle formation to dance. The location of a political rally and the particularities of those present determined the type of dancing that occurred. Though activists came from many different cultural backgrounds, they capitalized on the closely related circle-dance forms shared by a number of ethnic groups, such as chiwoda, which was popular in the Nkhata Bay District. These genres were similar enough that most women could easily join in.

Chibambo was very explicit that in organizing women to participate in the NAC's women's league, she intended women to be full participants in the political process. She perceived singing and dancing to be something they did as part of larger political strategies, not the primary form of their participation. She clarified this point to me in our exchange on February 4, 2000:

> CHIBAMBO: I had this feeling that women should be organized, not just for the sake of dancing. That was not what I had in mind. No. The idea was that women should be part and parcel of the whole movement, even of running the country. Women should be involved in decision making. That was my aim. That was why I said that women should be involved in politics.

AUTHOR: It sounds to me like dancing was just a way for women to express themselves.

CHIBAMBO: Yes!

AUTHOR: It didn't matter what else you were doing; it made sense to also sing and dance?

CHIBAMBO: Exactly! That is how you can really put it; the dancing was merely a question of expressing. It's just what I explained before. The women expressed their joy. It is part of our tradition. You express joy. You express sadness. In most cases, you sing, and so on. It wasn't just for the sake of dancing. And this makes me sad up to this day. That women, later, later, women were turned just to dancing.

In the second trajectory of political dancing, which occurred later in the movement, political leaders invited established dance groups to participate in rallies as performers. Unlike the informal dancing of women activists, single- or mixed-sex dance ensembles—what I call "established dance groups"—that existed outside of the political sphere were invited to perform. As did nationalist leaders across the continent, NAC leaders brought together dance teams representing the country's different cultural and regional groups to perform at rallies, creating opportunities for people to share their cultural practices with others from different areas, which in turn created a sense of unity and contributed to the development of a national identity based on difference (Kertzer 1988: 21–24). As Thomas Turino wrote about similar events in the Southern Rhodesian movement, rallies that integrated performances from different ethnic groups helped to "bring the imagined [unified nation] into being by presenting the possibility (of the object nation) in a concrete, perceptible form" (2000: 179).

Dance performances in the "established dance group" model were different from the women activists' informal dancing because party leaders actively sought out and organized the established groups' performances, exerting more control over participation and outcomes. Individual dancers had varying levels of commitment to or consciousness about the political cause; many came primarily as entertainers. Similarly, when party officials organized a rally, local NAC leadership invited local dance groups to perform. According to Chiume, the national leadership frequently told the local leaders what kinds of messages these dancers should convey; the performers then adapted existing songs or composed new ones that were appropriate (Chiume, personal communication, February 20, 1999).

Already, women and girls constituted a larger presence than did men and boys within this political performance realm because they danced at political rallies within both trajectories. As remembered by Mayi Mphase, political organizers went door-to-door in her community, urging people to attend rallies. Once there, she joined other women in spontaneous singing and dancing. Other women participated as members of established dance groups invited by political organizers specifically to entertain, and some did both. Men, on the other hand, mostly performed only with established teams. Asked specifically about the emphasis on women's dancing, Chiume answered that while male dances, such as the malipenga or *beni*, a dance form of the Yao in the southern region, attracted a lot of people,

> [y]ou must understand, you must appreciate . . . that even in the developed world, despite the fact that there are some gender activists against this sort of thing, who raise their voices against it, I think it is more attractive to have women dancing because they do attract a lot of attention.
>
> Later he added:
>
> Just as in the Western world or the developed world, women seem to be a much more effective element in advertising. And here, too, I think that dancing women tended to attract more of a crowd than perhaps just mere men. (Chiume, personal communication, April 21, 1999)

Chiume was suggesting that women's performing bodies were especially effective for drawing a crowd and advertising the NAC. Eventually, this same attitude led to women performers becoming the embodied advertisers for the nation.

Nation Building

Creating a national movement in Malawi was challenging given that the territorial boundaries of Nyasaland were arbitrary and had nothing to do with existing social or cultural groupings. Within Nyasaland, as in most other colonies on the continent, lived diverse groups of people who did not identify with one another; what they shared was their residence within the territory demarcated by the colonial power (Liebenow 1986: 50; Young 1994: 225). The leaders of the nationalist movement therefore instigated what Anthony Smith termed "territorial nationalism," creating a supra-ethnic political culture that allowed for and incorporated ethnic difference (1991: 84, 112). Activists capitalized on the NAC as the vehicle through which to both mobilize the population and imagine the nation (Anderson 1991 [1983]). Because the political constructs of "party" and "nation" were not part of local knowledge or political practice, for people in Nyasaland to accept, support, and ultimately join the movement for independence through the NAC, they first had to accept the political party as an identifiable entity.

David Kertzer posited that modern political organizations depend on rites "to create political reality" and that it is through participation in political rites that "the citizen in the modern state identifies with larger political forces that can only be seen in symbolic form." Most of modern politics exists on an abstract level. Through symbolic behavior, political organizations are reified, political leaders come to embody higher status than the people they lead, and people feel an emotional connection to both political entities and their leaders (1988: 1–2).

Correspondingly, NAC activists strategically developed a national political culture rich with symbolic behavior through a process that Eric Hobsbawm and Terence Ranger (1983) called the "invention of tradition." Common usage of *tradition* or *traditional* refers to cultural practices that are considered to be directly connected to the past: superorganic, bounded, static, transgenerational "things" or practices that can be inherited and passed from generation to generation.[5] The Chitonga term that is usually translated as "tradition" is *ujavi wapai widu*; the Chichewa equivalent is *chikhalidwe cha makolo athu*; both translate as "the way(s) of our parents/ancestors."

Many contemporary scholars writing about tradition recognize that cultural practices do not exist as superorganic, bounded, static, or transgenerational things. Rather, the concept of tradition is rooted in social life. Dell Hymes explained that people endow certain cultural elements with symbolic meaning by linking them to a primordial past. When people label a practice traditional, they elevate it to a special status, and then members of the group often feel an obligation to repeat the practice in order to perform their identity and meet the requirements of that group, a process that is often self-conscious and selective, what Hymes called "traditionalizing" (1975: 353–54). At any given moment, groups of people recognize any number of practices associated with the past; they select only some to continue and to endow with that special meaning (Handler and Linnekin 1984, see also Williams 1977: 115; Glassie 1995: 395).

Hobsbawm and Ranger (1983) argued that political strategists sometimes develop new or select existing cultural practices to achieve political goals. By subsequently cloaking the practice in rhetoric of its traditionality and ensuring its repetition through time and space, members of a population eventually come to call them *tradition* and thus endow them with special value (see also Ranger 1983). Responding to criticism levied against the work he did with Hobsbawm, Ranger (1993) revisited the idea of the "invention of tradition." He recognized that these "invented traditions" often had local antecedents, in that those involved often drew from or built upon local cultural practices. He maintained, however, that in specific historical periods, people have also created new practices rather than selecting existing customs as strategies to meet their goals.

In their development of a national political culture, NAC leaders capitalized on the value associated with tradition and both invented some symbols and practices and selectively drew from, appropriated, and extended local customs for use within the national political realm. NAC activists took it upon themselves to create a set of traditions and symbols to be associated with the party and by extension the movement and the nation. These symbols included visual signs, such as the national flag and images of the rooster and dawn, symbolizing the anticipated new beginning or independence, and slogans, such as *kwacha*, the Chichewa word for "dawn," symbolizing the awakening that would follow attaining freedom from colonial rule (Tangri 1975: 278; Chiume, personal communication, February 20, 1999, April 21, 1999). Additionally, NAC leaders selected from local customs in their integration of such things as singing and dancing into the political culture.

Turino emphasized that emotion was a key element in Southern Rhodesia's nationalist struggles. Citing nationalist leader Nathan Shamuyarira, Turino noted "how music, clothing, prayers, and other cultural gestures were used to generate attendance at the early rallies, to infuse them with meaning, and to create enthusiasm for a cause" (2000: 172). Correspondingly in Nyasaland, singing and dancing were an effective choice for nation building because not only did they bring people together and serve as methods through which to spread messages, but they were already laden with symbolic value because of their associations with tradition. Given the cultural diversity in the territory, activists could showcase the musical and dance practices of multiple ethnic groups at a single event to communicate a national identity built on and celebrating cultural difference. The role of dancing in such constructions of national identities has been important in other countries as well. Stephanie Urdang, for example, explained that in the struggle in Mozambique, people from different localities "learned the culture of their neighbors, people they might have regarded as threatening or alien," and enjoyed opportunities to move "to the rhythms of each other's dances." Leaders of Frelimo or The Liberation Front of Mozambique, the political party through which indepence was fought, hoped that through this exchanging of "the varied and rich cultures of Mozambique, unity could be forged" (Urdang 1989: 42). Similarly, Chiume explained that "when you feel that the people from Karonga with their music are part of us, you begin to wonder whether you don't belong to the same country!" (Chiume, personal communication, February 20, 1999). Or, as Sue Tuohy wrote, making music together is an "active means by which to experience the nation, by which to feel and act national" (2001: 108). Song texts in Nyasaland's movement affirmed this national solidarity:

Tiyende pamodzi ndi mtima umodzi!
Tiyende pamodzi ndi mtima umodzi
Eeee, A Banda tiye! Tiyende pamodzi!
A Chipe tiye! Tiyende pamodzi
Eee, A Chirwa tiye! Tiyende pamodzi!

Kanyama tiye! Tiyende pamodzi!
Tiyende pamodzi ndi mtima umodzi

Let's march forward in one spirit!
Let's march forward in one spirit
Banda, let's march!
Chipe, [Chipembere] let's march!
Let's march forward in one spirit
Chirwa, let's march!
Kanyama, let's march!
Let's march forward in one spirit!
(Chirwa, W.C. 2001: 8)

W. C. Chirwa explained that the phrase *tiyende pamodzi* "was like an anthem of the nationalist struggle" (2001: 8).

Music and dance were also good choices in the process of inventing a national identity because they contrasted with European cultural practices. Though the performance practices of different ethnic groups in Nyasaland were distinct, they were similar enough in contrast to British colonial culture that they could be used to symbolically represent a shared "African" identity in opposition to the colonial one. Many early missionaries and Europeans involved in the colonial enterprise referred to local dance practices as something to be "abhorred" (Sindima 1992: 79), "immodest" (Johnston 1969 [1897]: 408), "debased" and "disgusting" (Cullen Young quoted in Forster 1989: 59), "vile" (Fraser 1925: 30), and one of the "chief obstacles in the way of Christianity" (Mills 1911: 228). Given this history of disdain, the embracing of dance by activists in Nyasaland was a highly symbolic gesture valuing African cultural practices as something to be celebrated and as a source of power. Activists involved in independence movements across the continent were similarly capitalizing on local dance forms for their highly symbolic value as "African" as opposed to colonial European forms and as evidence of the vitality of African cultures. Francesca Castaldi, for example, explained that activists involved in the Négritude movement who lived in France during the colonial era recognized the value of using African artistic practices to performatively assert the presence of African cultures in Paris: "The artists and intellectuals of the Négritude movement knew that the act of speaking (writing/singing/dancing) in an African idiom within the institutions of white culture, at the very center of Europe, was a defiant form of social protest." And shortly after Senegal's independence, the new president and an important figure in the Négritude movement, Leopold Sedar Senghor, hosted a Pan-African festival in Senegal that "celebrated African arts as proof of the concrete achievements of African cultures and a clear sign of the greatness of past African civilizations" (Castaldi 2006: 51). Christopher Waterman similarly explained that Yoruba nationalist leaders in Nigeria in the 1950s hired performers of local musical genres to perform at their rallies and fund-raisers, poignant expressions of Yoruba identity (1990: 88–89). NAC leaders in Nyasaland participated in Pan-African activist networks during this period and shared many ideologies and strategies with their counterparts in other territories. As did Négritude and Yoruba activists, they understood the symbolic value of promoting local dance practices (see also Askew 2002: 13).[6]

Political rallies were important to this process of nation building in Nyasaland because they provided the population with embodied experiences of the developing national culture, the NAC party, and the leadership of the movement. Meetings became stylized performance events composed of formulaic elements (Short 1974: 150). At rallies in Nyasaland, party symbols were worn on participants' bodies, radiated from banners, were shouted in slogans, were proclaimed in speeches, and were disseminated repeatedly through kinetic and verbal communicative channels during dance performances. Through the performance practices—both the rally and its constitutive parts—the party became a recognizable part of people's social environments. Through knowledge about and displays of these symbols, people could express their allegiance to the nationalist cause (Moore 1977: 154; Kertzer 1988: 6). Here it is important, as Regina Bendix cautioned, to recognize that the process of nation building did not occur through a top-down process, but rather was the product of ongoing negotiations among all actors involved (Bendix 1992; Askew 2002: 12, 272–73; Ranger 1993). As Kelly Askew rightly contended, "No amount of rhetoric can construct a nation if it fails to find resonance with the state citizenry. There must be some degree of mutual engagement for nationalism to flourish" (2002: 12). The success of the nationalist movement was ultimately contingent on the shared frustration with the colonial administration and widespread desire for change combined with the highly effective strategizing of the movement leadership.

In preparation for Banda's arrival in 1958, the young intelligentsia spearheaded an intense propaganda campaign throughout Nyasaland promoting the prospective leader because, in Chiume's words, "you build a thing if it is not there already" (personal communication, February 20, 1999). In his autobiography, another one of the young leaders, Chipembere, related that in his letter inviting Banda he explained that "human nature is such that it needs a hero to be hero-worshipped if a struggle is to succeed" (2002: 300). In another, he warned Banda that "he must not be frightened . . . if he was heralded as a political messiah." Chipembere explained to Banda that this publicity could be "used with advantage" and that it "would cause great excitement and should precipitate almost a revolution in political thought" (Short 1974: 87).

NAC leaders traveled around the country, spreading the word of Banda's return and transforming him into a symbol for the movement. It was at this time that the strategic use of music and dance as political tools really flourished. Chiume explained that the NAC made a concerted effort to organize local performance groups to spread the word about Banda's identity and imminent return. This was the time period that triggered the memories of elderly women and men I knew in Nkhata Bay Districtwho explained that it was when Banda came that they really began dancing. Along with projecting him as the political savior, song texts publicized his virtues: he had been supporting and providing guidance to the party for years, though he lived abroad; he had a high level of education; he had experienced life in European countries; and he had expertise in Western medicine. In addition, they emphasized his advanced age (around sixty), an important factor in respect and leadership in the region (Chanock 1975: 344). They coined terms of adulation for him that resonated with local praise practices, referring to him with the exaggerated titles of lion, savior, and *ngwazi* (conqueror). The propaganda was intended to convey that Banda "was 'the Doctor' who would cleanse Nyasaland of the cancer of *Chitanganya*-Federation; the Moses come to lead his people from bondage; the Messiah; the Christ-figure who would deliver Nyasa from oppression" (Short 1974: 92). It emphasized his multiple degrees and certificates: after he arrived, the young leaders would address him at meetings with his full quota of qualifications: PhD, MD, LRCP, LRCS, LRFPS, and later DOF (Destroyer of Federation) (Lwanda 1993: 20).

Upon his arrival, Banda readily stepped into his role as the charismatic embodiment of the leader of the movement and a symbol of hope for freedom. Banda's role as a symbol for the newly emerging nation fit a pattern for nationalist movements across the continent at the time. Kwame Nkrumah served a similar function in Ghana, Julius Nyerere in Tanzania, Kenneth Kaunda in Zambia, Jomo Kenyatta in Kenya, and so on. In his autobiography, NAC leader Chipembere commented that "it was fortunate that the man whom we wanted to turn into a messiah was himself keen to play such a role" (2002: 303). By this time, the ritualization and formulaic structures of rallies were solidly in place. According to Philip Short,

> The meetings followed a set pattern. The people would begin arriving, by bus, by taxi and on foot, hours before Banda was due to appear. While they waited, members of the local Women's League branch would perform traditional dances. Later, cheer-leaders would take over, exchanging slogans with the crowd until excitement reached a fewer pitch. Then Banda would make his entrance, and give out the Party rallying-cry: 'Kwacha! Kwacha! Freedom! Freedom! Ufulu! Ufulu! Ntendere! (1974: 150)

This formula became the framework for all subsequent rallies from the independence movement through the most recent election campaigns and foreshadowed the shift in Banda's relationship with women dancers that would occur soon after independence.

Emerging Economic and Political Gulf

Political scientist Gus Liebenow explained that elite politicians in Malawi, as in other sub-Saharan African independence movements at the time, "had to convince the more traditionally oriented masses that the leadership's embrace of western education, religion, and lifestyle was not a rejection of African culture per se. It was the colonialists and colonial rule—through the imposition of the color bar and other racial restrictions—that constituted a rejection of African values and institutions" (Liebenow 1986: 212; cf. Anderson 1991 [1983]: 116). Through speeches and song texts, political leaders emphasized that they were bipolitical. They had to convince the populace of their abilities and legitimacy as leaders in addition to convincing "colonial powers of the cultural parity between Africans and Europeans" (Askew 2002: 171). NAC leaders promoted themselves as members of traditional culture (i.e., through their knowledge of local singing and dancing traditions) and authority systems; at the same time, they advertised their education, English-language skills, and knowledge of how the colonial administration functioned. In so doing, they projected the image that they could rule people based on systems already in place while at the same time working within new systems that had been imposed by the British. Banda was the ultimate embodiment of a bipolitical leader, expressed through the symbolic items he wore and carried with him in every public appearance. He always wore a black suit and black homburg hat and carried an English cane in his right hand—symbols of status in the European world, and dress appropriate for a European doctor. At the same time, he carried a fly whisk in his left hand, a symbol of status and also a totem of many traditional African healers, which he is said to have received as a gift from Jomo Kenyatta. He also always made a big point of joining the dancers, an enactment of his identity as a Chewa, Malawian, and African (Lwanda 1993: 44; Liebenow 1986: 213; Mphande 1996: 81).

The embracing of bipoliticalism contributed to class, cultural, and gender divisions that continue into the present between politicians, who are often associated with European ways of doing things (e.g., English-language skills, high levels of formal schooling, European-style housing and transport), and the majority of the population, who are more closely tied to "African" lifestyles (cf. Matiki 2001). Through their dancing, for example, women activists performed identities associated with what was considered "traditional" more so than did their male counterparts, thereby contributing to the emerging equation within the political realm between women and culture and Africa, on the one hand, and men and intellect, leadership, and Europe, on the other.

Political leaders took it upon themselves to inform the populace of what was wrong with the colonial system and explained the possibility for a better future. In selling the idea of self-rule, activists appealed to people on the level of their daily experience rather than with more abstract ideological or political issues: They demonized the colonialists and focused on their negative attributes while putting forth only the positive aspects of self-rule. Songs texts and other communicative channels conveyed that the colonialists were bad and were taking advantage of the African population. There was a possibility for a better future where Africans would lead themselves under the leadership of the NAC (Liebenow 1986: 213–14).

The disparity between the activists who took the position of political leaders and the general population contributed to the emergence of a level of dependence by the masses on their leaders for information and direction. These relationships combined with local patrimonial social and political systems contributed to the paternalistic relationships that would develop between politicians and the "led" (Liebenow 1986: 214). As in many contexts in sub-Saharan Africa at the time, the gendering of political leadership, which was largely dominated by men, created a foundation for a gendering of political relationships in the country in which men were more likely to play the role of political patrons, while most women fell into the category of the "led," or clients (see Kirkwood 1993, Staudt 1987). It is not difficult to see how these types of relationships between the majority of the population and political leaders easily led into authoritarian rule, even if that was not the intent of political organizers at the time. The general population was already used to hearing directives about how to think and what to do for their own good. With the dictatorship that followed, the addition of coercion into the picture shifted the power dynamics dramatically.

Performance and Power

Activists used dance in the movement for independence as an explicit strategy for resistance and rebellion against their colonial rulers. Implicit in much scholarly treatments is that acts of resistance are inherently positive and libratory. However, James Scott, whose work has been influential to many scholars of resistance, acknowledged that these "weapons of the weak" are "unlikely to do more than marginally affect the various forms of exploitation which peasants [applicable also to many subordinated peoples] confront" (1986b: 6). A careful examination of situated contexts reveals that relationships between resistance and liberation are often ambiguous, and acts of resistance can sometimes work to perpetuate existing or create new inequities. Systems of power are complex, and no individual lives within only one relationship of power (Ortner 1995: 177). When an individual resists against one situation of domination in her or his life, it often has implications for other relationships within which she or he also operates. Lila Abu-Lughod explained that in their resisting against one group of people, resisters can unwittingly enmesh "themselves in an extraordinarily complex set of new power relations" (1990: 52; see also Reed 2005: 362).

The power dynamics negotiated by women activists and their performing should be considered within two frames: the colony of Nyasaland and the NAC organization itself. Within the first frame, women were political actors in their own right and had control over their bodies: Their performances were a liberating force as they struggled against colonial rule. At the same time, they were marginalized within the second frame, the power structures of the NAC. Within the frame of the NAC, most women activists were subordinated, and thus their contributions were to some degree limited and controlled by those in the main bodies, who were almost exclusively male. The members of the women's wing to a great extent contributed when and where the main body found it permissible and advantageous. Because the focus was independence, resistance against male dominance within the movement received little attention and probably would have been seen by many as an unwanted, even unforgivable distraction from the more important goal of independence. Ultimately, this unequal gendered system, institutionalized through the organizational structure and activities of the NAC, provided a framework for continued gender stratification after independence. Similar patterns have been identified in revolutionary struggles throughout the world, for example, in Tanzania's movement for independence (Geiger 1997) and in the Iranian revolution (Tohidi 1991: 252–53).

Furthermore, though many individuals who danced were politically motivated, others, especially those of established dance groups, participated primarily as performers or members of dance teams. Even young children danced, though they may have been too young to understand the political implications of their actions. The NAC leadership's coordination of dancers to promote Banda elucidates the ambiguities of performers' motivations. Roger Tangri rightly cautioned that "we must, of course, not exaggerate the level of consciousness of the rural masses or discount that the Congress [NAC] leader's connexions with rural protests were, at times, opportunistic" (1975: 279). Turino similarly noted that there was much debate about the extent to which the masses were integrated into the nationalist movement in neighboring Southern Rhodesia (2000: 170). The songs glorifying Banda preceded his popularity, which implies that many of the performers who advertised him probably had little direct experience of him and so were probably not expressing their personal points of view. The incentives to dance during the nationalist movement were a combination of people's feelings of commitment to NAC's goals, dance groups accepting invitations to perform because doing so conformed to cultural expectations, and the effectiveness of the energy and charisma of the activists who asked the dancers to perform. Individuals had varying levels of understanding or commitment to the political contexts to which they contributed, which suggests that already some dance groups and dancers were being organized by leaders as political tools regardless of dancers' individual political commitments.

Notes

1. See Pachai 1973: 225; McCracken 1977: 257–85; Rotberg 1965: 116; Tangri 1968: 150.
2. Cf. Berger 1999: 49; Geiger 1987, 1997.
3. From my interviews with Rose Chibambo, I compiled a narrative of her political involvement (Gilman 2000b, 2000c, 20001d).
4. E.g., Gondola 1997: 76–77; Geiger 1997; Mlama 1995.
5. See Ben-Amos 1984 for a review of scholarly treatments of tradition within this vein.
6. Moreblessings Chitauro, Caleb Dube, and Liz Gunner mentioned in passing that after the popular Southern Rhodesian (now Zimbabwe) recording artist Dorothy Masuka was forced to leave Southern Rhodesia in the early 1960s because her political songs were deemed dangerous, "she moved first to Malawi, where she sang for the Malawi Congress Party," after which she went to Tanzania to help TANU raise funds (1994: 125). Unfortunately, they provide no dates. Their use of the post-independence name "Malawi" suggests that this stay in Malawi could have been after independence, though it is not clear. Regardless, this example is interesting because it suggests that politically active performing artists moved across borders to perform in movements in neighboring countries, providing more information about regional cross-influence in political performance practices.

3

Dance and Social Control During Banda's Presidency

In February 1999, during the height of the chilimika dance season, Mayi Ma. Longwe, an avid chilimika dancer, invited me to come to her home village, Nsanje, to meet and watch her team rehearse. Nsanje is relatively isolated, accessible from the nearest town of Nkhata Bay only by boat or a several-mile trek up and down hillsides.[1] We traveled with about thirty other passengers on a small wooden motorized taxi boat that bumped its way north, hugging the lakeshore as it dropped people off at fishing villages along the way. After about two hours, we arrived in Nsanje. Later that day, Mayi Md. Longwe, a woman in her late sixties or early seventies, who had heard about my interest in dance, came by the house to welcome me. The next day, February 17, 1999, I sat on the porch of her very small mud-brick house overlooking the lake; fishing canoes dotted the greenish blue water, providing a picturesque backdrop for the stories she shared about her political life. People in Nsanje still remembered Mayi Md. Longwe as the district chairwoman for the women's wing of the Malawi Congress Party, who had coordinated women in this community to dance during Banda's rule and who had often been selected to travel far to perform at national events and even once to perform internationally. Mayi Md. Longwe explained that it was after independence "that the meetings really started. Then there were different dances: masiawe, malipenga, football matches, people celebrating. It was then that we sang in praise of the Ngwazi [Banda] for leading us into freedom." As with Mayi Md. Longwe, many elderly women I met vaguely recalled political dancing before independence; all remembered that it was after independence that it really became a regular part of their daily lives.

The Political Culture after Independence

In 1961, leaders of the NAC, now called the Malawi Congress Party (MCP), drafted its first constitution, and in the first elections for African representation, MCP candidates won the majority of parliamentary seats. On July 6, 1964, Malawi officially became independent under the leadership of Prime Minister Banda. Prior to independence, Banda was already consolidating power and repressing dissent (Williams 1978: 205–11). Shortly after, following a series of incidents commonly referred to as the Cabinet Crisis, Banda declared the former young leaders of the movement—including M.W.K. Chiume and Rose Chibambo—traitors to the state and threats to national security.[2] Fearing for their lives, they and many of their family members and supporters fled into exile (Short 1974: 209–10). The country became a republic in 1971, and Banda followed in the footsteps of many of his colleagues across the continent by formalizing through the constitution that Malawi would become a single-party state (cf. Adamolekun 1976; Young and Turner 1985). Banda became the life president of the republic in addition to the position he already held as life president of the MCP (Short 1974: 281). The Cabinet Crisis set a precedent for silencing anyone who disagreed with or otherwise threatened the president through detention, loss of jobs, exile, and in some instances death (See Zeleza 1996; Forster 1994: 477; Mphande 1996: 91).

After the Cabinet Crisis, Banda continued the process initiated by NAC leaders and used the MCP party as the structure through which to crystallize a single unified entity within the country that could be controlled and manipulated by one leader. Because the idea of a nation had already been created and reified through the NAC during the independence movement, the MCP was the obvious structure through which Banda could consolidate power (McMaster 1974: 55; cf. Liebenow 1986: 221–28). Following trends across the continent, the government required that all Malawians—though only those of "indigenous African origins"—belong to the MCP, which required buying a party card and demonstrating allegiance to the party and its leader (Constitution of the Malawi Congress Party 1965, Article 2, Section 4). Membership in the party also implied membership in the nation and by extension the state.

Murray Edelman explained that "the governments which most often outrage their citizens or force unwelcome changes in their behavior plainly have the greatest need for reassuring symbols" and that it is therefore not surprising that "all totalitarian states involve their populations intensively and almost constantly in discussions of public affairs" (1985 [1964]: 9). Correspondingly, the Banda government developed a mass political culture in which it required all Malawi citizens to participate. Building on the nationalist culture already established during the independence movement, the government emphasized certain symbols as belonging to all and being representative of the nation.

One of the most prominent was that of Banda, whose role as a symbol of the party and state was ossified into law in the state constitution. His name, image, nicknames, and even the word *president* were protected along with other state symbols under the Protected Flag, Emblems and Names Act (*The Laws of Malawi* 1968: chap. 18:03). Symbols distributed through numerous channels reinforced Banda's position at the apex of the country's pyramid power structure. The image of Banda became commonplace in newspapers, on party fabric ubiquitously displayed on women's bodies, on T-shirts, and on photographs in offices and businesses. He was always seen wearing his black suit and the matching homburg, and waving a fly whisk, each signifying his power and authority. Even at his death in November 1997, he was buried in his full attire, complete with a fly whisk at his side.[3]

The symbols established during the independence movement furthered the aims of the authoritarian state. The rooster and the slogan *kwacha* (dawn) now referenced the awakening Banda brought the country by leading the fight for independence. The color red represented the blood of martyrs who died during the struggle for independence, and green represented Malawi's natural environment and economic reliance on agriculture. These symbols, along with the flag, the four cornerstones of the party (unity, discipline, obedience, and loyalty), the national anthem, national holidays, and most relevant to this study all women of Malawi as Banda's praise performers, became important tools through which the government required the population to experience and express their commitment to the party, nation, and state. Added to this was an attempt to impose to some degree the culture of Banda's own ethnic group, the Chewa, as the national culture.[4]

As with the NAC before independence, the Malawi Congress Party continued to have a youth (League of Malawi Youth) and women's wing (League of Malawi Women), in addition to its main body. Responsibilities were divided among the three branches to ensure that all government activities were effectively carried out. The women's and youth wings were ancillary to the central governing structure, called the main body, which was dominated by men (Constitution of the Malawi Congress Party 1965, Rules and Regulations: 9). The existence of these wings along with the paramilitary organization, the Malawi Young Pioneers, at every level of the party structure—national, regional, district, area, and branch—enabled the government to easily communicate with the populace in addition to monitoingr people's behavior, tracking people's critical statements, and forcing people into compliance with government policy and law (Chirwa 2001: 10–11). The president's speeches were replete with these messages, as in the following example, from October 1966:

> In order to make sure that Chipembere does not even make a nuisance of himself, watch everybody who comes back from Tanganyika,

> or Zambia or even Rhodesia or South Africa. Watch everyone of them! See what he is doing, listen to what he says. If he says anything like: "Chipembere is coming," report him to the police, to the Youth League, to the Young Pioneers, to the Chairman of the League of Women, and see that they go to Dzeleka [Prison]. (Quoted in Chirwa, W.C. 2001: 10–11)

The government successfully engineered an environment of fear in which many people were afraid to voice their opinions even in the privacy of their own homes or with their closest friends and relatives (Muluzi et al 1999: 122–23). Even many Malawians living abroad were afraid to criticize Banda in publications or other public forums for fear that relatives in Malawi would suffer on their behalf (Zeleza 1996: 14).

The praise cult that was built prior to independence continued to be used, this time to legitimate Banda by enveloping him with never-ending adulation. The government established a number of national holidays—May 14 (Banda's birthday); July 6 (National Independence Day), and October 17 (Mother's Day)—each of which was celebrated with large national events, usually held in a stadium in one of the urban centers. These events usually comprised a sequence of activities that always included a long entertainment component featuring performances by numerous dance groups from across the country in addition to other types of performances, such as choirs and skits; speeches; and sometimes army and police processions; and they almost always ended with a soccer match. Groups of women performing circle dances always dominated the entertainment component. While these national meetings were held in one of the country's two largest cities, Blantyre or Lilongwe, each district frequently produced similar events on a smaller scale, bringing the country together in shared activity, connecting the center to the periphery (cf. Moore 1977: 154, Kertzer 1988: 23).

Politicians had to open every official speech by praising Banda and affirming his supremacy. He was always to be addressed by his official title, "His Excellency the Life President Dr. Hastings Kamuzu Banda, the Ngwazi." Any speech that failed to do so could be taken as a sign of disloyalty and could result in dismissal from the party. Schoolchildren were required to regularly express their adulation of Banda, and meetings in nonpolitical contexts often started with words of praise for the leader, while images of the president looked down from the walls of all businesses and offices (Muluzi et al. 1999: 122–23; Mkamanga 2000: 51–65). Banda's yearly crop-inspection tours created additional opportunities for the population to experience his leadership and authority. As he visited districts across the country, he was always welcomed by throngs of women who danced and sang his praises. Cédric Jourde, explaining the importance of such presidential tours in countries around the world, wrote that "the central element of touring is the very presence of the polity's supreme leader." These tours are crucial for the ruler "because his physical presence in different localities made his power more tangible" (2005: 423).

Banda's *Mbumba*

Writing about women across the continent and relevant to the Malawi experience, Gisela Geisler explained that "all too often, however, women's involvement in nationalist movements and liberation struggles led to no marked improvement in their rights and their ability to acquire influence in newly independent states" (2004: 13).[5] The leaders of the MCP co-opted the League of Malawi Women, transforming it from the political body for female activists that Chibambo and others had developed before independence into a peripheral organization that contained women's participation and largely restricted them from decision-making power. Through this process, the political singing and dancing of women activists, once used for liberation, was appropriated by the Banda government into both one of the most salient national symbols and a tool for repression controlled by the government through the party. Johannes Fabian noted that "colonial rulers and their successors have been aware of these threats and challenges and often have, with true Machiavellian determination, encouraged performance as entertainment and a way of channeling or co-opting social protest" (1990: 17). By hijacking women's political and performative bodies, Banda's government indicated awareness of their power and potential threat and attempted to control them.

Banda's government drew from a tradition of several of the matrilineal ethnic groups in the country, most notably the Chewa, of which Banda was a member (cf. Chirwa 2001: 15–17). In these matrilineal systems, a special relationship exists between a woman and either an older brother or sometimes a maternal uncle. The male relation is the authoritative male figure in a woman's life. It is to him she goes for help and support. When she wants to marry, her intended spouse discusses the possible marriage with this male figure. When marriage problems emerge, it is to this person that she goes. The woman in this relationship is called *mbumba* and the male is the *nkhoswe* (Mitchell 1956b: 146). As president, Banda declared himself the Nkhoswe number one to all Malawian women, making them his symbolic mbumba (Mkamanga 2000: 36–38; Mphande 1996: 82). In an interview on May 30, 2000, Nicholas Dausi, who served the Banda government in several capacities, the last of which was press secretary, explained, "As the Head of State, he could not have taken care only of his family at Chiwengo [Banda's natal home], he also had to take care—defend, protect, enhance, and develop the minds—of the women of Malawi together, without segregation [differentiating between them]." While some, such as Dausi, frame Banda's extension of this familial relationship to all women in Malawi as indicative of his commitment to the population, others were more critical. Emily Mkamanga contended that Banda's symbolic appropriation and application of this relationship to himself and all Malawian women was exploitative, paternalistic, and grounded in patronage (2000: 37).

Though she felt that this relationship was later used strategically, Rose Chibambo thought that initially, Banda may not have used the term as an exploitative strategy. She remembered first hearing Banda call the women his mbumba when he returned to Nyasaland in 1958. At the time, she interpreted it as a sign that Banda was concerned about the well-being of the people he had come to lead, especially the women. She felt strongly at the time that Banda understood the importance of women's involvement in politics (personal communication, February 4, 2000).

As their nkhoswe, Banda symbolically became their responsible relative or benefactor, a relationship grounded in asymmetrical power relations. A number of women interviewed long after Banda lost power continued to use this rhetoric in reference to both the Banda government and the party. MCP supporter Mayi Mhone was twenty-seven years old when I met her in Blantyre in 2000. A widow with five children, she engaged in small-scale business, selling charcoal and sometimes beans. She served at the time as the vice secretary at the area level of the MCP's women's league. When asked what the MCP had done for her, she responded, "I should just say that they [political leaders] are like a parent to all of us, and we are supposed to listen to what a parent says" (Group Interview with MCP Women, May 16, 2000; see Appendix B). In many of his speeches, Banda explicitly expressed his commitment to be a good patron and promised to look after and care for women. At a New Year's Celebration in 1992, Banda said, "This is what your Kamuzu wants—people to eat well, dress well and live in better houses, particularly Kamuzu's *mbumba*" ("Life President Joins Mbumba in Traditional Dances" 1992). As the women's nkhoswe and patron, he often took the credit in his speeches for having improved their lives, as is evident in the following quote, where he claims that before he came in 1958,

> [w]omen were trampled down by everybody . . . everybody. . . . Nobody thought about women except to make them cook for them. That's all. . . . So, I made up my mind even before I came that I was going to do something about my women. Therefore when I see my women happy and singing and dancing with their heads high, their necks bent with pride like that . . . it makes me happy, very happy. (Quoted in Chirwa 2001: 5)

Because the distinction between Banda and the Malawi Congress Party was not clear-cut, in the same way that the women were Banda's mbumba, they were also the MCP's mbumba. And as the party and the state were hardly distinguishable, they were also the nation's or state's mbumba. To have all female citizens, more than half of the population, at least symbolically tied to the state in this way was a very powerful political tool in maintaining autocratic rule, a pattern also evident in other parts of the world (see Anthias and Yuval-Davis 1994: 313).

In exchange for his patronage, Banda's mbumba were required to regularly express their gratitude and commitment to him. The women were organized through the League of Malawi Women, to which party women, meaning all women in the country of "indigenous African origins," had to belong. As party members, they had to own uniforms and be perpetually prepared to dance and sing Banda's praises at the frequently scheduled rehearsals, local and national functions, any gathering attended by the president, and various other occasions.

In the time I spent in the Nkhata Bay District and then later in the city of Blantyre, I met many women who had played important roles in the League of Malawi Women during Banda's rule. Mayi Mphase, Mayi Md. Longwe, and others who held important leadership roles explained how MCP officials used the organizational structure of the party to coordinate women's political dancing. At the smallest branch level in both rural and urban settings, the chairwoman of the League of Malawi Women organized regular practices, which occurred once or twice a week, every other week, or once a month. The frequency of practices and dancing varied throughout the country because the president passed through some areas more often than he did others. In remote areas in the north, such as Mayi Md. Longwe's home in Nsanje, women practiced and performed less frequently than in most other areas because they were not invited as often and government officials rarely came to their communities. The mother of my research assistant Simeon Nyirenda, Mayi O. Mhone, who had been the chairwoman in the branch where we lived with the Ngwira family near the town of Nkhata Bay, remembered that they had rehearsed once a week on Saturdays. In large cities and populated areas in the central and southern regions, practices were more frequent, sometimes as often as twice a week. Though the frequency differed, the party required all women to devote a significant portion of their time to rehearsals, during which they learned songs and developed and perfected complicated dance moves.

At practices, party leaders selected women to be dance leaders or chairwomen of their locales. The selection process was formalized in that leaders in the national hierarchy selected those at the regional level, who selected those at the district, and so on. Criteria for selection varied. Some women were selected because of their leadership skills or commitment to the party. Mayi Kondowe was a leader within the League of Malawi Women and a dance leader in the Nkhata Bay District. We met in March 1999 at her house in Kalambwe on the road leading into town. Her house was larger and better built than those of most of the women I interviewed in the district. It had several bedrooms and a large sitting room. Mayi Kondowe was very committed to and active in her Catholic church. In addition to providing for her own family, she regularly hosted schoolchildren who attended a school near her home. I met her because she was hosting Martha Tembo, a secondary student and daughter to famed performer Zabweka Tembo, whom I discuss later in this chapter. Martha Tembo usually spent the school year with Mayi Kondowe so that she could attend a secondary school far from her home in Nkhwali. Mayi Kondowe had been a committee member at the district level of the women's league and a dance leader during Banda's rule. She explained that in choosing women's league leaders, she had often considered how well a woman cared for her family and received visitors in her home, indicators of whether she would be a good leader. Others, such as Mayi E. Mhone, a woman in her early seventies who lived near us and had been an active dancer throughout Banda's rule, were chosen for their performance skills: "They [MCP officials] saw that we danced very well. They were happy with that, so we were chosen [in the 1970s] to be leaders" (personal communication, February 9, 1999). Others were selected so that they could be monitored. The late Mary Chiume, a sister of M.W.K. Chiume, lived in the town of Nkhata Bay during my 1998–1999 stay there. Unlike some of his family members and political associates, Mary Chiume did not follow her brother into exile, but continued to live in Malawi throughout Banda's presidency. Banda's speeches frequently vilified her brother and other political dissidents, and song texts frequently invoked violence against him. She and other family members had to suppress their political views and support of their brother under the watchful eye of the authoritarian state. At one point, she explained that the district leadership of the Chitukuko Cha Amayi M'Malawi, a suborganization of the League of Malawi Women, selected her to be a district committee member. Asked why she thought she was chosen, she explained that it was part of an investigation to determine whether or not she supported the government (personal communication, January 18, 1999).

Along with groups that were created at the branch levels, the League of Malawi Women also organized groups of dancers in schools and large companies (Mkamanga 2000: 54–55). At primary and secondary schools, girls were called "bornfrees" rather than mbumba, though their activities and functions were virtually the same as those of adult women. Queen Gondwe was a teacher for many years, later a headmistress, and then a minister in Banda's government. At the time of our interview, on June 13, 2000, in her home in Blantyre, she was running a human rights organization, the Promotion of Women in Politics, which she founded after the transition to multipartyism. She explained that she was troubled when she first moved to Malawi from Zambia, where she had grown up:

> I was asked to be in charge of the girl's section at a boarding [school]. And it was new to me to find that when any visitor came, the headmaster would come to me [and say], "Ms. Chirambo, we want the girls to go and dance." [I would respond,] "To go and dance, now at night?" [He would answer,] "Yes." So, the girls would go and dance. They would dance the whole night until the morning. The next day, they would be fast asleep, and they would miss their lessons. So, I got angry with that. I said, "I don't think we are going to promote anything here. These girls will be failures if they keep on dancing. For every person [government official] that comes here, you call them to come and dance. What for?" But then I was told, "You have to be careful. This is not how we behave here."

Similarly, Chancellor College, a branch of the University of Malawi, had a group of dancing mbumba, as did the main hospital in Lilongwe. According to David Kerr, mbumba dance groups were also organized in Zambia and Zimbabwe, countries with large populations of migrant laborers from Malawi (1998: 38).

In the week preceding a national event celebrating the Banda government, the official newspapers at the time, the *Daily Times* and *Malawi News,* teemed with stories describing the preparations transpiring across the country. Newspapers published on the day of an event, especially Banda's birthday and Independence Day, carried advertisement after advertisement from local companies congratulating the president. For days following the event, photographs of and stories describing dance groups, mbumba groups, singing choirs, and Banda's speeches reminded the population of the significance of the event, and reinforced that Banda held power and authority in the country. Events were also broadcast on the radio so that people in the most remote districts could experience them firsthand. Recordings of songs continued to be broadcast on the radio long after the event itself. Even after Banda was no longer president, street vendors continued to sell cassette recordings and videotapes of the mbumba performances.

When an event took place at the regional or national level, the party (government) provided transportation for women and other performers, sometimes on buses, but usually on big open-bed trucks upon which organizers would squeeze the maximum number of people, and then add a few more. This transportation was usually neither comfortable nor safe. People still tell stories about accidents that occurred during these trips, some of which resulted in fatalities (Mkamanga 2000: 49). Mayi Kondowe related one that happened on her way back from a celebration in Blantyre:

> I was involved in bus accidents three times. . . . The third time we were coming from Chikwina; then the bus stopped. My friend wanted

> to relieve herself. The bus started back up and hit her. She died instantly. This was at Dedza after we had bought some chips [French fries], but I didn't see my friend. I told my other friends that I couldn't see my friend, but then looking around, we saw that she was already dead. (Personal communication, March 12, 1999)

The transport provided was often not paid for by the government. The party frequently required individuals to volunteer their vehicles (K. Phumisa, personal communication, April 24, 1999; Dzimbiri 1998: 89). Along with performers, several members of the League of Malawi Youth and Malawi Young Pioneers were appointed to each vehicle to maintain control and security, or, as a former Malawi Young Pioneer and my research assistant the late Simeon Nyirenda put it, "to maintain peace there, that the women should be free" (personal communication, February 12, 1999).

In Lilongwe or Blantyre, dancers were accommodated often in schools, where the party provided them with food. Sometimes women and other performers received adequate accommodation; sometimes it was even good. In the following quote, Mayi Kondowe remembered one time that she was invited to fly from her home in Nkhata Bay to perform at the presidential residence, Sanjika Palace, in Blantyre. There, she was treated exceptionally well:

> When they [party officials] called, we met at the resthouse in Nkhata [Bay]. We went to Mzuzu, where we stayed in a hotel. They gave us baskets with our lunches. We boarded the plane, but they took our luggage. When we arrived at Chileka [airport in Blantyre], that is when we saw our luggage again. There were cars waiting for us. We got off the plane; then we got into these cars. We went to the Grainmil Hotel; others went to Mount Soche Hotel. . . . They took us and gave us keys. My room was number 22. They took us to this thing that we didn't know. We got on it, and [she simulates the sound of an elevator motor]. Then we were at the top. . . . We could call on the telephone, and just sit on the floor, and the food would arrive. (Personal communication, March 26, 1999)[6]

At other times, numerous women slept together in one room with little besides their *zitenje* (rectangular pieces of cloth; singular, *chitenje*) between them and the floor. There was frequently no running water for them to bathe or use for cooking or drinking. Sometimes there was not adequate food. If a woman did not have money, she could not eat (Mkamanga 2000: 45).

When Banda and other party dignitaries traveled throughout the country, much effort was made by the local party leadership to prepare for receiving the guests. Mayi Kondowe shared her memories of organizing for Banda's visits in Nkhata Bay District:

> When Kamuzu was coming, letters were written. From region to district, from district to area, from area to branch. We invited each other and formed a committee for receiving the visitors. There was a committee for looking after accommodations; another was a food committee. Members of the food committee slaughtered a cow and distributed it among leaders of the areas who contributed additional food items to cook a sumptuous feast for the visitors. The accommodation committee organized places for them to sleep. (Personal communication, March 12, 1999)

As Banda's mbumba, not only did they have to welcome MCP officials well; women also had to appear at all public functions cloaked in uniforms made of party cloth. This uniform, called the "national dress," consisted of a head scarf, a blouse, and a chitenje, a rectangular piece of cloth wrapped around as a skirt that reaches from the waist to the ankles, made from matching fabric depicting multiple images of Banda's face surrounded by the other party symbols of a rising sun and a rooster, as shown in Figure 3.1. (cf. Phiri 1998: 160). Judith Perani and Norma H. Wolff discussed the roles played by cloth and symbolic dress in African political contexts. Though they claimed to be writing about Africa generally, their focus is clearly on West African contexts, where elaborate traditions of cloth making and usage exist. About political power, they wrote, "[I]t is hard to imagine an African society where cloth in its many forms does not support leadership" (1999: 39; cf. Martin 1994: 402; 1995: 155–58). Though their descriptions of political leaders who collect luxury fabric and wear layers of handmade cloth to emphasize their "bigness" have little resonance in Malawi, cloth commemorating leaders and events has had important functions in Malawi as in other African countries (Spencer 1982).

When I asked Rose Chibambo the history of the MCP uniforms, she explained that the wearing of cloth with Banda's portrait was introduced after independence. In the 1950s, predating the arrival of Banda, the women in the executive of the NAC women's wing selected fabric with which they made matching outfits. She showed me a photograph in which she and other activists, probably sometime in the late 1950s, were at the airport welcoming a visitor from the U.S. State Department. Chibambo and the other women were wearing zitenje made from fabric decorated with a floral design, with a matching sash. In the photograph, she drapes a piece of fabric in the same design over the shoulder of the American wife of the dignitary, signifying solidarity between the foreign guest and the women activists. She explained that women in some of the NAC branches followed the lead of the leaders of the women's wing and selected their own fabric designs, so that they were identifiable as a group (personal communication, February 4, 2000; cf. Mkamanga 2000: 41). The wearing of uniforms made of matching cloth by female members of different types of organizations is common in this part of Africa. Margaret Strobel, for example, explained that members of women's *lelemama* dance association in Mombassa in the 1920s to 1940s wore outfits made from identical cloth (1976: 187). Similarly, Ch. Didier Gondola explained that members of La Reconnaissance, a woman's organization in the city of Léopoldville (now Kinshasa) in what is now the Democratic Republic of the Congo, in the late 1950s wore uniforms made from matching colorful wax prints to their gatherings (1997: 74). In contemporary Malawi, at weddings in urban areas, women relatives and close friends of the bride or groom sometimes wear outfits made out of the same fabric design. Similarly, members of many women's church groups wear matching uniforms (Henderson forthcoming; Henderson and Gilman 2004). Activists therefore drew upon existing dress practices to express affiliation with one another and the NAC organization.

After independence, the fabric that women were required to wear to party functions came in different colors, mostly green, blue, and red, and were always covered with the ubiquitous images of Banda. The color uniform a woman wore depended on the district in which she lived. In addition to the regular uniform, specialty cloth was printed to commemorate special occasions, such as the government's silver jubilee. Emily Mkamanga contended that the government introduced new fabric designs each year as a profitable economic venture (2000: 41). When this cloth was fashioned into the required uniforms, Banda's visage shone from the fronts and backs of blouses and the front and back panels of skirts.

Strict rules about the placement of the president's likeness were enforced. It was forbidden to wear clothing in which Banda's face was cut or had a seam running through it. The cloth skirt had to be carefully worn so that the portrait was prominently positioned in the back when a woman danced, but upon which she would not sit. Writing about the uniform requirement, Lupenga Mphande contended that Banda's obsession about the placement of his face [on women's breasts and buttocks] "reveals not only the bizarre dimensions of Banda's aesthetics, but also the way he expropriated capitalist advertising conventions to turn (female) body and (male) body-politic into circulating advertisements of himself" (1996: 82).

As with the one described by Philip Short in the last chapter during the latter part of the independence movement, the political rallies—large ones at the national level and smaller ones at the regional or district levels—followed a formulaic structure:

> By mid-morning on the day of the event, thousands of women gathered at the site, often a stadium. When Banda arrived, women lined both sides of the road, sometimes for as far as two miles, welcoming him with their singing and dancing. After Banda was led to his guarded stand, a Protestant minister came to the podium and asked "God to give Banda a long life, good health and wisdom in order for him to rule

> for eternity." The prayer was followed by a short address by the Mistress of Ceremonies, usually a high-level figure in the League of Malawi Women. After her speech, she invited one performance group after the other into the arena to entertain the President as well as the rest of the audience; the entertainment segment averaged about five hours. (Mkamanga 2000: 45–49)

Mayi Kondowe described the dancing that took place at more localized gatherings in the town of Nkhata Bay:

> The Young Pioneers used to line us up from here all the way to Chinteche turnoff [approximately 1 mile up the road from her house]. We were there when the helicopter landed. We welcomed Kamuzu with our dancing. We danced alongside him as he walked from where he was dropped off to where the rally was. We sat on the ground in front of the platform for him. Then, welcome remarks were made. After everything that was important was said, they would announce that there would be dances for him. They called malipenga, chilimika, Nkhata Bay chiwoda. When they called Nkhata Bay is when my friend Nyamphase [Mayi Mphase] and I led the songs. (Personal communication, March 12, 1999)

The performances conformed to the two trajectories for dance outlined for the independence movement. The first was the dancing by the mbumba. The second was a series of performances by established dance groups—male, female, or coed—that existed outside the political arena and showcased genres from across the country.

As described by Mayi Kondowe, dancing mbumba framed the event: Women clad in Banda regalia escorted the president to his seat upon his arrival and back to his car at his departure, all the while singing and dancing. Women also sang spontaneously throughout the course of the event, and multiple groups of mbumba danced during the entertainment segment. Figure 3.1 depicts women wearing red party uniforms dancing in celebration of National Independence Day on July 6, 1989.

Regardless of where a rally occurred, building on the practices of activists during the independence movement, women performed variants of female circle dances, common to many ethnic groups in Malawi and neighboring countries. Because women danced these styles so much during the Banda era, there was much interinfluence among variants. As a result, a somewhat generalizable form, though still sometimes distinguished as identifiable genres, emerged that many Malawians refer to as *gule wa chipani* (the dance of politics) (Kerr 1998: 38). The genres comprising *gule wa chipani* were similar enough that a woman familiar with one could easily participate in another,

Figure 3.1 Women in full red Banda regalia dancing on July 6, 1989, at Kamuzu Stadium, Blantyre, to commemorate National Independence Day. *(Courtesy of Clara Henderson.)*

enabling women of different ethnic groups to perform together. Women at a small, localized rally would usually dance the variant associated with the dominant ethnic group in that area. Women party members in Nkhata Bay District usually danced the Tonga-variant chiwoda, whereas in the Ntchisi district, Chewa women danced the variant *chimtali*, and in the Rumphi district, Tumbuka women danced *mbotosha*. For those ethnic groups that did not have a variant already in their repertoires, women often danced the form either of a neighboring group or of the dominant group in their district. Ngoni women living in the Ntcheu District, for example, danced the Chewa chimtali, whereas those living in the north often danced the Tumbuka mbotosha. At large-scale rallies that brought together women from different districts and ethnic groups, women from one district often performed the dance forms associated with the dominant ethnic group from their home districts. Though generalizations are problematic, for the sake of clarity, I refer to all such variants as "chiwoda-like," only because chiwoda is the variant associated with the Tonga women in Nkhata Bay District, where I conducted the bulk of my research.

Chiwoda-like dance forms are especially suited to political events because of their flexible format and because they are relatively easy to learn. No specific number of women is needed, though dancers and audiences usually prefer having more because they energize a performance. As few as ten women can dance together, or at very large events, as many as several hundred. Women, usually of marriageable age and older, perform chiwoda, though girls and women of any age can participate within the circles, which rotate to the rhythms of male drummers beating conical drums built from long cylindrical wooden bodies, whose drumheads are made from an animal skin stretched over one side. Women usually wear their daily clothing (though never trousers) covered by a cloth (*chitenje*) wrapped around to make a long skirt, and they may also wear a cloth tied into a head covering; the costume is thus also easily adaptable to the political arena.

Several bootlegs of videos filmed and edited by the Ministry of Information during Banda's rule were still sold by street vendors in the country's cities at the time of my research. One, titled *Some Malawian Dances*, documented main events that took place in 1992. The video began with scenes of several groups of women performing chiwoda-like dances at Sanjika Palace in Blantyre, the regional center of the south and the country's largest city, to the voiceover of a male narrator: "The year started on a good note of affection between the Life President and his mbumba from the southern region who performed traditional dances at Sanjika Palace in Blantyre as they do at the start of each year." A group of about seven dancers, all teenage girls, dressed from head to toe in Banda cloth, moved rhythmically to drumming by two adult men wearing dark suits. That a video about national events began with images of female dancers covered with Banda's image and with this narration was evidence of how important the dancing mbumba were to the symbolic portrayal of the country. Footage of young men dancing *gule wamkulu*, the dance of the Chewa Nyau religious society, cut in. Grass skirts tied around waists, grass tufted around shins and ankles, heads covered in large feathered headdresses, the dancers kicked the ground athletically, occasionally dropping dramatically to their knees, only to bounce back up to continue kicking. Behind them stood a group of between five and seven adult women clad in colorful Banda regalia singing next to the male drumbeaters, the term usually used to refer to drummers in Malawi.[7] The lyrics, only partially audible on the video, clearly praised the president. Footage of a second group of women dancing a chiwoda-like genre quickly cut off the footage of the Nyau dancers; this time a much larger group, two to three hundred adult women fully clad in their green mbumba uniforms moved rhythmically around two male drummers dressed in trousers and T-shirts. Slightly bent forward at the waist, the dancers rotated around the drummers clockwise, their arms extended forward, sometimes swinging back and forth; their feet stepped synchronized patterns while their hips and buttocks moved seemingly independently from the rest of their bodies.

The video then documented one important event after the other in the year: the visits of heads of states from neighboring countries, Banda's annual crop inspection tour, his birthday, the Mother's Day celebration, and the MCP's annual convention. Regardless of the event, women clad in Banda regalia singing songs of gratitude and praise were omnipresent. The gendering of participation was especially evident at the party's convention. Important party dignitaries and members of parliament, male and female, sat side by side: The men all wore dark suits and ties; the women, regardless of rank, donned full mbumba regalia. Behind the spacious seating of the high-ranking convention participants, separated from the party heavyweights, hundreds of women all wearing their Banda uniforms squeezed onto benches and occasionally contributed to the convention by singing songs that glorified Banda. No similar presence of lower-ranking male party members was evident.

Another video called *Kamuzu Banda in Karonga*, also purchased from a street vendor, documented two political rallies held by the MCP during the campaigning for the first multiparty elections in 1993, one in the town of Nkhata Bay and the other in Karonga, a lakeshore town in the Karonga district to the north of Nkhata Bay. Though they occurred during the political turmoil leading to the first multiparty elections, these events nevertheless resembled those that took place throughout Banda's rule. The Nkhata Bay event provides a good example of a more localized rally at the district level. Performances by a number of established dance groups were featured at this event, though performances by groups of women dancing chiwoda dominated. Each group of chiwoda danced separately; from what I have learned about how women were organized, I surmise that each came from a different school, area, or branch within the district. In an especially energetic moment of one of the chiwoda group's performances, two women moved in place in the center of the performance arena, their backs facing the three drummers, who beat interlocking patterns on single-headed conical drums. Two of the drummers wore button-down short-sleeve shirts made from red Banda fabric; the third wore a red T-shirt. As the pounding rhythms soared, the two song leaders stretched their hands to either side, simulating the wings of an airplane; their nasal voices rose above the pounding drums to initiate a song that began:

Iyo Ndege	That's it, airplane
Iyo Ndege	That's it, airplane
Iyo Ndege	That's it, airplane
Yadera pa Nkhata Bay, iyo	It has landed in Nkhata Bay, that's it

The song referred to the aircraft that had recently delivered Banda to their town. The rest of the women, around one hundred, also covered from head to toe in Banda's image, danced in two concentric circles: each woman faced the backside of the woman in front of her, creating two rotating columns. The women circled around the drummers and the lead singers in close proximity.

With their arms outstretched, their hips jutted forward then thrust back; their buttocks rotated rhythmically as they slowly progressed, careful to maintain the circle formation. At one point, the dancers opened the circle, creating a wide pathway between the stage and the lead singers, now located in the center of the circle. They continued to move in place in this partial circle and sing while one of the song leaders, arms stretched to simulate airplane wings, danced to the end of the red carpet that led up to Banda's seat on the stage. Still moving in place, she summoned Banda to join her, an expected and exciting moment in every rally of the time. Supported by his cane, Banda looked old and unstable, yet still dignified in his black suit and homburg. With the help of an aid, he shakily descended the steps and progressed along the red carpet until he faced the dance leader. The other women's performances swelled feverishly, fervently moving back and forth, back and forth, as Banda swayed slowly, his fly whisk held high.

Fitting within praise song traditions and continuing the messages developed during the independence movement, mbumba songs extolled Banda to the status of a deity and gave him all the credit for leading the country to independence, either ignoring the roles of the other leaders of the movement or relegating them to dissidents. The following example was sung by a group of women at the Nkhata Bay rally in Chitonga:

LEADER:	*Amama imwe, tili mbumba za wa Ngwazi*
ALL:	*Yewo*
LEADER:	*Ati amama, imwe, amama, ise tili mbumba za wa Ngwazi*
ALL:	*Yewo*
LEADER:	*Yewo, yewo, eh, A Ngwazi wakakalipa*
ALL:	*A Ngwazi wakakalipa na ku Zomba, "Stupid federation wa charo ichi na"*
LEADER:	*Mwe tionge Nkhoswe*
ALL:	*Yewo yatiombola*
LEADER:	*Tionge wa Ngwazi*
ALL:	*Yewo, mtendere ku Malawi, eh*
LEADER:	*Ati, wamama, imwe a mama, ise tikutenge ku Sanjika na*
ALL:	*Yewo*
LEADER:	*Ati amama imwe amama ise tili mbumba za a Ngwazi*
ALL:	*Yewo*
LEADER:	*Yewo A Ngwazi wakakalipa*
ALL:	*Angwazi wakakalipa na ku Zomba, "Stupid federation na chalo ichi na"*
LEADER:	*Tiyiwonge Nkhoswe*
ALL:	*Yewo, yatiombola*
LEADER:	*Tiwonge wa dada*
ALL:	*Yewo, mtendere ku Malawi*

LEADER:	You women, we are the Ngwazi's mbumba
ALL:	Thank you
LEADER:	Say, you women, women, we are the Ngwazi's mbumba
ALL:	Thank you
LEADER:	Thank you, thank you, yes, the Ngwazi shouted
ALL:	The Ngwazi shouted there in Zomba, "Stupid federation in this country"
LEADER:	We should thank the Nkhoswe
ALL:	Thank you, he saved us
LEADER:	We should thank the Ngwazi
ALL:	Thank you, freedom in Malawi, yes
LEADER:	Say, you women, we should go to Sanjika
ALL:	Thank you
LEADER:	Say, women, we women, we are the Ngwazi's mbumba
ALL:	Thank you
LEADER:	Thank you, the Ngwazi shouted
ALL:	The Ngwazi shouted to those in Zomba, "Stupid federation in this country"
LEADER:	We should thank the nkhoswe
ALL:	Thank you, he saved us
LEADER:	We should thank the father
ALL:	Thank you, freedom in Malawi

Thirty years after the country attained independence, the songs continued to thank Banda for his role in fighting British colonialism, or shouting against the "stupid federation." Other songs at this event thanked him for his more recent accomplishments as president. Several, for example, expressed gratitude to Banda for encouraging Malawians to farm, a cornerstone of his domestic policy. Others thanked him for supporting women and several thanked him for sending women overseas on airplanes. A number of the songs simply repeated several ways of expressing gratitude.

Examples of songs from other sources illustrate the scope of the song messages. The following sung in Chichewa likens Banda to Moses:

Mau anu a Ngwazi, mau anu
Mudamenya leki Malawi
Taoloka Yorodano, taoloka!
Taoloka lero taoloka
Taoloka Yorodano, taoloka!
Mose waku Malawi
Ndiyo Kamuzu Banda
Adamenya leki Malawi
Taoloka Yorodano, taoloka

With your words only, with your words only
You hit the waters of Lake Malawi
We have crossed Jordan, we have crossed!
We have crossed now, we have crossed
We have crossed Jordan, we have crossed!
The Moses of Malawi
Is Kamuzu Banda
He beat the waters of Lake Malawi
We have crossed Jordan, we have crossed!
(Chirwa 2001: 15)

Others were used to vilify dissidents, such as this Chitonga song:

Afyengi wija, afyengi wija
Akulimbana ndi moto, Ngwazi!
A Ngwazi mbachatonda
Ndi muomboli mu Malawi

They will burn, they will burn
Those who play with fire, Ngwazi!
The Ngwazi is a hero
He is a saviour in Malawi
(Chirwa 2001: 13)

In this example, threats were expressed toward all dissidents. Others were directed toward specific individuals, including M.W.K. Chiume, who was the target of much vilification. Other songs, such as this Chichewa one, advertised the MCP logo, symbols, and slogans:

Tambala akamalira!
Kokoliko ooo oooo
Tambala akamalira!
Kokoliko ooo oooo
Tambala akamalira,
Kokoliko, liko, liko, kwacha!
Amalawi?
Amalawi ayamba, Kunyadira?
Kunyandira Kamuzu
Filidomo? filidomo, kwacha!

When the cockerel crows!
Crows, crows, crows . . . [cock-a-doodle-doo]
When the cockerel crows!

Crows, crows, crows [cock-a-doodle-doo]
[When the cockerel crows!
Crows . . . it is dawn]
[Malawians?]
Malawians are proud[?]
They are proud of freedom
They are proud of Kamuzu
Freedom [?], freedom, it's dawn!
(Chirwa 2001: 9)[8]

In the second trajectory of the political use of dance, the entertainment segment of the Nkhata Bay rally comprised performances by "established dance groups"—all male, all female, or coed—in addition to occasional choirs, acting groups, and comedians. As during the independence movement, by bringing together performers from each district in the country for national events, the government disseminated messages of national unity and projected Banda's legitimacy. For smaller rallies, such as this district-based Nkhata Bay example, organizers brought together performers from across the district, which gave everyone in the population direct experience of the party and contributed to expressions of local and national unity. In this trajectory, performers belonged to organized groups outside their political participation and were invited because of their entertainment skills rather than their membership in the party, though, as with all Malawian citizens, they were required to be MCP members. Unlike the mbumba, who wore the national dress, performers in this category usually wore the costumes appropriate to their specific dance forms, though they sometimes integrated pieces of Banda fabric into their costumes. They also adapted their song texts to include praise for the president and the party. Though men as well as women participated as dancers within this framework, it differed significantly from the dancing by the mbumba. All women had to participate as mbumba regardless of their dance abilities, while male dancers were invited only as members of highly skilled dance groups. It was considered an honor to be selected and for the most part was not a product of large-scale coercion.

At this Nkhata Bay rally, numerous local groups participated in the entertainment segment. A number of choirs, mostly composed of children from local schools, sang songs praising Banda, as did a group of men from a local church. Their songs thanked Banda for his visit and praised him for what he had done for the country. A group of about fifteen elderly men clad in skirts and accessories made from strips of animal skins stamped their feet dramatically as they performed *ingoma*, a signature dance form of the Ngoni. The Ngoni did not constitute a substantial ethnic group in the district. The inclusion of Ngoni performers suggested that they were brought to this rally by regional party organizers, or that Ngoni men who happened to be living in the district were invited because of their dance abilities. Zabweka Tembo—an important leader in his community and church and a famous performer—entertained Banda with his idiosyncratic group, the School Band, whose members were schoolchildren in his home in Nkhwali. For one song, the children, their bodies held rigid dressed in school uniforms, lined up in row-and-column formation; they held hand-carved wooden toy guns at their sides. Mr. Tembo shouted, "When the blood fuckin' Kanyama Chiume can be found here, Soldiers, what can we do?" The children responded by positioning their guns on their shoulders, ready to fire, and energetically retorted, "We can shoot!" while they shook their shoulders and hips dramatically and shouted "wa, wa, wa" representing the sound of exploding firearms.

The entertainment segments of rallies were followed by gift-giving sessions during which attendees gave material offerings to Banda. A series of speeches by politicians followed in an established order of precedence as dictated by the MCP constitution, an enactment and reinforcement of gradations of status (Constitution of the Malawi Congress Party 1965):

1. The Life President
2. Members of the National Executive Committee
3. Ministers
4. Parliamentary Secretaries
5. Regional Chairmen
6. National Chairmen of the Leagues of Malawi Women and Youth
7. Chairmen of District Committee of MCP
8. Members of Parliament
9. Chairmen of District Councils

Note that the national chairmen of the Leagues of Malawi Women and Youth had lower status than the regional chairmen of the main body, an indication of the lower status of the women's wing to the main body, or as Queen Gondwe put it, the "men's body" (personal communication, June 13, 2000).

Banda's speeches always included much self-praise as well as admiration of and thanks to the dancers, especially "his" mbumba, who pleased him so much with their expressions of happiness and gratitude. His rhetoric was resplendent with his dedication to promoting traditional culture, and he often pointed to the dances performed at these events as proof of his commitment. Banda's rhetoric contested the idea that African dancing was sinful, a sentiment frequently expressed by European missionaries. He declared that Europeans were wrong: Not only was there nothing inherently sinful about African dancing, but these dance forms should be celebrated:

> When I came in 1958, our traditional dances were dying because the missionaries of all denominations, particularly the missionaries of

> my own church, the CCAP [Church of Central Africa Presbytery] told my people that dancing was sin. . . . Do not let anyone make you believe that if you dance your own dance you are not going to heaven. . . . There is nothing wrong with dancing any African dance. That is what I have said many, many times. Here, men dance by themselves, women there. But in Europe and America, when I was there, what did I see? A married man with another man's wife, a married woman with another woman's husband. . . . If God is going to burn anyone for dancing, he is *not* going to burn you. He is going to burn the white man—the Americans, the British, the French and the Germans. . . . They have their own dances. So why should *chimdidi* be sin? Why should *chioda* [chiwoda] be sin? Why should *Ingoma* be sinful? Do not believe anyone who tells you that. If anyone tells you that, say Kamuzu says: "*you are a liar*!" (Quoted in Chirwa 2001: 15)

Banda's position valuing local cultural practices in opposition to European ones resonated with those of some of his colleagues in other African countries, including Kenneth Kaunda in Zambia (Crehan 1994), Mobutu Sese Seseko in Zaire, now Democratic Republic of the Congo (Fabian 1990: 270), and Léopold Sedar Senghor in Senegal (Castaldi 2006). Kelly Askew distinguished between African presidents who after independence promoted local cultural practices as a response to the cultural devastation of colonialism—such as Senegal's Senghor, Zaire's Mobutu, and Tanzania's Nyerere—and those who emphasized political developments over cultural, such as Ghana's Kwame Nkrumah (2002: 170). Banda did a combination of both.

Banda's speeches also reiterated whom the current enemies of the state were, warning people to watch out for them as well as to report any dissenting behavior. These messages were repeated in song texts, such as in the example of Zabweka Tembo's School Band.

Banda's mbumba always welcomed him and saw him off when he traveled internationally, and the airport was a common site for the expression of rejoicing at the accomplishments of the leader. Hundreds, sometimes thousands, of women lined up in their full mbumba regalia along the tarmac, singing praise as Banda and other MCP dignities took off and landed. Live recordings of these airport scenes were broadcast nationally on the radio, allowing others in the country to participate in the jubilation.

Sometimes the party transported women by plane to Blantyre or Lilongwe to perform at national events, contributing to the association of airports with political festivities. Mayi Kondowe explained that she flew on an airplane because when Kamuzu came to the north, the women sang the following song:

Tikumba kukwera ndege bwana	We want to ride a plane, sir
Tikumba kukwera ndege bwana	We want to ride a plane, sir

Having heard his mbumba's wish, Kamuzu sent a plane. Mayi Kondowe told me about her plane ride. "I sat down. They passed out sweets. I wasn't scared. I was so happy. I was so happy that I was singing in the plane." Without Banda's generosity, she explained that "she would have died without experiencing going on a plane" (personal communication, March 26, 1999).

On several occasions, Banda sent women, complete in their Banda attire, overseas to Britain, Germany, or Taiwan. According to the late Horace Somanje, a journalist and Banda supporter whom I met through mutual friends in Blantyre, Banda sent these women abroad because "he wanted his mbumba to be educated. And to him, he said, education is not only going to college, but also traveling" (personal communication, January 5, 2000). Yet, a number of the women I interviewed who had the opportunity to travel internationally as part of a mbumba contingent lived in poverty when I interviewed them, having gained little long-term benefit from their international exposure. Mayi Md. Longwe was one of the select few who visited Britain as one of Banda's mbumba, an opportunity she never would otherwise have had. At the time of our conversation, on February 17, 1999, her poverty was apparent. Her mud-brick house was small and slowly eroding from the heavy rains. My hosts in Nsanje told me that Mayi Md. Longwe's husband lived away from her in the town of Nkhata Bay, leaving her to provide for her divorced daughters and their many grandchildren. Her poverty was striking in relationship to her story of having once boarded a jet airplane, passport in hand, and able to see another part of the world, something most Malawians were too poor to ever experience. The opportunity provided her by Banda's government seemed to have left her mostly with happy memories. A more plausible interpretation for why Banda flew mbumba to other countries was that it was part of his larger effort to impress the international world that he enjoyed popular support and was accepted as the legitimate ruler by Malawians despite international criticism of his dictatorial practices (cf. Kertzer 1988: 33).

As Banda's mbumba, all Malawian women were lumped together into a single identifiable unit regardless of education, professional status, or political position. Speeches by government officials and Banda and references in newspaper articles frequently referred to "the mbumba," ascribing them with a single opinion, which each individual could not have shared (e.g., "Malawi One-Party State through Ballot" 1992). Considering all women as one entity implied that their primary significance was in their largely symbolic capacities as mbumba rather than as individuals with varied skills and potential for contributing to the state. As the mbumba of both Banda and the nation, Malawian women became the embodiments of "the traditional" or "African" way of life, while the men in leadership positions, dressed in their suits and speaking English, represented European ways and wielded status and ultimately the greatest power (cf. Geisler 1987). This gendering within the hybridity of the emergent state culture was detrimental to women, contributing to a binary and hierarchical system. The majority of women were ultimately positioned in the less powerful category, though symbolically they upheld the highly valued "tradition," making it difficult for them to contest their roles, a point I return to in Chapter 6 (Gilman 2004; Henderson and Gilman 2004).

Mbumba, Sex, and Banda

Banda was unusual among African leaders for having never officially married and for holding the presidency without a wife to fill the position of first lady, though Cecilia Kadzamira, more popularly known as "Mama," served as the official hostess. Banda was known for having very strict notions about sexuality and the impropriety of displaying or even discussing anything that might be construed as sexually suggestive.[9] His attempts to control eroticized behavior and displays, especially those of women, were expressed through his official dress code, which in 1971, through the Decency in Dress Act, legislated against women wearing trousers, short skirts, or skirts with slits (Short 1974: 280; cf. Hollander 1993: 312; Bastian 1996).[10] These prohibited clothing items drew attention to a woman's thighs and buttocks, two areas considered particularly erogenous in Malawi, as in many other parts of the continent. The dancing women wore long zitenje that reached to their ankles, concealing the definitions of their bodies and symbolizing sexual propriety. At the same time, their dancing consisted of eroticized hip and thigh movements directed toward the male politicians, notably Banda himself, expressing the opposite of what was intended by the long skirts. The dance movements in interaction with the dress had a transformative effect on the message: from one of modesty to one of explicit sensuality and sexuality.

Banda always made sure that he had the optimum view of women's dancing bodies. Anthony Mawaya and Nandini Patel quote a male member of Parliament describing the life president's attitude toward women dancers:

> The view between the life president and the dancers must not be distracted in any way. It is a directive from His Excellency the Life President that is why anyone obstructing the view it is not that one sitting who suffers it is the poor Regional Chairman . . . who is told in a very angry mood to run and correct the situation. . . . . sometimes we are scholded in the presence of our wives . . . H.E. [His Excellency] has said that dancing means the feet, the legs, the arms, the neck, the head. If you cannot see all these you will not enjoy it. Now, he has said it personally. When these women are sitting make sure they are not obstructing, the beautiful feet of the game [*sic*], the leg,

> the body, the arm. . . . The moment you see that someone is obstructing the feet, your duty is there. The whole body must be seen. (1995: 9)

This quote illustrates the extent to which party officials were directed to ensure that Banda enjoyed the best view possible of the dancing women's bodies.

As mentioned in the earlier description of the Nkhata Bay event, during a rally, Banda always entered the throng of undulating women, waved his fly whisk high, and selected a woman with whom to dance. There was a possible contradiction between Banda's emphasis on sexual propriety and his obvious pleasure in viewing and interacting with women's bodies, a topic that still evokes much speculation in contemporary Malawi. Banda's behavior also suggested that controlling women's dress might have had more to do with a strategy to control women than it did with any sincere concern about their well-being (cf. Hollander 1993: 312).

The sexual dimension of women performing was not always limited to dancing. Pervasive allegations suggest that one of the responsibilities of leaders in the League of Malawi Women was to select young women to be the sexual partners of ministers and other important government officials when they traveled within the country. Some women purportedly not only were dancing for the party, but also were expected to offer sexual favors (Mkamanga 2000: 81; Lwanda 1996: 203; Chiume, personal communication, January 18, 1999).

Repression

The institution of praise performances during Banda's rule was repressive: The government and party officials forced women to dance in the service of Banda, the MCP, and the state, regardless of women's individual political leanings, economic levels, health, special needs, desires, and so on. Women in Malawi still tell stories of their suffering during this time, such as the following narrative told by Mayi Masekesa, a UDF supporter when I interviewed her in Blantyre on April 25, 2000:

> There was a certain time when I was about to collapse at the stadium. . . . I had just had an operation at the hospital. I had just been discharged. My baby was only one month old. They came to tell me that I had to go to the stadium. My husband went outside and told them, "My wife is still recovering from a C-section. How can she participate?" They said, "It is not your concern. We just want your wife to go and dance. Modern operations are no problem. So she

> should go to the stadium. The baby is okay, isn't she?" So from there, I went to the stadium. They forced me to dance the songs. I was about to collapse. I had pains from the healing wounds. Afterwards, I fell down. . . . They took me aside and later told me to go home because they believed that I was really okay. My husband was about to be implicated, had it not been that a certain woman intervened. They wanted to arrest him because he was interfering with the affairs of women, which were not his concern. He was called to appear before the MCP area chairman, to be warned of his interference on the affairs of women. He was told that if he did that again, he would be arrested. . . . So after that, he stopped interfering, and we used to go and dance.

A woman could not use poverty as an excuse for not owning a uniform. Asked what would happen if a woman claimed that she could not afford the fabric, Mayi Mphase explained that if another woman had two uniforms, party officials would take one and give it to the person who needed it (personal communication, March 12, 1999). Loveness Schafer, a Malawian friend and colleague of the author's living in the United States, explained that members of the Malawi Young Pioneers would come to a woman's house and take "anything from your house, [saying] 'we won't give it back to you until you buy the cloth'" (Schafer, personal communication, November 14, 1995). Asked about these allegations, former Malawi Young Pioneer and current UDF dancer Mayi Chapola, whom I interviewed in Blantyre on May 2, 2000, answered, "Yes, we were doing that . . . sometimes we felt sorry. We would warn a house and tell their children to take care. If they could not afford to buy their children party cards . . . we could not continue. A guilty conscience would strike us, especially when they were our relatives."

Forcing women to sing and dance was part of a larger strategy of intimidation. Following the Cabinet Crisis and throughout Banda's rule, performers sang songs against the former ministers who were termed traitors to the state (Mphande1996: 91). In the northern region, where M.W.K. Chiume was from, songs against him were pervasive, while in the southern region, the home of Chipembere and Bwanausi, songs against them dominated. Mary Chiume remembered that she and her sisters had no choice but to sing songs, such as the following, that castigated their brother:

Chikanya, choka kuno, yayi	Big Kanya, get out of here, no
Chikanyama chaliya waka	Big Kanyama is just crying
Ise, mbumba za Kamuzu	We, the mbumba of Kamuzu
Muno m'Malawi	Here in Malawi
Tijuvwala salu za Kamuzu	We wear the cloth of Kamuzu

In a conversation at her house in the town of Nkhata Bay on January 18, 1999, Mary Chiume related how the chairwoman would come and stand next to her sisters and her to ensure that they were saying the words clearly, enunciating the name of their brother. Party officials frequently bullied her, saying that she had failed to do so. She would then have to defend herself by insisting that she had, and then she would sing "Kanyama" louder in the next verse. I asked how singing against her brother made her feel. She explained that eventually the words stopped having meaning. She knew that her brother was safe in Tanzania. She explained, however, that it upset her brother who could not believe that his own family sang against him. She elaborated that there was no way for him to understand that they had no choice, and that the words had become meaningless. Such use of song texts served as social control, further reinforcing social norms (cf. Strobel 1976: 193).

Through the heavy-handed control and censorship of performances, party leaders tried to stifle the possibility that women and other performers could use song texts as avenues for resistance. As explained in Chapter 1, in local praise singing practices, subordinates often sing songs that praise a leader while simultaneously expressing criticism of the same person. Through these songs, individuals fulfill their performative roles of panegyrizing while taking advantage of socially sanctioned opportunities to express criticism. Activists in the movement for independence adapted this practice. Rather than criticizing the same people or entities that they praised, praise was directed toward the NAC and its leaders while critical messages were reserved exclusively for the British and their imperial endeavors (White 1987: 217; Vaughan 1998: 174–75). This difference is significant because it ultimately restricted a mechanism that those in subordinate positions had used to communicate indirectly with their leaders. The movement's songs encapsulated only messages of unity, eliminating important avenues for communication between those at different strata within the NAC's hierarchical organizational structure. Further entrenching this adaptation, praise articulated in songs during Banda's rule was directed toward the party and president, while criticism was restricted to their opponents. As described by Mary Chiume, party officials listened carefully to all songs during rehearsals to suppress anything that could be read as dissension, whether through direct statements, metaphors, or coded means. This repression retracted local means of allowing controlled dissent within unequal power hierarchies, greatly reducing the potential for the socially sanctioned expression of criticism through song texts by subordinates. Nicholas Dausi, a high-ranking MCP official during and after Banda's presidency, thought that this stifling of criticism was one reason why the MCP eventually lost power. He explained that this "tendency of praising everything, it cost us because when people are not allowed to criticize, they suffocate." He recited a quote that he attributed to Socrates: "I am wise because

I know that I am foolish," and then explained that "you can only know that you are foolish when you are criticized" (Dausi, personal communication, May 30, 2000).

The relationship that Banda instituted between himself and all women in Malawi not only was repressive to the women, but also extended to Banda's relationships with men in the general population, as was evident in the narrative given by Mayi Masekesa about the party's response to her husband's concern about her health. Women were instructed that if their husbands went against the government, they should turn them in, as was explained by Kaliyoma Phumisa in an interview on April 24, 1999:

> There were certain families where you could not even trust your own wives because women had the best of the Malawi Congress Party. Not just getting money and things like that. But Kamuzu Banda used to call them, "My mbumba, my women, my women, my women. . . ." He used to encourage them. "Your husband is speaking something bad about me. You report that to my people! We will see what will happen." There are a few people who really suffered because reports were given to the party people by their own wives. There were women who would report against their own husbands, and then a Malawi Congress Party vehicle could come over here to their door and take away their furniture and explain that it was "because you are speaking bad about Kamuzu Banda"; [they would] take the furniture, take you away.

Similarly, David Kerr provided this song example:

> Husband, better buy me a dress
> How do I face Ngwazi (Kamuzu) without it?

Kerr explained that "the song contained an implied threat that she could have her husband detained (a not uncommon incident), if he refused to buy the uniform" (Kerr 1998: 39). This created a situation in which many men did not trust their own wives (Zeleza 1996: 14). In the following quote, my research assistant the late Simeon Nyirenda, a strong supporter of Banda and former member of the Malawi Young Pioneers, implied that Banda hoped to gain women's trust so that they would be more committed to him than to their husbands or villages and in effect become a spy network:

> He was doing that to make women be free. He believed that women can do so much more politics than men. Because, at least, a woman cannot hide anything, but a man can hide something in his heart or in his mind, doing it secretly. But the woman can reveal everything that has gone bad at home, or even in the village. So that's why, it was

> like a message to Dr. Banda that at least, if I can like women, then I can hear things more easily than with men. (Personal communication, February 12, 1999)

The party required families to accept that cultural norms regarding husband and wife as well as other kin relations were not as important as were the relationships imposed by the party. A man who complained that he wanted his wife home fulfilling her economic and domestic responsibilities rather than out rehearsing and dancing was considered a potential dissident. As a committed member of the party (and there was no choice), a person had to accept the situation (Chirwa, W.C. 2001: 17). When women were called to dance, they were expected to go, even when it meant leaving their husbands and children to fend for themselves for as much as one week. If a rehearsal or performance in a locality near a woman's home extended past the time she would normally be fetching water or preparing the evening meal, her husband was forced to accept the situation and make do. In addition to not fulfilling their household duties, when women traveled, they sometimes had more opportunities for romantic or sexual liaisons, further threatening their relationships with their husbands (Mkamanga 2000: 47). For these and other reasons, men sometimes tried to keep their wives from dancing. In these cases, the man could be brought before party leaders. Nyirenda explained that if a man forbade his wife to dance, the local chairman or chairwoman contacted the man and talked to him about it. If he continued to refuse, they brought him to the area leaders. If he still refused or "did not well understand," then he was brought "to the office where they were trying to talk to him so that he should understand" (personal communication, February 12, 1999). I can only imagine that this talking might have been less than gentle.

To Some, Not Oppressive

Critics of the Banda regime frequently juxtapose the limited responsibility of leaders of the League of Malawi Women with Banda's discourse about his commitment to women as evidenced by the high-level positions held by some women within his government (e.g., Mawaya and Patel 1995: 6; Semu 2002; Segal 1995). This criticism is justified, as only a minority of government posts were held by women and the responsibilities of members of the League of Malawi Women were more limited than were those of their male counterparts, who were charged with running the country, not just coordinating women's performances. At the same time, women's leadership roles within the league should not be undermined. Women's singing and dancing were an important facet of the MCP government's strategy. Women's league leaders were therefore making valuable contributions to the government; many women valued these leadership opportunities, and some were fully committed to Banda and his government.

Writing about Dan *ge* performers in Ivorian politics, Daniel B. Reed noted that the relationship between performers and politicians is mutually beneficial. "The members of the *ge* group are paid and are themselves honored to have been invited to perform at events associated with the most powerful chief in the land—the president" (2003: 56). Similarly, though most women dancing as Banda's mbumba were not compensated, many felt honored to perform for "the most powerful chief of the land." The women I interviewed who were especially active dancers during the period were proud of their performance abilities and proud that they stood out enough to be invited frequently to perform. Furthermore, the experience of dancing with hundreds of other women clad in the same uniform, rhythms pulsating, feet stamping, and drums beating, was emotionally intense. The moment when Banda descended into the dancing throng was a powerful moment that even some who did not support him were nevertheless drawn into. Schafer, who was very critical of Banda, conceded, "It was fun. I always say I didn't like it, but it was fun sometimes" (personal communication, November 14, 1995).

A number of women I knew in Malawi, in particular some who were especially active dancers, remembered Banda's rule with nostalgia. Some referred to Banda as a father figure who looked after and cared for them. They remembered the economic stability that had since disintegrated. Mayi Mphase remembered that following independence, Banda encouraged the population to farm. "He told us that people should farm. That is where the wealth is" (personal communication, March 12, 1999). Some remembered the pleasure of dancing, traveling, and being recognized for their performance abilities. A small minority remembered that they were remunerated materially, and many remembered a time when there was less crime and more political stability in the country. Asked why the Banda government forced them to dance, Mayi E. Mhone answered, "After independence everyone was happy. . . . It is the same if Mr. Chakuamba [MCP president in 1999] comes, we dance, and if Mr. Tembo [MCP vice president in 1999] comes, we also dance. These are Malawi Congress Party members, so we dance. We celebrate because we are party members. I do not know what you mean when you say that they forced us." Asked if she still dances at political functions, she answered that she would, but only for the Malawi Congress Party: "our old party, not that of Bakili, no" (personal communication, February 9, 1999).

The tensions in women's relationships with their husbands created by their relationships with Banda also created some fissures within which women could manipulate power to their advantage. A woman was empowered to make demands on her husband through her status vis-à-vis the head of state and the potential to turn her husband in as a dissenter. A woman who might not otherwise have been free to travel or perform so much within the authoritative structures of her family and relationship with her husband was empowered to do so.

Also important was people's varying access to information and thus differing reasons to either support Banda or not. Mary Chiume, for example, explained that during the period following the Cabinet Crisis, many people living in rural areas knew little about what the Banda government was doing. As an example, she explained that everyone had heard the reports on the radio and later in song lyrics that the ousted ministers, including her brother, had tried to overththrow the government. They also heard rumors about possible wrongdoings by the MCP government. She suggested that many in the general population had little basis to determine which of these rumors were accurate, so they chose to support the country's leadership.

Resistance

Scholars investigating oppression have increasingly turned their interpretations away from monolithic models of exploitation to more nuanced understandings of how people exist within unequal power structures. Rather than perceiving subordinate peoples as the passive victims of oppression, many now investigate ways in which people in disadvantaged positions creatively manipulate the resources at their disposal to increase their power, be it their opportunities to express themselves, their chances to improve their economic situations, or their opportunities to subvert the goals of those who wield power and authority over them. These various ways in which subordinates gain strength within adverse environments are often referred to under the rubric of "resistance." Authors have used the term to refer to acts ranging from those that culminate in an individual having a little more access to resources to more coordinated rebellions intended to transform power structures. This emphasis on resistance has inspired insightful scholarship that highlights ways in which oppressed people, often conscious of their oppression, are vigilant about opportunities to improve their situations by whatever means are available to them (e.g., Scott 1985, 1986a, 1986b; Raheja and Gold 1994; Radner 1993; Abu-Lughod 1986). My definition of *resistance* is broad and encompasses anything—sometimes action, though it can be an explicit choice not to act—that in some way increases a person's power or access to resources. By resisting, an individual may enjoy feelings of empowerment, satisfaction at having thwarted the aims of a dominating individual or group, economic gain, greater mobility, or opportunities for expression. Banda's government's attempts to control the population and repress dissent were not foolproof, and some people did find ways of resisting.

Interested in the ways that song texts have long been used to veil critical messages and to serve as socially sanctioned avenues for expressing dissent in this part of Africa, I asked numerous people with widely varying perspectives on the Banda government whether they had heard of songs used for resistance. In my many attempts to find examples, I have established that the government effectively created a climate of fear in which most people made great efforts to avoid resisting, afraid of the possible repercussions. Dausi, an MCP official under Banda, explained that if people could see that a cabinet minister who criticized the government could be killed, "then do you expect to see a woman, a simple woman sing against the president?" (personal communication, May 30, 2000). Only one person, notably M.W.K. Chiume, offered an example of a song that carried a veiled message that outwardly praised Banda, though it could be interpreted to be an expression of criticism:

> It was after Banda had established dictatorship. I lived in Dar es Salaam [in Tanzania]. My house in Usisya [in Malawi] was demolished. And the other one was bulldozed in Chikwina [in Malawi]. And one of the national women organizers of women's dancers and music was in Dar es Salaam when this thing was happening. And she saw me building a house in Dar es Salaam in a terrain that was similar to the one at home, but with a little anthill. And she composed a very, very interesting song, which she went to sing for Banda. And Banda was so happy about it. In short, she was saying, "You cannot compete with this man. You destroyed his property, but he has now built a much better house on an ant hill." Now, to Banda it meant, you know, Banda is an invincible man because he's built a house at Sanjika, which looks like an anthill. But actually, the dancers understood it to mean that you are wasting your time fighting against Kanyama. (Personal communication, April 21, 1999)

Unfortunately, I do not have the actual song text, nor have I talked to anybody besides M.W.K. Chiume who could provide me with information about this song, so I am not sure when or where it was sung or how others interpreted it. At any rate, it did have this veiled meaning at least for Chiume. Similarly, Reuben Chirambo (2001) provided some examples of coded messages critiquing the Banda government that were expressed through the songs of popular musician Wambali Mkandawire, suggesting that some veiled messages did seep through.

In *Power and the Praise Poem*, Leroy Vail and Landeg White referred to the Malawian poet Jack Mapanje's 1974 thesis, in which he provided some examples of songs performed by the League of Malawi Women that he interpreted as expressing veiled criticism through irony. Vail and White, however, qualified this example, suspecting that perhaps Mapanje and other Malawian fiction writers during Banda's era "were, if anything, overanxious to track down ironies in the women's songs and to appropriate to their cause anything that had the most innocent of double meanings" (1991: 298). According to Julius Ihonvbere, "There were pockets of opposition, though most of these were located outside the country and were often ineffective, especially in the context of solid Western tolerance and support for Banda's dictatorship" (1997: 225). No one I interviewed aside from M.W.K. Chiume could provide me with any examples, and most people stated that people were scared to express any criticism, so I have concluded that it was not a common practice. Chirambo's (2001) explanation confirms my perception; he said that songs encoding criticism really came to the fore in 1992, when open opposition against Banda surfaced.

More common forms of resistance included women feigning illness, hiding, or otherwise finding ways of avoiding rehearsals and party functions. A number of women claimed that they never danced for Banda or that they were able to discontinue participating at a certain time. This seems particularly common in the north, where Banda did not visit as frequently, though it occurred throughout the country. Mayi Kondowe, for example, explained that after witnessing so many deaths from car accidents during her journeys to dance, she eventually became frightened and avoided traveling. Jane Phumisa similarly claimed that she successfully avoided dancing for much of Banda's rule. Her husband, Kaliyoma Phumisa, was the director of Malawi Broadcasting Company during the early part of Banda's rule and was later fired by the Banda government and jailed. When he was released, his family moved to his home area of Ntcheu, in the central region, where they operated a successful business and stayed removed from politics until the transition. Soon after her husband was released, Jane Phumisa was hurt in a car accident and subsequently received a certificate from a doctor stating that she should not dance because of physical limitations. She used the certificate to avoid dancing long after she had healed from the accident. Kaliyoma Phumisa explained that he avoided participating as an audience member by claiming that his health had suffered so much while he was in prison that he could not sit in the sun for long periods of time (personal communication, April 24, 1999). It was therefore possible for some to manipulate the system and act out low levels of resistance. However, while some women successfully avoided participating, it is clear that many others felt that they had no choice. Women's dissatisfaction with having to devote so much effort to promoting the government regardless of their own political goals would eventually contribute to efforts to end Banda's autocratic rule.

Notes

1. Nsanje is also the name of a district is the southern region of Malawi.

2. For detailed descriptions of the events leading to the Cabinet Crisis, see Rotberg 1965: 319; Short 1974: 196–230; Ross 1997; McCracken 1968: 206–8.

3. See Adamolekun 1976 for a discussion of similar processes of identity formation by Sékou Touré in post-independence Guinea.

4. See Lwanda 1993: 9–11; Mphande 1976: 91; McMaster 1974: 66; Vail and White 1989: 180–82; Kaspin 1995.

5. See also Johnson-Odim and Strobel 1999: liii; Cullen 1994: 17; Staudt 1986: 208; Munachonga 1989.

6. Mount Soche is the most upscale hotel in downtown Blantyre and is often used by foreigners temporarily working in the country.

7. For more on Nyau dancing, see Schoffeleers 1992; Timpunza Mvula 1990; and De Aguilar 1995.

8. I completed the translation, which was incomplete in the original.

9. It is widely thought that Banda had long-term relationships with Mrs. Margaret French, a receptionist and nurse in his medical practice in England, and possibly with Cecilia Kadzamira in Malawi (see, e.g., Short 1974: 76–79; Mapanje 2002).

10. The dress code also prohibited men from wearing shorts or having long hair.

4

Dance, the Transition to Multipartyism, and Patronage

Waves of change spread across sub-Saharan Africa in the early 1990s, causing more than half of all African states to replace authoritarian regimes with multiparty systems of government (Lindberg 2006: 52). The end of the cold war precipitated changes in the global political climate, and in the early 1990s, the United States and European powers that had supported the pro-Western Banda during the cold war changed their tone. Donor countries and the World Bank refused Malawi economic assistance until "human rights were respected and a political liberalization agenda was announced" (Ihonvbere 1997: 227). Malawi's economy, already weak was further weakened by these measures, and many Malawians blamed the Banda regime. The pressure exerted on Banda from the international community widened extant fissures in Banda's control over the population: Activists at home and abroad took advantage of the moment to mobilize an extensive movement against him (Bauer and Taylor 2005: 28–30). This political ferment coupled with international pressure impelled Banda to hold a national referendum on June 14, 1993, at which time the population voted for a multiparty system of government.[1]

The institution of the mbumba was one issue against which the opposition rallied. In a conversation we had on January 18, 1999, Mary Chiume remembered that at the underground meetings held by opposition pressure groups (the associations that became political parties when multipartyism was legalized), women participants emphasized many issues directly related to political dancing. According to Chiume, women complained about being required to regularly rehearse and perform in addition to having to contribute food to feed the president and other government officials when they visited the area. Another big issue was the party's organization of sexual partners for its ministers. Throughout the campaign leading to the referendum, and then to the first multiparty general elections, which took place on May 17, 1994, new opposition politicians (mostly male leaders) responded to these concerns and promised that if they were elected, women would no longer be forced to dance and large-scale political functions would cease. In the aftermath of these first elections, there was a gradual increase in political dancing. By the time of the campaign for the second multiparty elections, which took place on June 15, 1999, the three main political parties at the time benefited from women's praise singing and dancing, which attracted people to their events and promoted their organizations. By the time of the end of his second term as president, Muluzi was notoriously associated with holding party and national functions decorated with throngs of dancing women, not unlike his predecessor.

The Transition to Multipartyism

In the campaigning leading to the referendum of 1993 and later to the first multiparty elections, opposition leaders emphasized the repression of the MCP. They promised the population that if people voted first for a change in the system of government through the referendum and then for new leaders in the first elections, the Malawian social world would improve markedly. The atmosphere of fear and the institution of the Malawi Young Pioneers would be eliminated; people would be free to hold and voice disparate political opinions, could belong to the party of their choice, and would not be required to buy party membership cards or provide gifts for party leaders; and most relevant to this study, women would no longer be forced or even expected to dance for the state president and other political leaders. Large national events that served the party and its leaders and for which significant sums of money were spent would cease, and there would be a separation between state and party affairs. The opposition promised that a multiparty system of government "would give power to the people, respect human rights, be transparent, and accountable" (Dzimbiri 1998: 92).

Harri Englund wrote about the central region and explained that young men were the first to adopt the multiparty cause. Opposition parties drove into villages to transport people to their rallies; young men were the first to pile on, singing *nyimbo za matipati* (songs of multiparty), including one that became popular: "Ndatopa Malawi kongresi," (I'm tired of the Malawi Congress Party) (1996: 120). A number of people involved told me that fewer women than men participated in pressure groups. Mayi Mfuni, whom I met through the Alliance for Democracy Party (AFORD) office in Mzuzu, explained that her late husband had been the personal secretary to M.W.K. Chiume before independence. Throughout Banda's rule, she neither supported the government nor enjoyed dancing for MCP events. She did not become active politically until three years after the transition because she had been anxious and did not trust that things had really changed. By the time of our conversation, on April 9, 1999, she was very actively involved in AFORD and told me that she now felt very free to talk and do what she wanted politically. Though men participated in greater numbers, women did participate, as is evident from Chiume's description of pressure-group meetings. Another woman who was active at this time was Mayi Nyirenda, probably in her fifties at the time of our conversation on March 23, 1999, who became active in the midst of the political turmoil that led to the referendum. She and her family had left Malawi during Banda's rule to go into exile in Zambia, where her husband eventually died. She explained that in 1993, when she heard that it would be safe to return to Malawi, she traveled to Lilongwe for a big opposition rally. Feeling confident that things were changing, she subsequently moved back with her family and became active in politics. Similarly, Mayi Mtayamanja, whom I interviewed in Blantyre on June 1, 2004, explained that she became active politically in 1994 after having been impressed when Chakufwa Chihana, a trade union activist who played a significant role challenging Banda's autocracy and then chaired AFORD, bravely spoke out against Banda. She said, "I saw him with my own eyes in court, and I thought that this person was really brave. His goals must be good. I will join him."

Though the use of women's dance as a political tool was an issue against which the opposition rallied, women in the opposition, used to expressing themselves politically through performance, sang and danced to promote parties and contribute to political strategizing. Opposition parties did not systematically coordinate their female supporters to do so; rather, women opposition supporters, including Mayi Mtayamanja, who were brave enough, came out against Banda. They reclaimed control of their bodies and subverted the practice that had legitimized Banda and symbolized his control over them, this time exploiting it to undermine him. These women manipulated many of the song texts that had become so well-known during Banda's rule, substituting words, so that they now praised his opponents and castigated Banda, a poignant sign that the MCP government was losing its control over people's personal expression. In his article "Dancing towards Dictatorship: Political Songs and Popular Culture in Malawi," W. C. Chirwa provided many examples, including the following:

A Kamuzu dziko la Malawi mwalizunza
Nanga tichite bwanji abale?
Dziko la Malawi mwalizunza
Onani! Gadama munapha
Onani! Chihana ku ndende ku Zomba

Dziko la Malawi mwalizunza
Onani! Matenje munapha
Onani! Aleke ku ndende ku Zomba
Dziko la Malawi mwalizunza

Kamuzu, you have tortured the Malawi nation
What do we do now?
You have tortured the Malawi nation!
Look! You killed [Aaron] Gadama
Look! You locked up Chihana in prison in Zomba
You have tortured the Malawi nation!
Look! You killed [Dick] Matenje
Look! You locked up Aleke [Banda] in prison in Zomba
You have tortured the Malawi nation!
(Chirwa 2001: 24–25)

Women used songs to rally support for a change in the system of government and for the new opposition parties who promoted it:

Tifuna yani lero? Matipate!
Tifuna yani lero? Matipate!
Winanso? Winanso ai! Winanso ai!
Matipate

Who do we want now? Multiparty!
Who do we want now? Multiparty!
Nobody else? Nobody else, no!
But multiparty
(Chirwa 2001: 26)

In addition to challenging the Banda regime, the opposition parties also vied with one another for popular support. Women's song lyrics promoted the leader of one opposition party while castigating those of others.

While the opposition campaigned heavily for multipartyism, Banda toured the country, using the established MCP apparatus, including the singing and dancing mbumba, which were still coordinated through the League of Malawi Women, to remind the population of all that Banda had accomplished for the country and to campaign against the "dissidents." He claimed that the attacks on him by his opponents were lies, and he warned the population about what would happen should the system of government change (Dzimbiri 1998: 93). Embedded in his speeches was incredulity about the oppositions' claims that he did not enjoy the support of "his people," as exemplified in the following quote from a speech he gave at a rally in Karonga, documented on the same videotape *Kamuzu Banda in Karonga* as the Nkhata Bay event described in Chapter 3:

> The dissidents and multiparty people are telling all kinds of lies against me personally, against Mama [Cecilia Kadzamira], against ministers, like Mr. Dereza, Mr. Tembo and all the ministers. All kinds of lies, I repeat! But I am happy, very happy indeed that from what the Regional Chairman here has said, you the people . . . do not agree with these people. Because everything these people say against me, against Mama, against all the ministers, then against mbumba, such as Mrs. Manjamkhosi, it's all lies, lies, lies, lies only! . . . Kamuzu is happy that you his people here in the north, as in the south, in the center do not agree and do not believe one word of what these people say.

Emily Mkamanga suggested in her book *Suffering in Silence: Malawi Women's 30 Year Dance with Dr. Banda* that many women at the grassroots level refused MCP directives and stopped dancing at political rallies during this period. She contended that, unbeknownst to Banda, MCP officials recognized this lack of enthusiasm and organized a group of mbumba whom they took to rallies across the country to maintain the illusion that he enjoyed popular support, specifically that of women. She referred to a rumor that after having heard that single-party advocates had lost the referendum, an incredulous Banda "queried the Electoral Commission to find out if all the votes from the women, his mbumba, had been counted" (2000: 16–19). I have met many female MCP supporters, such as Mayi Mphase and Mayi Md. Longwe, who danced during the referendum and continued to support Banda long after his death, suggesting that some of the mbumba during this period were avid supporters; others, as Mkamanga suggested, took advantage of the loosening of state control and refused to dance; still others might have participated mostly because they were organized to do so by the party. Regardless of their motivations, by donning their Banda regalia, dancing chiwoda-like genres, and continuing to sing many of the same songs they had been singing during his rule, praising and thanking him for virtually everything in the country, these women expressed continuity: Nothing had or would change.

MCP supporters also composed new lyrics that referred to what was occurring on the political front (Chimombo and Chimombo 1996: 110–12). Embedded in many of these songs were nostalgic affirmations of Banda's paternalism. In the following song performed at the Karonga rally from the *Kamuzu Banda in Karonga* video, women referred to themselves as Banda's children and promised him that they would vote against multipartyism:

A Ngwazi mwe zero	The Ngwazi you are wise
Mwe, Ngwazi yithu, mwe zero	You, our Ngwazi, you are wise
Eh, tawana muno	Yes, we children here
Tawana muno m'Malawi	We children here in Malawi
Mwe wati tikukana	You say, we refuse
Tikukana matipate	We refuse multiparty
Eh, wa Ngwazi m'Malawi	Yes, the Ngwazi in Malawi
Ngwazi yithu, mwe zero	Our Ngwazi, you are wise
Eh, tawana muno	Yes, we children here
Tawana muno m'Malawi	We children here in Malawi
Tikukana matipati	We refuse multiparty

Banda's physical presence presented conflicting messages. His aids led him slowly to the podium and stood by his side to bolster him physically and to guide him in moments of seeming senility.[2] Still, he continued to perform his paternalistic commitment to his mbumba, who swarmed before him decked in full Banda regalia singing songs of praise, as described in Chapter 3.

After losing the referendum, the MCP changed its tone. In campaigning for the first general elections, MCP officials explained that they were a transformed party committed to democracy and that they respected the choice of the population to change the system of government (Mkamanga 2000: 19–20). Some MCP officials, even those who held important positions in the MCP during Banda's presidency, supported the political transformations and were committed to political pluralism (e.g., Dausi, personal communication, May 30, 2000). Rather than denying the atrocities committed during Banda's rule, many distanced the blame from Banda, claiming that he was ignorant, and thus innocent, of the injustices carried out by his subordinates. They claimed that those actually responsible for the government's wrongdoings were the leaders of the opposition parties, bringing into question the latter's credibility (Dzimbiri 1998: 93). Bakili Muluzi, for example, who won the presidency, formerly held a high position in the Banda government until he was convicted in 1968 of theft of government money, an allegation he refuted (Lwanda 1996: 83). These stories were repeated in song lyrics as in the following example:

Ngwazi moto iyelei
Ife sitifuna Bakili iyelei
Angadzatibele iyelei
Chuma chathu

Ngwazi fire
We don't want Bakili (Muluzi)

He could steal from us
Our wealth
(Chimombo and Chimombo 1996: 118; my translation)

Bakili Muluzi's Presidency

After winning, Muluzi and members of his government explicitly expressed a commitment to transform the political culture and eliminate many of the practices and policies they had opposed during Banda's rule. Muluzi presented himself as a man of the people and rejected the type of personality cult that was so paramount during Banda's time. After his victory, his government did not organize large public events that cost the government significant sums of money and in which people were forced to dance, and the new president discouraged the practice of people lining up at airports at his departures and arrivals. Efforts unfolded to separate party and state events: The latter were no longer opportunities for advertising the party and its leaders, but were supposed to be nonpartisan national celebrations. After the 1994 elections, the praise singing and dancing subsided (Chimombo and Chimombo 1996: 125).

At the same time that it discouraged women from dancing politically, the new government articulated its commitment to "gender," following trends across the continent as countries responded to international pressures and internal activism (Semu 1993: 103). They promised women greater access to the political and social spheres and promoted projects and policies that would improve gender parity. The opening up of the social and political scene paved the way for the proliferation of nongovernmental organizations (NGOs) funded through international donor agencies. Some were watchdogs intent on ensuring that human rights improved in the country; others were more proactive, instituting projects that targeted specific populations or social issues. A number concerned themselves specifically with the well-being of women, for example, the Society for the Advancement of Women, the Women and Children's Committee of the Law, the Promotion of Women in Politics, Women's Voice, and CARER (Mvula and Kakhongwa 1997: 29).

By the second year of its first term, the UDF government communicated through local media that in its rejection of the policies and practices of the Banda regime, it had not adequately assessed the value of all they had eliminated. By the summer of 1996, two years after it took office, the government announced that it would hold its first large-scale celebration to commemorate National Independence Day on July 6 at Chichiri Stadium in the city of Blantyre. Many in the country were surprised and publicly voiced their criticism, questioning where the money to fund the event would come from and why Muluzi was suddenly advocating the very thing that he had vehemently opposed only a short time before. *The Nation*, a major newspaper that was at the time sympathetic to the UDF, carried numerous articles that defended the president. A frequently expressed explanation was that the government had underestimated the importance of these occasions, and specifically the performance of traditional dances, so central to the country's cultural heritage. One article referenced Shyley Kondowe, then the director of the Malawi Institute of Democratic and Economic Affairs, who was presented as explaining that when the UDF government took over,

> [i]t had not assessed what was at heart in Malawi's cultural heritage. "We do realize that the national celebrations were costly, but it became part and parcel of lives of Malawians." For the new government to ignore these festivities, they had in effect denied to accept historical fact. Kondowe said government has now realized that it has to build on what MCP had left. (Matiya 1996)

Opposition leaders criticized the president for his plans given that he had previously used the high cost of these events as a reason to do away with them. President Muluzi defended his decision by saying, "'[O]ur resources are very limited. We have other priorities. Commemoration of this grand scale will take place every five years until such a time when our economy picks up'" (quoted in "There Will Be Soccer Matches" 1996).

The organizers limited dance performances to those by the Kwacha Cultural Troupe, the coed national group whose members were full-time civil servants. Because the performers were professional and compensated, the government differentiated itself from the previous regime and protected itself against criticism that they were exploiting dancers. The choreographer of the troupe, Bernard Kwilimbe, arranged a program inclusive of dances from different parts of the country so as to promote and celebrate the diverse heritages of Malawi, once again a display through dance of a national identity built on difference. In addition, one hundred students from two Blantyre secondary schools performed alongside it. Though these students were not compensated, they also were not forced. Kwilimbe explained in a newspaper article that "the idea of involving the youth in the celebration show was to groom them into becoming better leaders of tomorrow armed with the country's cultural background" (Mita 1996a). The event organizers defended themselves against accusations that they were using these youth dancers in much the same way as had the previous government by explaining that

> [t]he schedule for the cultural show by the students was organized in such a way that there was minimal disturbance to their learning. . . . "No rehearsals took place during school hours to inconvenience students, therefore they had maximum time in class," said [Harry] Thom-

> son [chairman of the organizing committee] adding that the choice of HHI Boys and Blantyre Girls was also deliberate to cut costs. (Mita 1996b)

As with the celebrations during Banda's time, the event included a display of business-sponsored floats, an entertainment component during which the professional dance troupe and student dancers performed, displays by the police and army, speeches, and a soccer match as the grand finale. It was, however, largely nonpartisan. As mentioned in Chapter 1, the one exception was that a group of women wearing UDF fabric sat within the VIP stands and descended into the performance arena briefly to welcome President Muluzi's convoy upon its arrival with singing. Though they did not otherwise participate as performers and were not visually prominent in the celebrations, their presence at this purportedly nonpartisan function was a sign of changes taking place. Following this first large-scale public celebration and within the five-year period stipulated as event free by Muluzi, the UDF government orchestrated other national events featuring dancing, and there was a gradual increase in public rallies held by all political parties, with a subsequent increase in the performances of traditional dances at them all.

1999 Election Campaigns

The rise in political dancing was especially evident as campaigning gained momentum for the second multiparty elections. The UDF, MCP, and AFORD dominated the campaigns, though other parties also took part. The incumbent presidential candidate, Muluzi, led the UDF. Gwanda Chakuamba and John Tembo, MCP strongman during Banda's regime, were at the helm of the MCP. Chihana chaired AFORD (Dzimbiri 1998: 96–101). The MCP and AFORD formed an alliance and ran the MCP's Chakuamba as their presidential candidate with AFORD's Chihana as his running mate. Candidates from the two parties competed against one another for parliamentary seats.

As with the 1994 elections, each of these parties was associated with one of the three administrative regions (the UDF with the south, the MCP with the central, and AFORD with the north) and many people voted along regional lines (Phiri 2000: 73; Phiri and Ross 1998: 12; Chirwa 1994, 1998). Continuing the two trajectories of political performance established during the independence movement and entrenched during the Banda years, politicians in the 1999 elections used their female membership as vehicles for displaying and disseminating symbols and messages, and they invited established dance groups to attract people to their functions.

The most established political parties in Malawi borrowed the party hierarchy of the MCP and were organized into tripartite structures that consist of a main body—the overarching organization that oversees all the workings of the party—and two ancillary organizations—a women's wing and a youth wing. Each wing of the party is organized into a pyramid structure. At the top of a party's hierarchy is the national executive committee. The country is then broken down into three administrative centers: the central, northern, and southern regions. Each region is subdivided into districts, which are divided into areas, which are further broken down into branches. At each of the administrative levels (executive, regional, district, area, branch), three leadership committees exist, one for each of the subdivisions of the party (main body, women's wing, youth wing). Each committee ideally includes a chairman, vice chairman, secretary, vice secretary, treasurer, vice treasurer, and committee members.

The youth and women's wings function to integrate women and youth into active participation in party activities. Women do participate in the main body and youth wing, and some hold leadership positions. The majority of active members in the main body and youth wing and in most leadership positions within them, especially at the highest levels, are male. The membership of the women's wing is exclusively female—adult women and some teenage girls—and women fill all leadership positions within them from the branch to the executive levels.[3]

Women, Dancing, and Election Campaigning

Most of my time researching the 1999 campaigns was spent in the Nkhata Bay District, where I learned about political activities in rural settings. I also frequently traveled to the city of Mzuzu, the regional center of the north, to follow party activities at the regional level. Toward the end of my stay in Malawi, I left Nkhata Bay in April to spend two weeks following the campaign activities of Kaliyoma Phumisa in the Ntcheu District, located in the central region. Campaigning was time-consuming, exhausting, and very exciting. Those of us who traveled regularly from rally to rally experienced the elation of arriving when large crowds had already gathered. The ongoing singing, shouting of slogans, and electricity of hundreds of people gathered together were energizing. There was also often confusion, changes in scheduling, cancellations of meetings, frustration, hunger, and fatigue during long trips; all of which contributed to the buzz of the campaign experience.

Though the lives of women participating as performers in the contemporary political scene differed, the majority shared some economic and social characteristics. Most lived in villages in rural or urban locales or urban high-density neighborhoods. Most struggled financially and had low levels of formal schooling, limited political experience outside of the localized party, and little access to the country's means of production or resources (Mvula and Kakhongwa 1997).[4]

The lives of all women who danced politically were filled with home, occupational, familial, and leisure-time activities. A typical day of a woman living in a village in the Nkhata Bay District often began with obtaining water. Mayi V. Mwale was married into the Ngwira family, with whom we lived. Unlike some of their neighbors, who had access to piped water, Mayi V. Mwale began her morning by walking from her house down the steep hillside to a meandering stream where she filled her tin buckets with the day's water and then carried them back up the hillside on her head one by one. Children playing afoot and sometimes her young son strapped to her back begging to nurse, she continued her morning activities, scrubbing her house, pounding soaked and then dried cassava into flour, cultivating fields, chatting with the other women in the family, gathering firewood, and preparing meals. Women in this family occasionally sold firewood or wild grasses they gathered from a nearby forest to sell for small amounts of money. Other women I knew living in Nkhata Bay villages sometimes engaged in regular or intermittent small-scale commerce, selling such things as dried fish, agricultural products, soap, or rice either out of their homes, or along trails that link villages, or in town. Most men in the Ngwira family, like their peers in nearby communities, spent their days away from home in the nearby town of Nkhata Bay engaging in various moneymaking ventures. The patriarch of the family had a small shoe-repair stand in town, and several of his sons made and sold wood carvings to tourists. Many of those living on the lakeshore relied on fishing for some of their income. Women often spent the afternoons engaged in similar activities to the mornings, though often slowed by the heat of the sun. Naps and strolls to family and friends in nearby villages were common, and the reduced pace of afternoons allowed time for leisure pursuits, such as participating in performance activities or sports. Political rallies often took place in the afternoons, allowing women to fit them into their routines.

AFORD Campaigns in Nkhata Bay and Mzuzu

AFORD, the party associated with the northern region, garnered the support of a majority of northerners, both those currently living in the region and outside, for its leader, Chihana, and the party's parliamentary candidates. In 1999, many northerners also felt ambivalent because Chihana, so admired when he defiantly stood up against Banda in the early 1990s, had now forged an alliance with the MCP, a strategy to strengthen the opposition against the ruling UDF. Many questioned how he could associate himself with the same party and even many of the same individuals responsible for the repression he had so courageously stood up against only a few years before. Nevertheless, many I knew in the Nkhata Bay District prided themselves on their allegiance to AFORD.

Though the Nkhata Bay District was in the party's stronghold in the northern rergion, the party was poorly organized there. When I tried to find the local leadership, I asked around unsuccessfully until I finally met a man who, on December 14, 1998, led me to the home of the district chairman because there was no official party headquarters in town. My escort criticized the local leadership and told me the party was much better organized in his home in Mzimba.

Unlike those of the MCP and UDF, AFORD rallies in the Nkhata Bay District were not coordinated or even necessarily known about by a central district office. Rather, parliamentary candidates coordinated with leaders in their constituencies to organize rallies at the local level. In addition to scheduling a lineup of local speakers, party officials, usually at the constituency level, invited women supporters to join in dancing chiwoda and invited established dance groups to perform the genres active in that constituency. My friends on chilimika dance teams often told me about these events after the fact, indicating that dancers were not given much warning. I should clarify that I was unusual enough as the white woman who traveled across the district to attend and videotape dance performances that visitors from dance teams stopped by our house regularly, and acquaintances (and often strangers) I met in town and on rural pathways kept me well informed of dance activities. Had members of dance teams with whom I regularly spent time known about rallies much in advance, they probably would have notified me.

I did attend one AFORD rally on November 22, 1998, before the presidential campaigns really heated up. My host in Nkhwali, Zabweka Tembo, held a position in the party at the local leadership level and was largely responsible for organizing the event. His dance group, the School Band, which sang a song against M.W.K. Chiume during the previous regime, as discussed in Chapter 3, performed at this event for AFORD parliamentarian Austin Mwenda. The group adapted the lyrics of this same song for this event, and it no longer invoked killing Chiume, though the singing was too garbled for me to understand the adaptation. Two chilimika dance teams performed, one of which, Mweluzi, included three of Tembo's daughters, famous locally, as was their father, for their entertainment abilities. The rally also featured samba, a dance form from the Karonga District. It was performed by a group of young men who worked in the nearby Vizarra rubber estate. The inclusion of this non-Tonga and non-Nkhata Bay genre demonstrated the diversity of the area and the way in which any recognized performance group could be featured. Mwenda had also hired the Phaka Town Band, a honara dance team, which arrived on the back of a truck after the rally had already started, interrupting the performance by the Mweluzi chilimika team with their graceful accordion melodies and the dancers' elegance: eight men and five women, all probably over the age of forty, lined up in three columns with the women in the central one facing Mwenda. The men, dressed to the hilt—dark suits, handkerchiefs neatly peaking out of lapel pockets, eyeglasses, hats, and two in white leather shoes—gallantly waved their canes in the air and then lightly stamped them on the ground as they gracefully stepped in place. The women, in skirts with alternating panels of white and AFORD's blue color and white T-shirts, stepped vigorously yet gracefully, their hips swaying back and forth. A man standing near the accordion shook a steady triplet pattern from a shaker, while the accordion player sang and played a festive accordion dance tune. People in Nkhata Bay rarely saw honara, and this was my first time. The response to this highly stylized and polished dance group was enthusiastic; the audience clapped and ululated (see "AFORD political rally Nkhwali Village," http://purl.dlib.indiana.edu/iudl/eviada/5-E3922).

The party's signature color was turquoise, and its blue cloth was decorated with the dark blue letters *AFORD* surrounding a white image of their kinetic symbol, a hand signing *V* for *Victory*, as shown in Figure 4.1. Individual politicians distributed the fabric to supporters, and it was available for purchase in cloth stores in urban centers. At this rally, no one wore AFORD fabric, probably because it was before the campaigning really took off, and party officials had not yet started systematically doling it out to supporters. This was the only rally I ever attended anywhere that did not feature singing and dancing by party women, probably because it occurred before the campaigning picked up.

In contrast to the Nkhata Bay District, the nearby city of Mzuzu, forty-seven kilometers away, had a well-organized AFORD presence. The party's headquarters, visibly located on the main drag, was the site for organizing campaign trips, welcoming and seeing off party dignitaries, orchestrating primary elections, and registering voters. Men and women participated in all these capacities, though many, but not all, of the leadership positions were held by men. Women gathered in front of the office, rehearsing their dancing and singing routines in preparation for a campaign trip, were a frequent sight.

On March 23, 1999, I joined hundreds of AFORD supporters a little after lunchtime at the small airport in Mzuzu to welcome Chihana. He was scheduled to land in Mzuzu, where he would be picked up in a car to continue to Chombe, south of Mzuzu. Following the trend of welcoming party dignitaries at airports so ubiquitous in the previous government, AFORD supporters had converged at the airport to greet Chihana during his brief transition from plane to car. A large grassy field extended between the tarmac and the airport building. When I arrived, all the men stood in the shade under some tall plants that lined the building, while the women had already spent hours on the grass under the beating sun, alternating between enthusiastic dancing of mbotosha, the chiwoda-like dance associated with the Tumbuka, the majority ethnic group in Mzuzu, and sitting around bored and waiting. After being introduced to some male officials, the publicity secretary

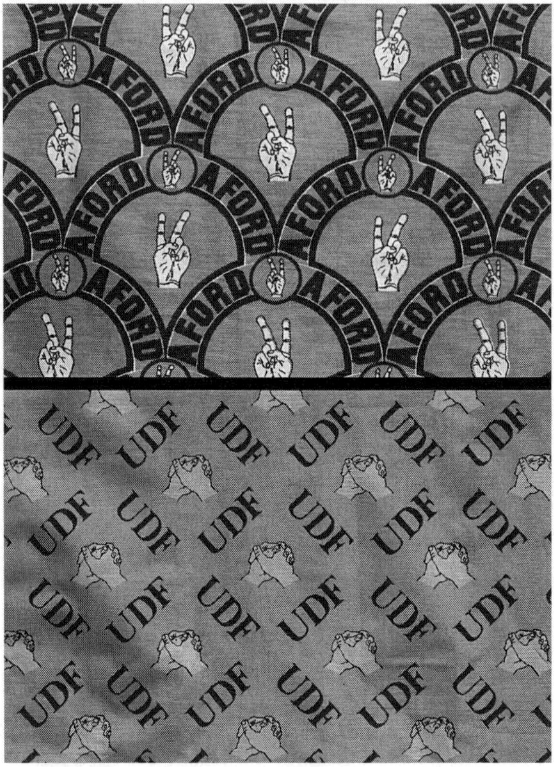

Figure 4.1 Turquoise AFORD fabric decorated with the party acronym and a white hand signing *V* for *Victory* and yellow UDF fabric decorated with the party acronym in blue and its symbol of clasped hands. *(From the author's collection.)*

walked into the center ring of the pulsating concentric circles and emerged with a woman, probably in her early fifties. He introduced me to Mayi Nyirenda, a committee member of the party at the district level, and I very briefly explained my presence. The next thing I knew, I was awkwardly following her foot patterns as I moved around with others among the inner ring of dancers. The other women watched and laughed as they continued to rotate and sing. Somebody wrapped a chitenje around me to cover my trousers. Soon, my attraction waned and no one paid me much attention. Mayi Nyirenda explained that the song they were singing expressed that they were tired of the current government, and that it was time to give the AFORD-MCP coalition a chance.

Later, as I was chatting with Mayi Nyirenda, one of the male organizers came to tell us that he had received a phone call that Chihana's schedule had changed and that he would go to Likoma Island before coming our way. At 4:15 P.M., another call came informing us that Chihana was now en route to Lilongwe and so would be even later. Another male organizer came to tell Mayi Nyirenda that she should tell the women that they should wait for his arrival and be prepared to sleep at the airport. After the announcement was made, the women started a new song that, as Mayi Nyirenda explained, expressed, "We are not going to stop." I was less committed than they, and I left shortly after.

Almost one month later, when Muluzi came to Mzuzu on April 17 to launch his presidential campaign in the north, as described in Chapter 5, the Mzuzu AFORD office was a hubbub of activity. While the UDF party successfully dotted the cityscape with its signature yellow color, AFORD members, both men and women, held rallies and sang in the streets, sometimes parading in large numbers and disrupting the flow of traffic, all the while singing songs criticizing Muluzi and other UDF politicians, contributing to musical articulations of the political contest. Though AFORD members disrupted Muluzi's rally briefly, the Mzuzu launch was nevertheless carried out with little trouble. AFORD supporters were more successful in the city of Karonga, where he went next. News reports indicated that Muluzi had to cancel his rally because of the protests and harassment of AFORD supporters.

UDF Campaigning in Nkhata Bay and Mzuzu

In the 1999 campaigns, the ruling UDF made its presence felt throughout the country. They distributed yellow paraphernalia to the most remote areas, gave yellow vehicles to party leaders throughout the country, painted their party headquarters bright yellow, and sent their most important dignitaries to campaign throughout the country, even those firmly associated with opposition parties, such as the Nkhata Bay District and nearby city of Mzuzu. Bright yellow fabric decorated with the UDF logo and kinetic symbol of two hands clasped and raised (see Figure 4.1) clothed women throughout the country and was especially salient at rallies.

The UDF headquarters in the district was located in the town of Nkhata Bay. It was highly visible, painted in the signature yellow with the party name in large blue letters. Though small, it was the only political office in the district that had a staff and was regularly open. The district chairman based at the headquarters kept track of and was involved in coordinating the many rallies that occurred throughout the district. His staff maintained a monthly schedule, which they generously shared with me. The national party leadership provided the district office with a brand-new pickup, also painted yellow with blue lettering, increasing the party's visibility and greatly facilitating campaign efforts in a district where only a small minority of people owned vehicles.

The chairman explained to me that the strategy of the district leadership was to orchestrate multiple rallies on the same day in nearby locations to increase the party's prominence in particular locales. Thus, on December 21, 22, and 23, party members from the headquarters went to three rallies a day, moving from one to the next, greatly aided by the ease of transport provided by the pickup. UDF supporters in the communities that held rallies coordinated many of the details of the events, including the speaker and entertainment lineups. In addition to UDF members from the community in which the event was held, women from the district level traveled from rally to rally, singing along the way and often dancing at events.

On December 23, I went to the UDF office and joined four women party members—the chairman of the women's wing at the district level, Mayi Chicago, and three district committee members—along with three male party members—the district chairman, deputy district chairman, district secretary—the full-time male office employee, and a male driver. In contrast to the women, who all wore full yellow UDF regalia, the men wore suits or approximations thereof: dark or gray slacks, button-down shirts, and sometimes suit jackets. The chairman, his deputy, and the driver, all men, sat in the cab, while the rest of us piled onto the back of the pickup. In the remaining space, the chairman offered rides to random others in need of transport, though they first had to say that they were UDF supporters, amidst much joking from all involved.

At around 10 A.M., we left town, the campaign spirit high as we rushed by villages and bus stops along the lakeshore highway. My companions eagerly sang UDF songs the whole way, raising their voices especially triumphantly as we passed people walking on the side of the highway, clasping their hands high above their heads in the UDF's kinetic symbol, and cheering and ululating enthusiastically when people responded in turn. We continued to pick up *matola* (hitchhikers who pay a small fee for transport), though they were not asked to pay. The chairman explained to one man who offered the regular fee that when they were on a campaign trip, they did not charge. He elaborated that if they were using the vehicle for fund-raising, as they had on other occasions, then they would expect payment. As riders pulled themselves onto the pickup bed, my UDF companions badgered each in good fun, asking if they were really UDF members or had just conceded because they wanted transport.

Later, when we were taking a break, the driver told me that on similar campaign trips around Mzuzu, they had not always been received so well, and had sometimes had to dodge the barrage of stones thrown by their opponents. He explained that many people were upset with the government because of the recent devaluation of the local currency and the subsequent price hikes. Though my companions were generally jovial, they were also aware of the potential for harassment and paid careful attention to the people greeting us.

Unfortunately, on this day, as we headed south and stopped at each place where a rally had been scheduled, we found it quiet. The area chairman in each locale told us a similar story: Each claimed that he had not received the letter instructing him to organize the rally. All also explained that the women in their communities had received UDF uniforms and had been taken to

Mzuzu to dance at other events. Disappointed, we returned to the town of Chinteche, south of the town of Nkhata Bay, where Mayi Chicago welcomed us to her home and prepared a generous meal of *nsima* (a thick cornmeal porridge), greens, and small dried fish to nourish our bodies and spirits, for we had been traveling for hours. The women, including myself, and the male driver ate in her house, chatting and joking convivially. The other men ate separately in the UDF office.

After eating, we made our way to the office, where we found a small group of women rehearsing outside, dancing chiwoda around a UDF flag and singing loudly about the UDF's strengths while two male drummers beat on conical drums. My companions joined in the dancing, contributing to the political soundscape of Chinteche. Though a number of my companions were from other ethnic groups, they sang in Chitonga, the language of the Tonga. They explained that they sing in the language associated with the locale in which they perform.

The next week, on January 2, I showed up at the UDF office at 9 A.M., having been invited once again to join officials from the party's headquarters, this time on a much longer journey, to the town of Tukombo in the southern reaches of the district, where Aleke Banda (no relation to the former president) was holding an especially elaborate rally. Aleke Banda was a controversial figure in the district. He was a youthful politician involved in the MCP at the time of independence and then a high-ranking MCP official under Banda who later fell out of favor and was imprisoned. After the transition, he aligned himself with the UDF when it became the ruling party. Many in the north were suspicious of him because though he was from the north, he had allied himself with parties that had not attended to northerners' needs.

As with the previous journey, a number of us piled onto the pickup truck, this time sitting in the drizzly rain, which dampened the campaign spirit. Two male party officials and a male comedian were my only companions as we left town. We sped down the lakeshore highway to the town of Chinteche huddled under umbrellas, trying to keep them from folding in the wind. In Chinteche, we found a group of women dressed in yellow waiting for transport to another rally, this one for the late Katenga Kaunda, then secretary-general of the UDF and an incumbent parliamentary candidate in the Chinteche area. About nineteen women, including Mayi Chicago, squeezed on, and we soggily made our way down bumpy mud roads to the village where the rally they were attending was taking place. This time, everyone focused on staying dry rather than singing and gesturing for the UDF.

After we had dropped off the women, I was invited into the dryness of the cab on our return to Chinteche. As we rode along, the district chairman explained that he was grateful that Muluzi had provided him with this vehicle that he could use to transport supporters. He explained that the government also paid for the car insurance and servicing in Blantyre on a regular basis. I asked if all the districts had similarly received vehicles for campaign purposes. He answered that they were all supposed to, but only two in the north had thus far.

When we reached Chinteche, we met Kaunda, who asked if we could trade vehicles because he did not want his shiny black Toyota luxury sedan to get ruined on the muddy roads. He took the pickup, and the rest of us had a comfortable, dry, and uneventful ride to Tukombo. When we arrived, the rally had already begun. We were escorted to the seating area, where we sat alongside important dignitaries, including Aleke Banda, the regional UDF chairman, the district heads of some national businesses and the police, the Nkhata Bay District commissioner, the local traditional authority, and a large number of village headmen and headwomen from surrounding communities. The presence of the leadership of important government and private organizations was far more common at the rallies for ruling party politicians than at those for opposition ones, enactments of the continued linkages between the government and ruling party. Several thousand in the audience crowded around the periphery of a large rectangular open space and watched the dancing, which comprised the bulk of this event (see "UDF political rally Tukombo," http://purl.dlib.indiana.edu/iudl/eviada/5-E046).

This rally was much more elaborate and included more entertainment groups than any other I attended. It was an unusual rally because the entertainment section of the event was presented as a dance competition. The man seated next to me was one of the organizers, and he showed me the list of scheduled entertainers, all of whom were from the southern part of the district. Three genres of dance were featured, the three most popular dance forms in the district at the time: chiwoda, malipenga, and chilimika. On his list were the names of each dance group and the name of its home village. One group performed after the other, intermixing the genres though the competition was between teams of the same genre: chiwoda dancers competed against other chiwoda dancers, chilimika against other chilimika performers, and malipenga against malipenga teams. As with intervillage competitions I had attended, each group was given a specified and equal amount of time to perform.

Having heard so much about chiwoda dancing during the Banda years and having witnessed it only twice in person—once at a relatively lackluster performance at a tourist lodge, and the second time, at a more, but still understated performance at the installation of a village headman—I greatly enjoyed the quality of women's chiwoda dancing at this event. Not having danced much since the transition, women, mostly adult women over the age of thirty, once again demonstrated their impressive dance abilities. For each chiwoda group's performance, two to three male drummers came out into the dance arena and pounded. Dancers in each team, anywhere from thirty to one hundred, most wearing UDF fabric, creatively maneuvered from the audience space into the dance arena in complicated formations that always ended up in a circle or concentric rings.

For one group, two adult male drummers came into the performance arena and positioned themselves behind the microphone stand. One wore a button-down short-sleeved shirt made of UDF fabric; the other wore no UDF paraphernalia. The two men beat on the single-sided conical drums characteristic of chiwoda. The man in yellow beat a steady triplet rhythm while the other alternated between repeated triplets that interlocked with the other drummer's and occasional improvised syncopated patterns that coordinated with the women's movements. As they drummed, about thirty women, all wearing UDF outfits, emerged in a single column and wound their way into a circle surrounding the drummers, their backsides facing the audience, including those of us in the VIP seating. They sang in a call-and-response style. The song leader stood behind the microphone singing the call line in her strong nasal voice. The rest of the dancers sang the response lines in unison in higher-toned nasal voices. The melodic structures of the two lines differed, though they shared similar melodic contours. Singers punctuated certain lines with hand claps. Their foot patterns corresponded with the first drummer's steady beat, while their buttocks and shoulders moved independently and polyrhythmically. At some points, they stopped rotating to face into the center of the circle and alternated between stepping side to side and gently kicking their right feet into the center, as shown in Figure 4.2. Their song affirmed that they would not vote for Chihana nor would they wear his AFORD cloth. When their short allotted time had passed, the MC interrupted their performance with the expected "*yewo, yewo, yewo*" (thank you, thank you, thank you), and called out the next performers, another group of chiwoda dancers. Members of this group, also wearing all yellow, emerged in two columns and similarly formed a circle around their two male drummers. The dance leader signaled changes in movement by blowing a whistle. This group danced to most of their songs facing into the circle, their feet stepping into and out of the center; their backsides moved rhythmically with two sideways shakes followed by a thrust of their right sides into the center of the circle, while they repeatedly sang, "*yewo, yewo*" to Aleke Banda.

The all-male malipenga dancers similarly entered the arena one team at a time. Members wore their best uniforms, matching white shorts and shirts, or khaki. Other costume items included black spats strapped to their shins, hats, and sometimes a single ostrich feather stuck from either a hat or a band around the head. No malipenga performers incorporated UDF paraphernalia into their costumes. Dancers marched into the performance space in row-and-column formation, mimicking a British military drill.[5]

As with most other malipenga groups, the drummers of one team entered the performance arena first. A man hit a steady syncopated rhythm

Figure 4.2 UDF women dancing chiwoda in circle formation dressed in party uniforms at a rally for Aleke Banda in Tukombo on January 2, 1999. *(From the author's collection.)*

with two sticks on a small handheld drum. Two other men emerged carrying a European-style marching band bass drum. It was constructed from a metal oil drum cut into one-and-a-half-foot rounds, over which was stretched a cowhide. It hung between them from a branch that rested on both men's shoulders, allowing them to face each other, though only one man played by hitting it on one side with the palm of his hand and on the other with a strong stick. His drumming alternated between establishing the pulse for the dancers and improvising around it in syncopated patterns. The all-male dancers, ages nine to around thirty years old, wore khaki shorts, white T-shirts, and pink, orange, and yellow dyed ostrich feathers that stuck out of handmade paper headbands. Once the drummers had established their patterns, the dancers emerged from the audience space, already in row-and-column formation. Their feet stepped steady syncopated patterns that interacted around the drum pulse and also correlated with the beats of the small drum. The four best dancers, positioned in the front row, waved fly whisks and rolled-up paper back and forth. The other dancers, a total of about sixteen to twenty, lined up behind them in four additional rows, and followed the movements of the front row. Unlike at intervillage competitions, where malipenga is most often performed, the dancers did not rotate around a central point in formation, but rather marched in place facing the VIP stand, their feet stepping in the exaggeratedly slow marching steps characteristic of Tonga malipenga.[6] Their bod-

Figure 4.3 Men dancing malipenga in row-and-column formation facing the VIP stand and dressed in typical malipenga costumes at a rally for Aleke Banda in Tukombo on January 2, 1999. *(From the author's collection.)*

ies bent slightly at the waist while their arms reached up and down and then to the sides. Their shoulders alternated between repeating a slow up-and-down pattern and a more choreographed circular movement that corresponded to changes in the stepping (see Figure 4.3).

Throughout their entrance, the dancers were singing more or less in unison. Once they were all in place and dancing well, two team leaders, one wearing white pants and a white long-sleeve shirt, the other in dark gray slacks and a sweater, moved in front of the formation and danced in place behind the microphone, where they initiated the call lines of their first song, which praised Aleke Banda for his commitment to development. The two dance leaders sang different vocal lines that supported each other heterophonically, while other groupings within the dancers either joined them or sang additional melodic lines, producing harmonies that interlocked melodically and rhythmically. Once the song was well established, the leaders reentered the formation to oversee that everyone performed their best while they continued to sing the call lines.

This event took place at the beginning of the chilimika competition season, so many chilimika groups had already been rehearsing for a month or two. As a result, their performances were polished and well rehearsed. The members of chilimika teams tended to be much younger (the youngest were probably nine, while the oldest were mostly in their late twenties) than the women who danced chiwoda. Some teams wore the same outfits they would usually wear at competitions—combinations of skirts, blouses, sashes, baseball caps, and sunglasses. Others incorporated UDF fabric into their costumes. All of the members of several groups wore skirts made from UDF fabric, indicating that they had received the fabric enough in advance to arrange for tailoring.

The performance of one group began when three men emerged into the performance arena before the women dancers: one beat a timeline on a cowbell; the other two played the same style handmade bass drum that was played for malipenga. The woman dance leader played on a screeching small metal whistle using the same timeline as the cowbell, though the whistle was offset temporally from the cowbell, producing interlocking rhythms. Her whistling signaled to the dancers to move from the audience space into the performance arena while the bass drum set the pulse that was then maintained by the dancers' foot patterns for the remainder of the song. The front row of five, always the best dancers, emerged first, wearing UDF hats in addition to their bright yellow skirts. The rest of the dancers, whose outfits replicated what they would wear in other contexts—blouses, belts, sashes, and sunglasses in addition to their yellow skirts—emerged in two lines following the dance leader, who was whistling and marching backward. The leader drew them out until they gradually formed a row-and-column formation behind the front row. As with the malipenga groups, they did not rotate in formation as they would have at other events, but moved in place, facing the politicians, as shown in Figure 4.4.

The dancers focused their eyes downward toward the ground, their serious gazes fixed while they waved handkerchiefs back and forth until the song leader indicated through a shift in her whistle pattern a change in movement. The dancers then reached their hands out in front of them in the UDF clasped-hand gesture and proceeded to very slowly move down into a crouching position, all the while swaying their hands in conjunction with the steady rhythm. They then gradually returned to a standing position, their outstretched clasped hands reaching into the sky when they were once again standing. They repeated this down-and-up pattern two more times before resuming their original positions and their handkerchief waving. Only then did a male leader of the group, wearing the all-white outfit typical of malipenga groups, who had up until then been stepping in place to the side of the formation, move to the microphone and sing the lead line of their first song in a low nasal voice that reassured "*A Kadona*," a term of respect directed toward Aleke Banda, that he and his party leader Muluzi were on fire with votes. The women dancers responded by finishing his sentence in unison. Their nasal vocal quality maintained a constant tension with little variation in pitch, which sounded almost like shouting within a pentatonic four-note range. Their singing contrasted with the dynamic quality of the drum beating, whose volume rose and fell. The energy of their

Figure 4.4 Women dancing chilimika in row-and-column formation facing the VIP stand and wearing skirts made from UDF fabric in addition to other typical chilimika costume items at a rally for Aleke Banda in Tukombo on January 2, 1999. *(From the author's collection.)*

stepping picked up as they instructed Banda to tell Muluzi that he was on fire in Tukombo, in Lilongwe, and at Sanjika. The audience responded enthusiastically with clapping and ululating. The first song bled into a second song, indicated by a change of beat and an increase in tempo by the drummers and in whistle blowing by the leader. This time, the woman leader took over singing the lead lines, which similarly reassured "A *Kadona*" that he should stop worrying because "we have already won votes":

A Kadona, lekani ku dandaula tawawina
Tawawina kali vote
A Muluzi
A Muluzi sekeliyani he
A Kadona
A Kadona, kondweliyani, eh!
Tawawina
Tawawina kai voti

Kadona, stop worrying we have won
We have already won votes
Muluzi

Muluzi smile today
Kadona
Kadona, be happy, yes!
We have won
We have already won votes

Notice that the song promoted both the local politician Banda and the party's presidential candidate, Muluzi.

Partway through the rally, the sky turned dark, and then darker, until thunder boomed and rain crashed, chasing us to find shelter. I crammed with hundreds of others in a nearby school in what felt like a sauna until the rain stopped and the rally proceeded.

At the conclusion of the dance segment, members of the VIP announced the winners for each dance group, and gave all the dance teams envelopes of money for their efforts, the winners receiving the most. From my estimates, the total amount distributed was about the equivalent of US$870, an enormous amount of money in Malawi at that time. Then came the speeches and the proud introduction of people in the audience who had recently converted to UDF, all of whom stood up and showed off their UDF hats and buttons to the cheering of all.

The next day, though exhausted, I made my way to another rally, this one for Kaunda. I joined a UDF staff member and took the bus along the lakeshore highway, and then walked on village trails under the beating sun for about an hour until we reached Sanga village ("UDF political rally in Sanga Village," http://purl.dlib.indiana.edu/iudl/eviada/5-E4475). In Sanga, I met many of the women I had come to know well on our previous travels and at rehearsals. As they waited for Kaunda's arrival, the rally organizers coordinated a quick run-through of the entertainment section of the event. The singing and drumming of the rehearsing groups drew a large crowd, ensuring a sizable audience for Kaunda and other speakers. Women in yellow also stood scattered along the path leading into the village, spanning about a quarter of a mile. When Kaunda's vehicle was spotted by those farthest away, they sent the message from person to person until it reached us at the rally space. A large number of women, some men, and loads of children then rushed to join the others on the path, where they surrounded Kaunda as he made his way into the rally space, singing a song that thanked him for coming to Sanga. Note the similarity between this welcome and the one for Phumisa described in Chapter 1 where I present the celebrated arrival from the perspective of the politician and his entourage.

As the singing and dancing throng came into sight, Kaunda's dignified graying hair emerged slightly above the crowd. The women continued dancing around him as they escorted him to a seat in the center of about eight upholstered chairs that had been set at the forefront of the rally space. They continued dancing until the rally organizers called out "*yewo, yewo, yewo*" (thank you, thank you, thank you) on the microphone and others nudged the dancing crowds back into the audience. Among the women dancing were the women from the district level, including Mayi Chicago, all of whom wore full UDF regalia. They sat in the front of the audience space, creating a visible yellow contingent. When it was their turn to dance chiwoda during the entertainment, their performance was by far more precise and energetic than anyone else's, an indication of the hours they had spent rehearsing and their commitment to the party. Toward the end of each group's performance, the seated male politicians stood up, almost in unison, as if they had done this many times before, and stepped forward to briefly dance facing the women, their movements reminiscent of the Banda years, and then, diverging from the practice of the previous head of state, they reached into their pockets to give monetary gifts to the dancers.

MCP Campaigning in Nkhata Bay and Mzuzu

The MCP did not have a strong presence in Nkhata Bay during the 1999 campaigns. The MCP campaigned mostly for the MCP-AFORD alliance presidential candidate, MCP leader Chakuamba, though some MCP candidates ran for parliamentary seats in the north. The district MCP office in the town of Nkhata Bay was located on the main road into town. It was neither marked nor visible. Many people I asked did not know where it was. Unlike the UDF office, it did not have a regular staff, and the man I often met there did not always have very reliable information about party activities in the district.

In contrast, the MCP headquarters in Mzuzu was large and well established, probably the same office that had been used during Banda's rule. Consisting of many well-equipped rooms, it sat on a large open field. In front of the building was a plaque on which was written, "Lest We Forget," a slogan coined after independence referring to the repression of the British colonial government. Large posters of Banda decorated the walls inside the building, coupled with posters promoting candidates running in the upcoming elections.

When I first went to the office on December 16, 1998, I met three high-ranking MCP officials in the region, including Wyson Mkotchi, the regional chairman, and the Mzuzu district secretary. The men all wore expensive dark double-breasted suits. The one woman I met, a high-ranking and very famous and important MCP personage, was also there, wearing the type of Western-style clothing usually worn by professional Malawian women, a shin-length colorful rayon skirt and blouse. I had gone to Mzuzu because I had been told there would be an MCP rally on that day. When I arrived, the chairman told me it had been canceled because they were concerned that the working people of Mzuzu would not be available to attend. This detail pointed to the differences in strategies for those campaigning in urban settings, where many people work salaried jobs, versus in rural areas, where most are small-scale agriculturalists and thus have more flexible schedules.

The officials invited me instead to join their convoy to Mzimba, a city south of Mzuzu, where Chakuamba was scheduled to hold a series of rallies on December 21 and 22. When I arrived at the MCP office prepared for the excursion, having woken up early to take a minibus from Nkhata Bay to Mzuzu, all was quiet. The regional chairman, who was the only one there, looked apologetic as he explained that the rally had been canceled because Chakuamba had collapsed and been rushed to the hospital during a rally several days before. I include these details because cancellations were frequent. Inasmuch as I traveled far and made great efforts to attend rallies, so too did party supporters and those invited to perform expend a great deal of time and often money, sometimes only to find that it was all for naught.

Unfortunately, I was out of the country when Chakuamba and Banda's former hostess, Mama Kadzamira, came to Nkhata Bay to campaign. I was told that the party invited women from throughout the district to come to town, where a large and enthusiastic rally took place. Many women MCP supporters who had not danced politically since the transition to a multiparty system of government entered the dance arena to support their party once again.

The only other MCP rally I had the opportunity to attend while in Nkhata Bay took place on March 30, 1999. My husband and I took a minibus on yet another gray, rainy, and dreary day and arrived in Chinteche around noon. We found a green flag stuck in the ground in front of some stores on the main street near the minibus stop. Some benches had been set near the flag, and a few people milled around. Eventually, a man arrived driving a large open-bed truck. He was one of several MCP candidates officiating the event. His arrival drew people to the rally space. A drummer appeared and started beating, and women formed a circle to dance chiwoda and sing. Soon after, a hired minibus showed up carrying important MCP dignitaries from the northern region, including the men and woman I knew from the Mzuzu office.

After the transition to multipartyism, one way that the MCP distinguished itself from the Banda past was by designing a new fabric that conformed to democratic ideals. Rather than having a picture of the party leader as its centerpiece, the new design featured the party's red and green colors and acronym, as did the cloths of other parties, signifying that the MCP was no longer identified with one person, but rather existed for all and that the leadership would be selected through a democratic process. According to MCP officials, the party had ordered this new design from the country's one cloth manufacturer, David Whitehead. Throughout the 1999 campaigns, the cloth was never printed. Mkotchi explained that the fabric company neglected to fill their order because "you know we [MCP] are not in control. As Muluzi was saying the

Figure 4.5 Women's spontaneous dancing during a speech at an MCP rally for Mr. Chirwa in Chinteche on March 30, 1999. Two women wear carefully preserved mbumba uniforms. *(From the author's collection.)*

other day, 'I've told David Whitehead to produce yellow cloth only from now on!' So, we are stuck" (personal communication, March 29, 1999). I heard this explanation from other MCP officials, though I was not able to verify that the failure to produce the MCP cloth was politically motivated. I did confirm that the cloth was not available at David Whitehead stores throughout the 1999 campaigns, during the 1999–2000 academic year I spent in Blantyre, or during my stay in the summer of 2004. Because there was no new MCP fabric, carefully preserved pieces of Banda fabric and random red and green fabric and clothing items dotted the symbolic landscape of MCP rallies instead, as shown in Figure 4.5.

As with other rallies, when the MCP officials arrived at this event, singing women escorted them to their benches as the crowd expanded. When the officials were seated, three male drummers entered the center of the empty space between the audience and politicians, and around fifty or sixty women soon followed, four to five of them dressed in their well-kept Banda regalia. The event was heavy with nostalgia for the Banda years, as was evident from the following song:

LEADER: *Mungaluwanga*
ALL: *Mungaluwanga*

LEADER: *Mungaluwanga*
ALL: *Mungaluwanga vyo wangukamba a Ngwazi.Mungaluwanga cha!*

LEADER: Don't you forget
ALL: Don't you forget
LEADER: Don't you forget
ALL: Don't you forget all that Ngwazi said. Don't you forget, no!

The leader repeated the simple phrase "Don't you forget" until the rest of the dancers eventually finished the statement, clarifying what it was that the performers and audience should not forget, the messages and accomplishments of Dr. Banda, the *Ngwazi*.

A long series of speeches, mostly by male parliamentary candidates, interrupted the dancing. The best-received speakers started by leading songs in well-rehearsed, strong voices, to which the women and others in the audience enthusiastically sang the appropriate response lines; many were the same songs that had been sung during the previous regime. The praise in some was directed toward Banda and the MCP rather than the current candidates. One of the most electric speakers was the woman I had met at the MCP office, who wore a well-tailored red Banda uniform. She began by entering the performance arena and enthusiastically shouting the slogan "Kwacha," to which the audience responded, "Kwacha," the same slogan, "dawn," coined by nationalist leaders in the movement for independence. Not receiving the desired response, she explained to the audience that when a rooster is crowing, he flaps his wings in the air, and so too should the audience wave their hands in the air while shouting this slogan. That she had to clarify what their response should have been suggested that most in the audience had not attended many other MCP rallies recently. She then started a song whose first call line was "Whatever hardships might happen, we will take the government," to which mostly women in the audience responded by singing, "We are behind Kamuzu." She interrupted herself again, this time to clarify how the audience should respond: The correct answer was "We are behind Gwanda [Chakuamba]," indicating the degree to which Banda continued to be the rallying symbol for the party despite its new leadership, and the extent to which Banda songs continued to be the basis for singing after the transition.

As the rally continued, I heard drumming from the other side of town, and then a car passed that resembled Kaunda's car, which I had ridden in months before, to Tukombo. I learned later that women UDF supporters were practicing not far away in preparation for President Muluzi's upcoming visit to Mzuzu. The drumming and singing from the two parties on either side of town was a sonic representation of the political landscape.

As the speeches wound down, swarms of women entered the circle and formed concentric rings, into which I was pulled, evoking much laughter and intensifying the spirit. They danced and sang nostalgically, a performative enactment of their memories of the political past under Banda as well as their support for the MCP.

Political Dancing after the 1999 Elections

In the 1999–2000 academic year, I lived in the southern city of Blantyre, which provided me with opportunities to increase my knowledge of political activities in an urban center. The UDF party was especially well organized in this city because the party's stronghold was in the south, and Muluzi's home village was in Machinga District in the southern region. I joined the regular gatherings of two action groups, committees of women organized through the UDF party that engaged in some self-help and charity activities, in the high-density neighborhood of Zingwangwa. Residents of Zingwangwa belong to a range of economic strata, including the very poor; those subsisting on steady, but small incomes; and up-and-coming professionals. This neighborhood had a bustling market district and active nightlife.

The relationships of these urban supporters to the UDF party were quite different from those of many rural women I knew in Nkhata Bay. With the exception of the women active at the district level, many of the Nkhata Bay women came together only when they were called to rehearse or perform. The Blantyre women came together weekly and participated in numerous events both within their constituencies and in the city of Blantyre. The large and very yellow district headquarters on the highway that cuts across Blantyre and connects Blantyre to the adjacent city of Limbe was often bustling with activity. Crowds of UDF women clad in yellow waiting for transport or rehearsing were often my signal that a political event was scheduled. UDF women often traveled great distances to participate in government events, private company functions (especially if the president was officiating), and national events (such as National Education Day), in addition to political rallies.

Though the election campaign period was over, the heightening of political organizing, specifically of women who were party members during the previous campaigns, was kept alive by the UDF leadership. Under the direction of the district leaders of the women's wing in Blantyre, the two action groups met weekly for short business meetings followed by dance rehearsals. At their meetings, they conveyed messages sent from the UDF headquarters, organized their trips to party rallies, and shared information about the needs of members of the group and community. Their rehearsals usually took place in front of one of their homes or at a neighborhood soccer field. One or two men from the neighborhood drummed for them while the women developed new songs and established dance moves. They danced chimtali, the chiwoda-like variant most popular in the central and southern regions.

Some of these women lived in multiroom houses with running water and electricity. The majority lived in less expensive houses constructed similarly to those most commonly associated with villages. Their morning activities resonated with those of their rural counterparts. Many shared the responsibilities of cleaning, caring for children, and preparing meals. Some had gardens to tend. Most who were married relied on their husbands or sons to provide money needed by the family, though many also engaged in small-scale commerce, selling such things as fresh vegetables, beans, rice, charcoal, and cooked food—*mandazi* (doughnuts), samosa (Indian fried pastry), banana fritters, boiled peanuts, or roasted corn.

The woman who introduced me to these groups was Mayi Kachoka, a neighbor of Praise Gondwe, who assisted me with my research in the neighborhood. Mayi Kachoka, a forty-two-year-old UDF member, supported herself and her family by making and selling crocheted covers for chairs. Her husband was a small-scale businessman who sometimes went to neighboring countries to buy things to sell in Malawi. She explained to me that when she was fifteen, she was forced to stop her schooling because she developed eye problems that made it difficult for her to read the blackboard, which subsequently limited her options. She danced at the regular practice sessions of her action group and at rallies when they were held in her neighborhood and when the president held mass rallies in Blantyre. As with many women active in political parties I met in Blantyre, she played a role in the women's association of the Catholic church she attended that was similar to the role she played in the party. Other women in Zingwangwa similarly struggled financially. Mayi Masekesa explained that when she had money for capital, she engaged in small-scale business, selling secondhand clothes. Her husband did not engage in any income-generating activities. Mayi Smoko sold doughnuts from her home. Mayi Mphande was widowed and struggled to support herself and her family selling dried fish.

I also spent time with MCP supporters in Zingwangwa who were active members of their women's wings. They too were organized into neighborhood-based committees and served important functions for their parties and one another. At their regular meetings, they shared ideas, discussed strategies for attracting other women into the party, and practiced singing and dancing. Their economic situations were similar to those of the UDF supporters. Mayi Kunthembwe, an elderly woman, explained that "money is a problem" and that she lacked any way to generate income (personal communication May 16, 2000). She relied on her adult children, who provided her with help when they could. Twenty-seven-year-old Mayi Mhone was widowed with five children and supported her family by selling charcoal and sometimes beans.

During my time in Blantyre in 1999–2000, the MCP was fraught with internal conflicts, as Chakuamba and Tembo battled over the leadership of the party. Each of the two heavyweights held many events to rally support for his side. Tembo's energies were directed mostly toward his home region in the center, while Chakuamba enjoyed more support in the south. I joined MCP women and leaders for two rallies, one organized by women in honor of Chakuamba's wife to express the women's support for her and her husband, and another presided by Chakuamba in a rural community in the Mulanje District. At these rallies, women danced chimtali and sang eagerly about the party's greatness. The party fabric still had not been printed, so some women wore uniforms made out of plain green or red fabric, while a few donned their well-kept Banda uniforms.

AFORD did not have a strong presence in Blantyre, though numerous supporters lived in the city and joined together for party activities as needed. Mayi Mtayamanja, whom I met on June 1, 2004, explained that AFORD supporters in her neighborhood in Blantyre met on Tuesdays and Saturdays to rehearse. When AFORD's leader, Chihana, planned to come to Blantyre, AFORD officials telephoned to tell them to practice and prepare to welcome him. Because there were no AFORD members of parliament in Blantyre, she explained that they did not participate in many AFORD rallies other than during campaign periods.

The perspectives of these Blantyre women and my experiences attending business meetings, rehearsals, and rallies in and around the city greatly inform the analyses in upcoming chapters.

The Songs

The songs sung at the rallies of all parties conformed to praise-singing practices associated with the political sphere, and the songs performed at the rally of one politician were often the same as those performed at the rally of a competing politician, but adapted to be appropriate to the specific context, making it important to consider the process through which songs were composed and spread.

Some of the songs sung at political rallies were already known to all the dancers, while others were newly introduced by an individual or group participating at a specific event. Some were variations of those sung during Banda's rule, others were adaptations of songs sung in nonpolitical contexts, and still others were new compositions. During the practices that occurred prior to an event, the group of individuals present rehearsed songs in their shared repertoires, changing song leaders according to who best knew and could best sing any given song. The song leader not only sang the call lines of the song, but was free to manipulate and change lyrics, making them context specific. These changes were usually straightforward—such as the replacement of a name, title, or political party—but they were also sometimes complex improvisations. Because all participants were familiar with the basic style of singing, respondents could easily contribute the appropriate response to the call line, altering it as needed. Sometimes the response line remained the same, allowing the leader to freely improvise. In other cases, the response line included the changed word of the call line. For example, in a song sung at the MCP rally in Chinteche, the leader began with the call line "*Isi iyayi kusatopa Bakili*" (It is not us who support Bakili), referring to Muluzi, which the group eventually responded to with the line "*Choka, choka, choka Bakili*" (Get out, get out, get out, Bakili). In a subsequent verse, the leader changed the line to "*Isi iyayi kusatopa Katenga*" (It is not us who support Katenga), to which the rest responded appropriately "*Choka, choka, choka Katenga*" (Get out, get out, get out, Katenga).

New songs were introduced either by individuals or by groups. Women from Nkhata Bay District, for example, when invited to perform in Mzuzu, sometimes heard a group from another district sing a song they liked. One or more women would remember the lyrics, and then later, the woman or women would teach the song to other party women, and thus the new song would be incorporated into the group's repertoire. New songs spread throughout a party's structure in much the same way. For example, rallies at the district level brought together women from branches within the district. At district-level practice sessions, women from each of the branches introduced songs that they taught to those at the district level, who then could integrate them into their repertoires (Mayi E. Nyirenda, personal communication, March 23, 1999). When women at the district level came together for regional or national events, they continued to spread the lyrics. Similarly, leadership of a party's women's wing at the district, regional, or executive level could spread song lyrics that were particularly suitable to the party's image and strategy by using the party structure, a top-down approach. At a regional meeting that brought together representatives from districts, regional party leaders could teach a song to women present, who upon returning to their respective districts, taught it to women in all the branches in their districts, until eventually, it was sung by people throughout the country, even in the most remote places.

The sharing of songs occurred not only within one party, but also between parties, creating multiple intertextual layers of significance. Women from one party could hear a song sung by another that they thought was clever. They then changed the lyrics to make it appropriate to their party and to the contexts in which they performed. The following songs illustrate this type of intertextuality. At the UDF rally held in Sanga for Kaunda, on January 3, 1999, UDF supporters performed a song in which they refused to wear AFORD fabric and proclaimed their commitment to wear only that of the UDF because "Kadona" (a title of respect referring to Kaunda) had forbidden it:

Salu yaku Chihana yo	Cloth of Chihana
Ndivwalenge cha	I will not wear
Nanga yingatowa ule	Even if it is beautiful
Nanga yisiki mutengo	Even if the price goes down
A Kadona wakana	Kadona has forbidden it
Ndivwalenge cha	I will not wear it
Salu za UDF	UDF cloth
Ndivwale pe	Is the only cloth I will wear

A variant of this same song was performed by MCP women at the Chinteche rally, in which they refused to wear UDF fabric:

Nsalu	Cloth
Tivwalenge cha	We will not wear it
Nanga yingatowa ule	Even if it is very beautiful
Nanga yisiki mutengo	Even if the price is very low
A Gwanda wakana	Mr. Gwanda [Chakuamba] forbids it
Tivwalenge cha	We will not wear it

In this song, the women claimed that even if they were given very beautiful cloth for free or at a low cost by the UDF, they would refuse to wear it because the president of their party at the time, Gwanda Chakuamba, forbade it. The song hinted that though the UDF tempted the women with its gifts, these women would not be so easily bought. The declarations in both of these songs that women's political affiliation was expressed through their choice of party fabric also references the singing during Banda's rule, for example, in the anti-M.W.K. Chiume song given me by Mary Chiume that ended with the line "We wear the cloth of Kamuzu."

When a new song was taught to a group of dancers, whether it was an original composition or a song learned from others, one person usually taught the rest the song. At one rehearsal I attended, the song leader stood up with the drummer, while the rest of the dancers sat. Accompanied by the drummer, the leader sang the lead line followed by the response line so that the group could hear it. The next time around, she sang only the lead line, and those who remembered sang the response. They continued in this manner until everybody knew the song. Once everybody was adequately familiar with it, the group stood up in a circle formation, and the leader showed the others the accompanying steps, which they practiced and further developed as a group. At subsequent practices or even at a performance, those who were not present when the song was first learned joined the group and followed what the others were doing. This process made it easy for anyone to join in whether or not they had previously rehearsed. The time for learning a song was also an opportunity for further refining a song's text or rejecting it. As the person introduced the new song, the rest of the group could interject words or lines that they thought would improve it. Sometimes, the group decided that the song was inappropriate or not very good. This collaborative process provided opportunities for creativity, but also for censorship in that the group's decision overrode opportunities for personal expression; I elaborate on this topic in Chapter 6.

Dance, Gender, and Party Affiliation

In my presentation of political dancing in Malawi, I distinguish between the chiwoda-like dancing, or *gule wa chipani*, the "dance of politics," by women party members and the dancing by what I call "established dance groups," which existed outside the political sphere. Many Malawians did not divide political dancing into these two categories; some disagreed that political dancing was gendered, pointing to the fact that men, such as performers of malipenga, danced during the entertainment segments of rallies. Certainly, the dancing in the two categories was similar. All the dance forms I describe were emically labeled "traditional"; all served similar functions of livening the proceedings up and providing opportunities for expression of cultural identities; and party officials relied on all to attract people to rallies and spread political messages and symbols. Furthermore, the songs accompanying all the dances usually conformed to praise-singing practices. I contend, however, and many in Malawi agreed with me, that the first category was distinct from the others because it was gendered: Only women participated in this capacity.

Men active in their political parties wore party paraphernalia, usually T-shirts, hats, and buttons. They shouted slogans, sang at various times, and certainly some occasionally moved their bodies rhymically. The male members of political parties, however, were not systematically organized to sing and dance as were their female counterparts. The participation of men (and women) in "established dance groups" was contingent on their affiliation with a dance group rather than a party. When men danced malipenga at rallies, they did not participate or display themselves as party members, but rather as performers. My inclusion of the chilimika example illustrated that not all women who danced at rallies did so in the same capacity. As with malipenga, performers of chilimika participated primarily as entertainers, and individual members did not necessarily support the party. The distinction between the two categories was also communicated through costume: performers of established dance groups usually wore the costumes appropriate to their dance genres, whereas women party members ideally wore the head-to-toe party outfit. Note that even within established dance groups, however, women were more likely to incorporate party cloth into their costumes, as in the example of the chilimika dancers in the Tukombo rally, further signifying the symbolic linkages between women and party symbols, so well established during the Banda years.

To confuse things even more, some women perform in both capacities. Mayi Chirwa, a chilimika dance leader in the village of Msani in Nkhata Bay District, understood the difference between the two categories: "This is a group for chilimika. In it, we have some members from UDF, AFORD, and MCP. When we go vote, we do so on an individual basis. But when it comes to dancing, we come together as does the chief; he does not choose [a political party]" (Mayi Chirwa, personal communication, February 8, 1999). An avid AFORD supporter, Mayi Chirwa joined her chilimika dance team, America State, to perform at the rallies of all political parties in the 1998–1999 campaigns. However, she participated with other women party members dancing *chiwoda* only at the rallies of the party she supported.

Another clear indication that the two categories are distinct is that even at gatherings where no dancing is explicitly organized, women party members still often show up or are invited by party officials to serve in the capacity of praise performers. For example, on February 26, 2000, the private company RAB Processors held a private function for the launch of a new food product, and President Muluzi was the featured speaker. I was not able to attend this event because it was invitation only, but I acquired a videotape from a friend of a friend. Although the event was held indoors, between the podium and the seats provided for invited guests, a group of women wearing UDF fabric sat on the ground, ululating and singing during Muluzi's speech. Men active in the general membership of their parties were not invited or allowed entry.

The singing and dancing by women party members is further distinct because it comprises the most visually and aurally salient dancing in rallies: It frames the beginnings and endings of events, embellishes speeches with interruptions, and is prominent during entertainment segments. It features in political discourse: Journalistic reporting of political happenings frequently mentions the presence of women in party paraphernalia singing and dancing. Little mention is ever made about male or female performers of established dance groups, evidence that women's chiwoda-like participation is considered by many to be distinct and symbolically important within the political culture and the discourse that surrounds it. In addition, many refer to women's political dancing by the name *gule wa chipani*, rather than by the name of the genre of dancing, for example, chimtali or chiwoda. By 2004, many Malawians called UDF women who danced at rallies *liolio*, because as journalist Pilirani Semu-Banda explained, "every time the president speaks, they go liolio" (mimicking the sound of ululating). No similar name for male dancers or their dancing exists (personal communication, May 27, 2004).

Gender, Dance, and Patronage

Continuing patterns established during previous phases of Malawi's political history, the use of women praise performers in the post-transition political scene is rooted in large class (economic, education, and political) divisions between politicians and the majority of the population and is characterized by paternalistic patron-client relationships. Political party hierarchies correspond largely to economic disparities evident within the population. Those at the highest echelons of parties, most notably elected officials and those in the executive leadership of the main bodies of parties, belong almost exclusively to the top 20 percent, and many to the top 10 percent, of the country's elite. A majority of those at the lower echelons, operating at the lower levels of parties' main bodies and within the youth and women's wings, including most of the women who dance, belong to the country's poor majority, what is often called *grassroots* in Malawi (Lwanda 1996: 19; *Second Integrated Household Survey* 2005).

As in most African contexts, characterizing the population along class lines in Malawi is problematic because distinct classes do not exist; rather, individuals with widely varying access to resources have strong interpersonal relations with one another. Most wealthy Malawians necessarily have close family members who live at lower economic levels; people of differing economic levels have access to those at higher and lower ones; and individuals may at different times have significantly different access to resources. For the sake of understanding the relationships between dancers and politicians, however, it is useful to superficially reify class distinctions, given the striking differences in the lifestyles and access to economic resources between most politicians and most women who participate as praise performers.

Similar to what has been documented in other African countries, the model for politicking and for much social interaction in contemporary Malawi is based on continual assessments of social relationships within a fluid political-economic pyramid structure of haves and have-nots. Irving Leonard Markovitz described class in Africa as "the question of who gets what, when, where, and why—and who gets left out" (1987: 4). In *The State in Africa: The Politics of the Belly*, Jean François Bayart contended that in Africa, the state is "a major manufacturer of inequality." He correlated having political power with having access to economic resources, which ultimately results in a small number of people gaining large amounts of both political and economic power while the majority of the population has little (1993: 60–83).

Access to economic power and access to political power in Malawi are often intertwined. Holding a governmental position is one way in which some people hope to preserve and expand their wealth (cf. Bayart 1993: 87–89; Monga 1999: 49; Tripp 2000: 3; Vaughan 1998: 183), and those in the economic elite not only enjoy economically superior positions, but also have greater social and political power than do the majority in the population. Séan Morrow described the patronage system in Malawi, epitomized by Muluzi, as "populist pork-barrel politics" that operate at the parliamentary, government, and popular levels (2006: 154). Harri Englund likened Malawi politicians to piggy banks: "a big man or woman who embodies the welfare of the dependants in his or her persona and who, as such, is constituted in him- or herself by those relationships" (2002b: 176). Muluzi exemplifies this image in his very corporality. Photographs of him before his presidency reveal a relatively thin man, contrasting markedly with his current robust frame, an embodied representation of his wealth and his status as the ultimate Malawian "piggy bank."

At the same time that many opportunistically gain materially from their positions, many politicians also promote themselves within a rhetoric of paternalistic generosity, perhaps to stave off criticism or even rebellion, but also as a strategy to maintain themselves in their positions of power. In the new multiparty system of government, a person needs his or her constituents' support through votes in order to hold political positions and ultimately to increase wealth (Bratton and van de Walle 1997: 62–63). To get votes, politicians must "nourish the clientele on which their power rests," which often means exploiting governmental resources to maximize one's ability to give (Chabal and Daloz 1999: 15). Because the majority of the population, including most women who dance, are poor, politicians and political organizers target these people in order to obtain votes and gain legitimacy. One way politicians attempt to sway individuals to vote for them is through gifting.

Neither women dancers nor most established dance groups are hired to perform with agreed-upon terms of service and compensation. Rather, they participate with the hope that politicians will provide them with gifts. In many dance contexts in Malawi, as in many other parts of Africa, audience members express their appreciation by entering a dance arena and giving small material gifts to individuals or groups whom they feel are performing especially well.[7] Since the transition to a multiparty system of government, politicians have capitalized on these customs by giving to both women party members and established dance groups. As described at the Sanga rally, politicians make grandiose gestures of entering the dance arena, often briefly joining dancers, and then handing the lead dancer coins, bills, or envelopes of money. At other times, they gift party fabric, bags of salt, sugar, or other basic needs.

The gifts given during dance performances outside of politics are usually small tokens of appreciation, usually a small coin or two or sometimes a snack or bottled soft drink. Politicians' gifting of dancers is framed as this same practice, though they give much larger amounts and more systematically. In the campaign leading up to the 1999 elections, the UDF party spent millions of Malawi kwacha, the local currency, to compensate performers. The source of the money for these gifts was ambiguous. All the politicians I interviewed told me that at least some of the money they spent was their own. The papers reported that donor countries contributed money to the parties so that they would have equal opportunities for campaigning. Yet, many contended that the opposition saw little to none of this money. Others claimed that President Muluzi and his UDF party received money from Muslim countries, raising a sometimes expressed alarm that the Muslim president planned to transform Malawi into an Islamic state (Chirambo 1998: 206–207).[8] Further rumors suggested that perhaps some of the money was counterfeit. Suspicions over the source of UDF campaign money persisted into the 2004 elections when the UDF amassed large sums to promote its presidential candidate, Bingu Mutharika, and many of its parliamentary candidates. In the ensuing battles between Muluzi and Mutharika, evidence emerged that Muluzi probably did illegally use donor money intended for development for political purposes (Malawi Agents Raid Muluzi's Home 2005). A leading UDF politician in October 2005, George Mtafu, made a public admission to Parliament that "K1.4 billion from various donors" was "deposited into party chairman Bakili Muluzi's personal account" and "was used for UDF's electoral campaign last year [2004]" (Sonani 2005). Mutharika too has come under fire for allegedly using state funds to finance his new DPP party (Malawi MPs Renew Impeachment Bid 2005). Whatever the source of the money, UDF candidates spent enormous amounts of money on pecuniary gifts to dancers, money unavailable to other parties.

Closely related to giving out money was the distribution of party paraphernalia before and during political rallies. Though this distribution was a strategy to spread party symbols throughout the country, it was frequently presented rhetorically as one more example of a party's generosity. UDF officials, for example, explained to people at rallies that their party was different from the former ruling party. During MCP rule, women had to provide their own party cloth, and they were required to bestow gifts on Banda. With the UDF, by contrast, not only were people free to choose which party to support and whether or not to wear a party's symbols, but the UDF gave women the cloth for their uniforms for free. The following song text, which I recorded at a UDF rally I attended in Ntcheu with Jane Phumisa on April 26, 1999, but which I heard at almost every UDF rally I attended, included "free cloth" in its list of benefits provided by the UDF government:

Feteleza wa ulele
Chimanga cha ulele
Nsalunso za ulele
Tijuthokoza pa zomwe mwatichitira

Free fertilizer
Free maize

And also free cloth
We are thankful for all that you have done for us

Women dancers representing the clients in these patronage relationships expressed their positions by publicly receiving gifts and singing songs, such as this one, of gratitude (Morrow 2006: 154).

The UDF's financial advantage over its competitors during Muluzi's presidency was also evident in its ability to have visible offices throughout the country, to hire staff, to paint its buildings, and to provide campaign vehicles. The Nkhata Bay District chairman's decision to offer free transport to *matola* seekers with the party truck was one more projection of the party as a generous patron.

These patronage relationships have become so much the standard in Malawian politics that all politicians I interviewed, regardless of their party affiliation, conceded that a person could not win an election unless he or she went along with the system and provided gifts to prospective constituents. As one prominent UDF male politician who wanted to remain anonymous explained on April 24, 1999:

> This is democracy. It is an expensive system, but we have all come to accept it. . . . You need to have money to please. They [constituents] don't think that an MP hasn't got any money. Anybody who says, I want to say such and such a thing [at a campaign rally], you should give [to him or her]. Because they don't expect you to say, "No, I don't have it." If you say you don't have it, they say, "Oh no, he is not good. He is mean." You see? So they want leaders that can help them to alleviate their own poverty. . . . It's hard times and . . . you have to dish out!

Similarly Patricia Kaliati, a UDF politician, explained after winning her second term in 2004, "You cannot . . . you cannot make it unless you have resources. If you won't give them money, you help them construct roads. You construct bridges" (personal communication, June 21, 2004). Correspondingly, a number of dancers I interviewed expressed their preference for a party because of what it had provided for them materially. UDF member Mayi Rojasi, who lived in the Zingwangwa neighborhood when I met her, explained that she liked the UDF because she received cloth or money when she danced for it, as is discussed in Chapter 6 (personal communication, May 2, 2000).

Even the highest-level politicians are involved in relationships within these patronage systems. The national chairs of political parties, for example, to a large extent assist some politicians and not others in their campaigns for office. In exchange, the lower-level politicians owe allegiance to the higher ranking ones. In an article in the Kenyan newspaper *The Nation* on March 27, 2005, the reporter explicitly blamed the conflict between former president Muluzi and current president Mutharika as resulting from the latter's refusal to act his role as client to his "patron" Muluzi, to whom he owed his success: "Mutharika's predicament stems from politics of patronage. The current president [Mutharika] is a beneficiary of patronage, or in other words, he owes his presidency to his predecessor, Muluzi. . . . Once in power, he [Mutharika] embarked on an anti-corruption mission that turned the heat on Muluzi's cronies. This move did not go down well with Muluzi who decided to come for his pound of flesh" (Ngunjiri 2005).

During Muluzi's presidency, many candidates from other parties felt that UDF politicians had corrupted the system. In giving monetary gifts during the 1999 election campaigns, many, such as Ophten Ebell Sinkhala, an MCP parliamentary candidate in Chitipa District whom I met in Mzuzu, felt that the UDF was trying to buy votes: "Bribery is evil. So, what our friends [in the UDF] are doing, giving money to those who dance with an impression of buying them is evil" (Group Interview with MCP Officials, March 29, 1999; see Appendix B). A number of politicians from AFORD and MCP told me that they did not feel that they should have to pay dancers to support them. Watson Kawirima Khonje, for example, an MCP parliamentary candidate I also met in Mzuzu, said:

> In our party, we don't [pay dancers]. We try to instill selflessness in our members, so that whatever they do, they do it . . . for the sake of the party. . . . What the ruling party is doing now, UDF. They have a lot of money to throw out. As a result, we still have a good message to deliver to our people. Money or no money, we do it, because the reward comes at the end. Let's fight with or without money. We'll get the reward in the end." (Group Interview with MCP Officials, March 29, 1999; see Appendix B)

Similarly, John Nkhwazi, AFORD area chairman within the city of Mzuzu, explained that for their party, dancing was voluntary. "Music and dance is part of culture. It is something people just do, not something they do for money. Maybe UDF pays money, tries to buy them. For AFORD, it is voluntary" (personal communication, April 9, 1999). Though in these quotes opposition politicians explained that they did not pay their dancers, evidence suggested that many felt obligated to try and occasionally did also give. Dancers with whom I spoke said that they had received monetary gifts from AFORD and MCP, though the amounts were much smaller than what I observed at UDF rallies. According to Mayi Chirwa, for example, her chilimika team received MK145 ($3.50, or about 10 U.S. cents per dancer) each time they performed for the 1999 AFORD incumbent candidate for their constituency (Mayi Chirwa, personal communication, February 8, 1999). Mayi Ma. Longwe from Nsanje told me her chilimika team had received MK10 (about 25 U.S. cents) for dancing at an AFORD rally also during the 1999 campaigns. These amounts were more in line with the tradition of giving token amounts to performers as demonstrations of appreciation.

Correspondingly, the other parties did not have the resources to produce and distribute as much party paraphernalia as did the UDF when it governed. Because MCP fabric had not been printed at the time of the 1999 election campaign, it not only was not available for advertising the party, but also could not be used as gifts. Barbara Momba was the southern regional secretary for the main body and the women's wing of the MCP when I interviewed her at the Blantyre MCP office on May 23, 2000. She explained that the MCP was at a disadvantage because it could not compete with the UDF's distribution of uniforms to women supporters. She explained that women from the different parties competed against one another through their uniforms, and that she thought some former MCP supporters had switched to the UDF only because they wanted "beautiful uniforms."

Though it was available for purchase in the David Whitehead fabric store in Mzuzu, I did not see AFORD politicians distributing the party's cloth during the 1999 campaigns, most likely because many AFORD politicians did not have enough resources to do so. At the AFORD rally in Nkhwali, Mwenda, the AFORD Member of Parliament for that constituency, promised to provide one of the dance groups that he particularly liked with T-shirts. Another AFORD parliamentary candidate who asked to remain anonymous and who won the election in his constituency told me that he had not been able to distribute much party paraphernalia during his campaign, though his opponent, with help from UDF, had distributed large quantities. Using his own money, he therefore made and distributed one hundred T-shirts to his supporters. He explained that his constituents were impressed with this act; it was a message to them that "I can do it; here is someone with little resources who is not in government, but this is what he can do! It was a morale builder." He felt that having and sharing personal resources was an important test of his dedication and ability to serve his constituents (personal communication, May 6, 2000). Notice that his explanation has more to do with the importance of demonstrating his ability to provide than it does with the distribution of paraphernalia as advertisements.

By the 2004 elections, the giving of material gifts at political rallies had become normalized, and most politicians gave as much as they could. Even the independent candidates in the 2004 elections produced some promotional materials to distribute, as is discussed in Chapter 7.

Notes

1. For detailed descriptions of the transition period, see Van Donge 1995: 3; Chimombo and Chimombo 1996: 25–26; Muluzi et al. 1999: 135–50.

2. Banda's birthday was not recorded, leaving much speculation about his actual age at this time. Popular opinion put him in his late nineties.

3. This organizational structure is similar to those in other African countries. Jane L. Parpart and Kathleen A. Staudt estimated that political parties in as many as forty-one African states have similar women's sections (1986: 9). See also Mba 1982, 1989; Munachonga 1989; Geisler 1995; Adamolekun 1976; Chazan 1989.

4. Cf. Mullings 1976; Robertson and Berger 1986; Bayart 1993.

5. The histories of malipenga and by extension chilimika, which was modeled on malipenga, intersect with World War I and World War II, which explains the militaristic themes characteristic of both genres (Ranger 1975; Kerr and Nambote 1983; Kamlongera 1986; Gilman 2000a.). In my research on chilimika, I was very interested in these connections, and I asked many people in Nkhata Bay about the militarism in both forms. Though historians and some elderly Tonga people make the connection, most in Malawi did not equate the dances with militarism, but rather associated the costumes and movements with ideals of dignity, respectability, and dressing well. Though I do not think that this militarism held any political significance in contemporary Malawi, the costumes and movements of a related dance form, *beni*, by the Yao people in the southern part of Malawi, more clearly resonated with contemporary law enforcement, and this dance was probably used at times to comment on or parody the contemporary political sphere.

6. The Tonga and Tumbuka both dance malipenga, though they are distinguished largely by the tempo of their stepping. The Tonga variant is exaggeratedly slow, and the Tumbuka one is much more fast paced and athletic. A stereotype of the Tonga is that that are obsessively concerned with their appearance and cleanliness, and many Tonga explained that their malipenga is slow so that they can preserve the cleanliness of their all-white uniforms. Many other ethnic groups in the region perform variants of malipenga, often called *mganda* or beni (see Jones 1945; Mitchell 1956a; Lambert 1962–1963; Koma-Koma 1965; Ranger 1975; Argyle 1991, Hill 2000; Nyoni 2000).

7. For examples across the continent, see Mack 2004: 48–49; Askew 2002; Kasule 1998: 45.

8. I should clarify that concerns about Muluzi's faith were relatively minor, and tensions between Christians and Muslims in Malawi have not been very politically significant. In my description of Muluzi's northern campaign launch in Chapter 5, for example, a Christian clergy member leads the prayer without evoking tension from Muluzi.

5

Power and Performance in Political Rallies

My focus now narrows to a single high-profile rally to illustrate how these performance events both serve the interests of political power wielders and yield opportunities for negotiations of power. This event, the launch of Muluzi's campaign for reelection in the northern region, which took place on April 17, 1999 in the city of Mzuzu, was the most elaborate of any campaign rally I attended. It was especially interesting because the focal person was the country's president, and the event took place in the northern region, many of whose residents felt that Muluzi had largely ignored their needs. UDF officials exerted great efforts, including transporting masses of women and established entertainment groups from throughout the region to come to Mzuzu to perform, to ensure that this event was a success. They also distributed enormous amounts of paraphernalia, effectively cloaking the event and much of the city in yellow.

Inasmuch as political dancing constitutes a performance, so too do the rallies of which it is a part. Rallies are complex performance events in that they comprise multiple primary genres—speeches, slogans, prayers, dances, songs, and costumes—each of which serves as a communicative channel on its own. These genres then interact with one another in the constitution of the whole event, in addition to referencing previous enactments intertextually. The women who dance play an especially important role in these communicative processes because through their participation, they embody numerous channels simultaneously: They appear in great numbers, wear yellow, shout slogans, sing, and dance, all of which contributes to the repetition of party symbols and messages. However, the multiplicity of channels and the potential for dialogism also produce the possibility for them to express multiple, and sometimes conflicting, messages. Examining the ways in which politicians capitalize on these communicative channels and the ways in which audience members can differently interpret what manifests during rallies yields insights into ways that power is articulated and negotiated through performance.

Muluzi's Campaign Launch in the Northern Region

After launching Muluzi's campaign in the southern and central regions, teams of organizers from the UDF came to Mzuzu to work with the district and regional level committees to organize the event in the north. Preparing for the event generated a buzz of activity across the region, and I joined many hundreds of Nkhata Bay UDF supporters who traveled to Mzuzu to participate. By the day preceding the event, President Muluzi gazed down from life-size portraits placed in central locations throughout the city. Bright yellow flags waved from vendors' stalls, and yellow banners draped the outside walls of businesses and other important institutions. UDF supporters—women dressed from head to toe in bright yellow fabric; men and boys wearing yellow T-shirts; and men, women, boys, and girls wearing various combinations of yellow hats, towels, scarves, and buttons—brought to the regional center from all districts in the north poured into the city, strolled the streets, and filled restaurants, hair salons, and rest houses. Yellow vehicles circulated the city carrying loads of yellow-clad supporters who shouted slogans and sang songs that thanked and praised the president and his party. Supporters swarmed the yellow-walled UDF regional office, distributing or receiving party materials, rehearsing, and helping to coordinate the week's events.

Having received permission from regional UDF officials, I joined several thousand people as they made their way to the airport on April 16 to welcome Muluzi, who was scheduled to arrive that afternoon on the presidential jet. A UDF official directed me to stand, video camera ready, alongside reporters very near the red carpet that would lead Muluzi from the airplane into the airport. The exterior walls of the building were lined with life-size portraits of the president and covered with yellow banners and flags. UDF supporters abounded, wearing multiple yellow items while carrying yellow banners and holding portraits of the president high overhead. As the time for the president's arrival neared, hundreds of yellow-clad women clustered in groups lined the tarmac, as shown in Figure 5.1. Each group moved rhythmically in place, singing its own songs, which produced a cacophony of melodies. Muluzi's accomplishments and greatness rang through the air in mosaics of song texts. Behind me pushed hundreds of male party supporters, probably members of the youth wing, all dressed in yellow T-shirts and other party paraphernalia.

Figure 5.1 Women dressed in UDF uniforms line the tarmac at the Mzuzu airport on April 16, 1999, waiting to welcome President Muluzi. A red carpet leads into the airport, and life-size posters of Muluzi decorate its walls. *(From the author's collection.)*

When the presidential jet was sighted in the distant skies, party and government dignitaries, mostly men dressed in black and gray suits, lined the red carpet, preparing to welcome and greet the president; the crowds hushed, allowing the women's singing voices to rise above the din. As their singing reached a fevered pitch, Muluzi emerged from the airplane, wearing a black suit with a small yellow flower peeking from his left jacket pocket and a bright yellow UDF button fastened to his left lapel. Ushered by male UDF officials clad in dark suits and plenty of security staff, he walked along the red carpet, shaking hands with each of the almost exclusively male dignitaries awaiting him, who stood just in front of me. Behind me the hundreds of men pressed forward. As Muluzi neared the airport building, two security officials raised yellow umbrellas to shield him as he disappeared into its entrance (see "President Muluzi's welcome at the Mzuzu airport," http://purl.dlib.indiana.edu/iudl/eviada/5-E7025).

The next day, yellow-clad crowds made their way to Katoto Freedom Park (see "President Muluzi's campaign launch in the northern region," http://purl.dlib.indiana.edu/iudl/eviada/5-E5559). To one side of the large grassy field, a yellow shelter erected during the preceding days shaded a platform on which were rows of chairs. To the fore was a podium draped in UDF fabric. To either side of the platform, but on the ground, and without shelter, were several more rows of folding chairs. VIP guests—regional party leaders, UDF parliamentary

Figure 5.2 UDF women situated in the center of the entertainment arena spontaneously stood up, burst into song, and danced during a speech by President Muluzi at his northern region campaign launch in Mzuzu on April 17, 1999. *(From the author's collection.)*

candidates, the spouses of prominent UDF politicians, important traditional authorities and village headman, the press, and I—gradually filled these seats. The general audience, consisting of entertainment groups and hoards of people in the same yellow regalia seen for days created a semicircle in front of the seating area, leaving a large open space between them and the VIPs.

As the time for the president's arrival neared, the female master of ceremonies stood up and yelled over the microphone in Chitumbuka, the language of the Tumbuka, majority ethnic group in Mzuzu: "Ladies, ladies, we should be, we should be singing over there. We should sing because the boss is about to arrive. Ladies, ladies, we should sing." A group of about thirty women in head-to-toe yellow positioned themselves in the middle of the empty performance space, where they remained for the duration of the speech making that followed, as shown in Figure 5.2. Standing behind a microphone, they began to sing, only to be interrupted soon after by sirens in the distance, signaling the president's arrival. The TOT Band, a Tanzanian ensemble hired by the president for the campaign period, positioned on a stage behind the general audience, burst into the theme song of the president's campaign. The audience and many already seated in the VIP stand enthusiastically joined in repeating this strident, catchy melody over and over:

President Muluzi
President Muluzi
Palibenso ofananaye
President Muluzi

President Muluzi
President Muluzi
There is no one comparable
President Muluzi

It graced party dignitaries and presidential security as they descended from vehicles, and women ushered them to their reserved seats, the most central and best chair offered to the smiling president, who was wearing a bright orange-yellow shirt.

The MC officially began the rally by initiating a well-known UDF slogan. She shoutied "U," and the crowd, led by the yellow-clad women still seated in the center of the arena, yelled back, "DF." The MC proceeded:

MC:	*UDF*	UDF
CROWD:	*Boma leni leni*	The real government
MC:	*Kumpoto?*	In the north?
CROWD:	*U*	U
MC:	*Pakati?*	In the center?
CROWD:	*D*	D
MC:	*Kumwera?*	In the south?
CROWD:	*F*	F
MC:	*Dziko lonse?*	In the whole country?
CROWD:	*UDF*	UDF

After greeting and paying her respects first to the president and then to all the important guests in order of descending status and prestige, the MC called the Reverend Overton Mzunda to say a prayer because "the president, who is God-fearing," is "heading the party, which also fears God." Following the prayer, the regional chairman took the microphone to invite all UDF parliamentary candidates in the northern region to parade in front of the audience, accompanied by the Phaka Town Band, the same honara group that had performed at Austin Mwenda's rally months before. Members of the group played the accordion, sang, and danced alongside the shadow MPs, who mimicked their dance steps. Once all were seated, the regional chairman stood up to make a short speech. Immediately, the yellow-clad women spontaneously rose and burst into song:

Boma, boma ili
Bomali lachitukuko
Ati amayi?
Amayi kuyenda opanda mantha, ee!
Bomali lachitukuko
Ati abambo?

Abambo kuyenda opanda m'sonkho, ee!
Ati anawa?
Ana akupita kusukulu
Bomali lachitukuko

Government, this government
This government is development conscious.
What about the women?
They move without fear, yes!
This government is development conscious
What about men?
Men move without poll tax, yes!
What about the children?
They attend school [without paying fees]
This government is development conscious

Eventually stopping their singing, the MC thanked the women, asking them to sit down so the parliamentary candidates could proceed with their presentations.

Then speaker after speaker rose to talk, each one alluding to the role the president played in the transition to a multiparty state, emphasizing the weakness of the opposition, pointing to the UDF's accomplishments during its five years of rule, and intermittently shouting slogans. The yellow-clad women in the arena periodically stood up and burst into song, responding to and interrupting speeches. On occasion women seated within the VIP stand—some politicians or political organizers, others wives of politicians, most dressed in full yellow uniform—descended from their VIP seating to join the singing and dancing women.

The last person to speak was Muluzi, who was welcomed by the singing women, who were again interrupted by the Tanzanian TOT Band singing the president's theme song. Muluzi began his address by shouting in his characteristic low, booming voice: "*Zinthu zathani*?" (What have things done?) to which the audience roared, "*Zasintha*!" (They have changed!) He then made some attempts to address the crowd in Chitumbuka, the language most commonly spoken in the north, instigating much ululation and clapping by the women in the arena and the general audience, positioned farther away. After greeting all the honored guests—"the country and UDF's vice president, executive members of the party, members of Parliament and parliamentary candidates, traditional authorities, church officials, and all ladies, gentlemen, boys, and girls present"—he began his speech. He emphasized his accomplishments during his term of office, explained the government's shortfalls, made promises for the future, and criticized his political adversaries. Singing women intermittently interrupted his speech with songs that alternated between praising him and castigating his opponents. He ended by pleading with people to vote for him and the UDF parliamentary candidates in the upcoming elections, warning them that if they did not vote for UDF candidates, they should not be surprised if after elected, he did not visit their areas or see to their development needs. Women accentuated the conclusion of his speech with shrill ululation, clapping, and more singing.

The entertainment portion of the event followed. One after the other, dance groups and a few choirs took turns coming into the performance arena. Most women dancers wore full yellow party uniforms, while most of those men and women performing dances with more specialized costumes incorporated bits of yellow. When the MC called for Rumphi women to dance mbotosha, three women in yellow UDF T-shirts and yellow skirts made from UDF fabric (zitenje) crouched at the microphone while three drummers, all wearing yellow UDF T-shirts, arranged their drums behind the women. One drummer pounded a triplet pattern, which the other drummers quickly took up with interlocking patterns. The three women stood and started the call line "*Rumphi-i-i iyo*!" (Rumphi, there it is!). They stepped in place three times, and then kicked their right feet out in front of them while their hips moved to the triplet patterns of the drums, with occasional pelvic thrusts as accents. Their arms reached high into the air and waved back and forth. As they sang, the rest of the group, about one hundred, emerged in three columns, each of which followed a dancer, moving backward who drew the column into a large concentric circle. As they stepped, kicked, and thrust their hips, they sang the call line repeatedly in unison until they had formed three rings of concentric circles, at which point they took up the rest of the song:

"Rumphi-i-iyo!"
Ona step iyo
Mayi wa ku Rumphi
Awo wona m'nyako

Matipati ndi boma
Ndimphalilani
Wanyina chipani wapinyoliska
Wapinyoliska
UDF ni boma, wanyinu chipani

Rumphi-i-iyo!
Nati nimphalilani

Muluzi ku Malawi wawinengeso
Wawinengeso
Chipani Chambula boma

Chikhalenge cha
Wawinengeso
Muluzi ku Malawi wawinengeso
Tamvotera Muluzi ise-wo!

Rumphi, there it is!
See the steps
Women from Rumphi
Watch your friends

Multiparty government
Let me tell you
Your friends have sold their party
They have sold it
UDF is the government, your friends have sold their party

Rumphi, there it is!
Let me tell you

Muluzi in Malawi will win again
He will win again
A party without government
Will not stand
He will win again
Muluzi in Malawi will win again
We will vote for Muluzi!

As with every other group that performed, halfway through the first song, the VIP stand emptied as men in dark suits, a few women in elaborate versions of the party uniform, and President Muluzi, flanked by male security guards, also in dark suits, descended from their elevated stand, walked across the open space, and approached the dancing group deposit money into waiting hands. The MC thanked them and called the next group, a malipenga group from Rumphi. As each group performed, the politicians paraded down to give money, so much so that bills and envelopes often tumbled out of the receivers' hands, challenging them to maintain their performance while deftly reaching to the ground to gather them up.

As it got later, the MC rushed groups into and out of the arena as quickly as she could, calling out "*Nyengu yamala,*" (Time is running out). The entertainment segment was cut short when the rally was called to an end at around five o'clock, and the president and other dignitaries made their way back into their vehicles and departed ceremoniously in a convoy with the presidential siren blaring, women's singing voices still in the background.

Rallies as Complex Genres

Malawians classify events such as Muluzi's launch within the generic category of political rally. Because a rally is a recognizable genre, people expect certain structural and ideological conventions when they attend one (Bakhtin 1981; Bauman 2004: 3; Barber 1999). The ideological conventions for this event included that power was centralized within the party and politicians sponsoring the event, and that the event was explicitly about promoting a party, its members, and its activities. The structural conventions included that it took place in a public arena, followed a formulaic sequence of events, and was multigeneric.

Building on Bakhtin's argument about speech genres and using examples from Northern Ireland, Ray Cashman (2007) argued that by their very nature, certain performance genres are monologic, while others are dialogic. Malawian rallies, such as the one discussed in this chapter, were intended to be monologic: All messages should serve the single goal of promotion by reifying, legitimating, and advertising a party and its leaders in addition to spreading information about the weaknesses of opponents. To some extent, they could be analyzed as scripted performances (Jourde 2005: 430–37). Party officials worked hard to try to ensure that all involved participated in this event in the way they had planned, and that they disseminated only those messages desirable to the party. An AFORD politician interviewed in April 1999 described this process when he explained that composers were told that songs performed at AFORD's rallies should (1) praise the party's leaders, (2) disseminate the party's manifesto and policies, and (3) educate audiences about important health or economic issues. Similarly, at the regular rehearsals for UDF women in Blantyre I attended in 2000, officials from the district office regularly attended to make sure that dancers were fulfilling party directives.

Though organizers of the Muluzi launch event in the north attempted to control the messages disseminated, the possibility for the articulation of multiple concurrent messages during the enactment of individual genres, in addition to the dialogic potential of different genres interacting with each other, allowed for contradictory messages to be disseminated simultaneously, ultimately resulting in semiotic cracks often outside the control and sometimes even awareness of rally organizers (Bakhtin 1981: 276–77, 1986: 62; Bauman 1991). The dialogic interaction of the numerous communicative channels operating within a single complex performance engendered webs of signifiers that could be variously interpreted by participants based on the foci of their attention, their relationship to various aspects of the performance, their past experience, and so on. Furthermore, because many actors were often involved in the production of the primary genres, the locus of control was diffuse, and messages that could be variously interpreted by participants could leak out (cf. Fernandez 1986). The manifestation of power and the types of meanings various actors attached to what transpired in rallies were therefore not nearly as centralized or monologic as they might have appeared to be.

Pre-Event Hubbub

The UDF leadership went to great efforts to coordinate the prerally buzz through the ubiquitous display of party colors, the singing party supporters paraded about on top of open-bed trucks, and the singing and dancing women rehearsing throughout the city in the time preceding the event. As with the rallies described in Chapter 4, organizers coordinated performers' early arrival at the launch as part of a strategy to attract an audience. The performers themselves were members of the audience: The more performers the organizers invited who attended, the larger their audience would be.

As people arrived, they were immediately enveloped within an escalating emotional atmosphere saturated with multisensory messages about the greatness of the soon-to-arrive politicians. Murray Edelman explained that "political symbols bring out in concentrated form those particular meanings and emotions which the members of a group create and reinforce in each other" (1985 [1964]: 11). The political symbols at this Malawian rally, already concentrated with meanings and emotions, were intertwined with energetic and culturally valued music and dance practices. Bruce Kapferer wrote that music and dance have a central role in Sinhalese rituals because "they mold all subjective experience to their form" (1986: 198). Whether or not they mold *all* subjective experience, there is no doubt that direct experiences of collective music making can impact a person's emotional state. As Steven M. Friedson asserted, the experience of people making music together is "an intense, intersubjective experience" that brings participants "into an existential immediacy unparalleled in quotidian or ritual life" (1996: 7; Turino 2000: 56). All those present, whether performing or observing, participated as the rhythmic vibrations moved from the ground through their bodies, and their sensory receptors became alert and focused on the surrounding heightened atmosphere.

Of those who attended this rally, as with other rallies, some came because they were committed party members. Through their presence, they expressed support, and they came prepared to listen to what the party had to communicate to them. Others came because they were politically undecided and wanted to hear what those sponsoring the event had to offer. Others may have been opposed to the party but were interested in hearing what it had to say. Some came only because they were invited as performers, or they came primarily to be entertained. Others came in the hopes that they would receive material gifts. Regardless of why an individual attended, she or he contributed to the dissemination of messages about the party: A large turnout communicated symbolically to politicians, voters, and opposing parties that the party enjoyed popular support (cf. Kertzer 1988: 119).

The Arrival

Muluzi's arrival in Mzuzu a day before his launch provided the opportunity for two welcomings: one at the airport and the other at the rally. The arrival fanfare was a display of the presiding politicians' legitimacy and status. In the case of Muluzi's arrival by airplane, air travel within the country of Malawi was rare, and the distance between cities was small, making air travel usually unnecessary. His airport arrival was a loud statement proving that he was presidential material, given that he already had access to the presidential jet. At all rallies, politicians' ceremonial arrivals in private vehicles (or airplanes) is also a performance of their status as part of the country's elite, their economically and politically superior position to the people they address in speeches, and, indirectly, articulations that they have adequate resources to provide for their current or prospective constituents.

When Muluzi emerged from his vehicle at the launch into a dancing mass, the women welcoming him sang:

Tialandire, kudzatiwona	We welcome you, you've come to see us
Tialandire	We welcome you
Anduna athu, tialandire	Our leader, we welcome you
Abwera lero	He has come today
Tialandire	We welcome you
Kudzatiwona	To see us
Tialandire	We welcome you

Welcoming guests properly to one's home is very important culturally in Malawi, and failing do so can cause great offense. Through songs, women conformed to these cultural conventions and symbolically enacted their roles as the representative hosts for the region. They welcomed Muluzi warmly on behalf of all.

The relationships between the guest(s) and the dancing women, expressed kinetically and through song texts, were clearly ones in which the guests were in more authoritative and powerful positions and deserving of special attention.[1] For example, being offered a seat in Malawi is a signal of being a welcomed and honored guest. When I was welcomed into people's homes, status differentials were clearly enacted. As a well-educated foreigner, I was automatically granted a certain amount of status. In most cases, the person receiving me greeted me and provided me with seating. The status of the person then determined whether or not he or she joined me. It was fairly common that after I had been received, the person greeting me would disappear. However, if the person receiving me shared similar status, she or he often sat on a chair with me. In the case of political rallies, women welcomed guests and then left to sit on the ground in the audience space, or at the Mzuzu event in the middle of the performance arena, thus signifying their respect for the guests in addition to their lower status. UDF officials who greeted the guests, by contrast, joined them in the VIP seating, enactments of their similar social positions.

These welcomings also played an important role for politicians faced with the challenge of promoting themselves at these events. The enthusiastic displays could affect the psychological states of both the people already there and those who were arriving. I did not speak with Muluzi about how he felt at this event, though I do have information from other politicians about their experiences at other rallies. In my travels with politicians, the rides were often long; sometimes meals were skipped. When the rallies took place in rural areas, the roads were often bad, making the trek even longer and more tiring. The throng of women swarming around the car, expressing excitement and happiness at our arrival, invigorated and energized us so that by the time we emerged from the car into the singing mass, we too had smiles on our faces; enthusiasm for the event returned. Politicians interviewed expressed that these performances often empowered them to lead the event. Ophten Ebell Sinkhala, an MCP parliamentary candidate in Chitipa in the 1999 election, explained, "Sometimes when you prepare to have a public meeting somewhere, you feel very weak spiritually. You have all the facts with you, but you feel very weak. But after hearing some dancing and some singing, then power comes on you. You speak with power, which you did not expect to have when you started" (Group Interview with MCP Officials, March 29, 1999). The greeting of guests and their ushering to specially arranged and reserved seating contributed to the warm welcome: They received the communication that they were wanted in the area, certainly information important to someone presenting him- or herself as the locale's current or prospective representative.

Spatial Relationships and Orientation

The spatial arrangements at the Mzuzu events as well as at rallies more generally created an immediate visual and physical representation of power and class divisions (cf. Stoeltje and Bauman 1989: 167). As Muluzi descended from the airplane, the relationship between Muluzi, parading on the red carpet, and the rest of those present, standing on the tarmac, articulated gradations of status. Immediately along each side of the carpet were those elites, almost all adult men wearing dark suits, privileged enough to occupy the space closest to that reserved for the president, with whom they were also entitled to physical contact: The president shook each of their hands as he advanced toward the airport building. Immediately behind were people a few rungs down the status ladder, including myself, categorized between the elite and the general population. The male youth were positioned in organized clusters behind the higher-level participants. The women dancers lining the edge of the tarmac were visually prominent, yet also farther away, fulfilling their specialized roles as praise performers.

The organization of space at the launch was similar to that at other rallies I attended, though on a far grander scale. The VIP area at rallies always included some type of seating, though the quality and quantity differed depending on the occasion and location. The highest-status politician, often the one for whom the event was organized, in this case Muluzi, sat in the best seating, positioned in the center and front. To his immediate right and left was lesser-quality seating reserved for his immediate entourage, officials at the next status level. Less comfortable seating and benches were placed beyond and behind (cf. Kertzer 1988: 31). At the Mzuzu event, the attendees with the highest status not only received comfortable seating, but also sat under a canopy. Those of us in the less exalted seating area enjoyed the comfort of chairs but suffered under the beating sun. The thousands of other people present, performers and general audience members, sat on the hard, dusty ground or stood for hours, many of them fanning themselves with pieces of party paraphernalia.

Access to the VIP seating space at rallies was for the most part limited to political leaders and other elites, except when people in the general population escorted politicians to and from seats, greeted them, or delivered messages. The spatial division between politicians and the general population was especially pronounced at the Mzuzu event, where the president and the other highest-ranking elites sat on a stage above ground level and far removed from the audience, whose positioning was controlled by security personnel.

The performance arena was an open though restricted domain that either remained empty or was occupied with individuals or groups who entered to perform. At most rallies, women party members filled this space with their singing and dancing before rallies began. Once a rally officially started, the area usually remained empty except for the designated entertainment segment and when women spontaneously entered it during speeches. In the scripting of the Mzuzu event, officials coordinated women to sit in the middle of the entertainment area. They were the only ones sanctioned to fill this usually empty space in order to fulfill their prearranged roles as exemplary audience members: They were positioned to be the quick respondents to initiations of slogans or comments from the podium. Anyone else attempting to enter this space was quickly ushered off by the many security personnel.

The use of the performance domain was most formalized during the entertainment segment, when the MC invited one performance group after the other into the space for a limited amount of time. The MC called each group by name, officially giving them access to the space; each group moved in quickly and subsequently acted its praise for the party. When the MC felt that the group had performed enough or that it was not fulfilling its role appropriately, it was told to leave the space through the MC's repetition of the words "Thank you, thank you, thank you," either in English or in Chitumbuka, followed by the immediate introduction of the next group. During the performance segment, politicians and guests of honor accessed the performance space to gift and join dancers. Had they entered it at any other time, it would have caused confusion.

The centralization of power at this and other rallies was contingent on all participants complying with the rigid spatial and sequential structures established and controlled by party organizers. Failure to appear or to leave the performance arena, singing or shouting slogans at inappropriate times, or entering a space to which one was not permitted or at the wrong time could disrupt the rally or subvert the messages intended by organizers. During a speech by Manoah Chirwa, a leader during the independence movement who was forced into exile shortly after independence, a group of young men, probably AFORD supporters, disrupted the event by noisily emerging from the audience space and shouting slogans against the UDF. The response to this disruption was quick. The MC quickly took the microphone from Chirwa and loudly shouted "U!" The audience was supposed to respond "UDF!" but the MC did not get much response. She then shouted, "Sit down everybody. Take your positions. Nothing has happened! Sit down! Nothing is wrong!" A man then led the women located in the performance arena in a song while the security personnel hustled the rabble-rousers away.

The use of space also provided opportunities for dialogic messages. The movement into the entertainment arena by VIP guests to join dancers was a symbolic act because the VIPs transgressed the spatially established identity divisions. While the dancers and the VIPs were dancing together, class divisions were briefly overridden by shared cultural identifiers. When VIP women joined women dancers, they expressed shared gender identity and solidarity. When asked about joining dancers during her rallies, Bertha Masiku, a successful UDF parliamentary candidate in the 2004 elections, explained that it was to "make them feel that I am part of them. Yes, you see. I did not want to just sit on the chair and then look at them. I join them, make them feel that I can dance. I can also dance traditional dances" (personal communication, June 16, 2004).

These displays of gender solidarity communicated complicated messages about class and status. As Laura Fair wrote, differences in dress can be examined for the ways in which they articulate intersections of gender and class (2001: 64–109). On the one hand, they expressed cultural solidarity tied to shared gender identity. On the other hand, conflicting messages emerged through the vast contrasts of the visual images presented by the dancers and the female VIPs as they shared space. The latter were often heavier, a signifier in Malawi of wealth, well-being, and beauty, and had smoother, shinier skin because of greater access to cosmetics and less time spent working under the beating sun. Their dress, hairstyles, and footwear also differed markedly. The uniforms of most dancers tended to be made with minimal amounts of cloth and usually lacked any extra ornamentation. The dancers' footwear was usually cheap, worn-out, and sometimes missing. In contrast, women VIPs, especially at an event like the Mzuzu launch, usually wore elaborate outfits. They were tailored in the same basic clothing style and made out of the same party fabric of the same quality produced by the same cloth manufacturer. However, their outfits were visibly of higher quality and more expensive. They often included a second-layer of fabric, fancier tailoring, and additional adornments, such as ribbons or lace. When the VIPs wore head wraps, they often wore wigs under them, making for more flamboyant and stylish headpieces, and many wore fancy sunglasses, showy costume jewelry, and stylish high-heeled footwear. When elite women entered the dance arena to perform, the two categories of women dancing together communicated to some extent unity based on shared gender: All were women wearing party uniforms and dancing together, yet, at the same time, their actions and contrasting dress pointed to striking differences in economic status.

Opening of the Event

The moderator for the Mzuzu event was a woman MC who ushered speakers on and off the stage and performers in and out of the performance arena. It was also her job to bring the crowd's attention back to the official activity when there were disruptions and to gracefully stop women from dancing or singing when their spontaneous performances was deemed to have gone on long enough. The selection of a woman for this particular event was a calculated demonstration of Muluzi's commitment to women's rights, as was clear from the MC's opening speech:

> The women have sent me, Mr. President, to thank you for the great party platform that you made public at Mount Soche the day before yesterday when you unveiled the manifesto, especially when you said that women should take part in development work, work in the business sector, work in the education sector and other areas, especially in politics. *As you can see for yourself today, I am the Director of Ceremonies.* Secondly, Mr. State President, my friends sent me to thank you because it is only the UDF that has ten women as shadow MPs in the upcoming general elections.

In response, the women in yellow seated on the ground in the performance arena broke out into hand clapping and ululation. The convention during the Banda era was for the MC to be selected from high-ranking members of the League of Malawi Women, suggesting that the selection of a female MC for this event may have had more to do with the traditionalization of the practice than Muluzi's commitment to women's rights. Also note that ten female MPs comprised about 5 percent of the parliamentary seats at the time, not a very significant representation of women, and positions to which the applauding women seated on the ground could never aspire, given the lack of opportunities for poor women to move up politically. The paternalistic relationships so ingrained within the political sphere were also implied in the MC's speech. She thanked the president for all he had done and would do for women, portraying the president as a benefactor empowered to bestow upon women their rights. She thanked the president alone for the party manifesto, certainly the product of a great number of people's efforts, in much the same way as he was panegyrized in song texts.

The prayer that followed the opening of the launch was a standard feature of rallies. The male clergyperson who led the prayer was from a local Christian church; he prayed loudly so all could hear him give credit to God for having safely brought the guests to Mzuzu, communicating that the politicians were watched over, and hence legitimated on a higher cosmological plane.

Symbols

The preponderance of UDF symbols before and during Muluzi's campaign launch in Mzuzu was striking given the regionalism of Malawian party politics. People in the north overwhelmingly supported AFORD, yet one of the biggest cities in the region was covered in UDF yellow. Party colors and symbols disseminated through visual media served the party in several ways. When a party creates and spreads its name and symbols throughout the country, it becomes a real entity, something tangible with which people have regular contact (Kertzer 1988: 6; cf. Blomqvist 1987). The presence of these symbols not only on inanimate objects, but also on bodies, further reifies the party, visually demonstrating that it has real people as members. It is also through the wearing or displaying of party symbols on personal property that people can publicly proclaim allegiance to an organization. All those displaying party symbols contribute to the goals of the party. The frequency with which people see the symbols can increase a party's perceived legitimacy, as it becomes ever present and gives the illusion that it enjoys support (Kertzer 1988: 17). In the following quote from his speech, Muluzi demonstrates his understanding of this process:

> We want to know who belongs to the UDF. We don't just want yellow here and there. If a person is a preacher, he is supposed to move with

> a Bible in his pocket. Who knows? Maybe he will find himself at a funeral. What would he do then? The name of the father, son, and the holy spirit, yes! [Laughter.] People should know that you are UDF! Look yellow!

There is also a psychological dimension to getting people to display and enact their allegiance to the party. The fusion of some dance forms in contexts throughout Africa with supernatural beliefs and practices has made dance an especially powerful and sometimes dangerous mechanism for political use. Reed, for example, explained that *genu,* masks of the Dan in Côte D'Ivoire, mediate between the spiritual world, where the ancestors reside next to God, and the world of humans. *Ge* dancers are valuable to politicians because they are the "ultimate manifestation of earthly power and authority" (2003: 55). Similarly, in the Mande world, the words of griots and griottes are laden with *nyama,* a powerful force associated with the occult that according to Patrick McNaughton "is a prerequisite to all action and it is emitted as a by-product of every act" (1988: 14–15). Barbara Hoffman explained that the griot's (*jeli*) performance "stimulates the person to whom it is addressed, wakes him/her up, makes him/her vibrate with the energy of *nyama*" (1995: 39). These powerful performers variously invoked the spiritual world to bring power to politicians in these contexts, and they could also use it dangerously against opponents. In Malawi, some dance forms are linked to occult power in similar ways, for example, the masked dance form, *gule wa mkulu,* of the Nyau male secret society of the Chewa people. David Kerr, for example, explained that Banda used gule wa mkulu dancers to intimidate the supporters of the exiled ministers (1998: 37). The dancing by women party members at this rally was not associated with the occult in these ways. It could nevertheless evoke powerful emotional reactions useful for achieving political goals. David Kertzer explained that "by engaging people in a standardized, often emotionally charged, social action, rituals make these symbols salient and promote attachment to them" (1988: 40; cf. Stites 1987: 23). The meanings people attribute to symbols are often influenced by the sentiment they associate with it. For example, if a person experiences a symbol within a context of intense positive emotion, for example, at a rally with its pervasive singing and dancing, they may associate positive attributes with that symbol (Elder and Cobb 1983: 37).

Political leaders at this as at other rallies strategically attempted to give potential supporters a positive embodied experience of their parties in the hopes that it would invoke such feelings of unity, solidarity, and membership, and later translate into votes. Edelman explained that "ritual is motor activity that involves its participants symbolically in a common enterprise, calling attention to their relatedness and joint interests in a compelling way" (1985 [1964]: 16). By being together at a rally, participating in the singing, dancing, slogan shouting, and wearing of symbols, individuals engaged in motor activity of togetherness, and significantly a togetherness that was specifically identified in relationship to the party. An MCP regional official for the south gave me a schema that described the party's strategy for attracting supporters that relied on providing opportunities for people to experience the party firsthand. In the first step, they provided people with knowledge of the party. Once a person learned about the party, she or he should have direct experience of the party, which could include attending or participating in a rally. They hoped that this experience would influence her or him to bond with the party. The process for bonding in their schema was detailed as "I know, I see, I was helped, I trust." Once an individual bonded with the party, he or she should identify with the party. Once the identification occurred, then the person should register to vote. This bonded, identified, and registered person was then somebody who could potentially convince others to also vote for the party (Dausi, personal communication, May 30, 2000).

The distribution of party paraphernalia at rallies continues to function when people display them outside the context of party events. Even people who do not actively participate in politics are nonetheless involved in politics to the extent that they live in a political environment and monitor political happenings through their interactions with political symbols and activities in their day-to-day lives. Though this involvement may be passive, it "involves actively assessing continuities and changes in one's political environment" (Elder and Cobb 1983: 10). In a country such as Malawi, where most of the population lives outside of urban and administrative centers in remote rural communities, if there were no political symbols paraded about, those not already engaged with the political sphere could easily live their lives with little idea of its existence. The presence of bodies clad in party symbols both in the context of rallies and outside them provided a constant stream of information about the political world that even those with little interest nonetheless perceived. The UDF hoped that by having many more symbols of their party on display, they would communicate to these passive participants that its party dominated.

The association between a party and its visual symbols is especially important in Malawi, where the majority of the population is nonliterate; visual symbols are therefore used to identify political parties on ballots. UDF supporters therefore exhibited the clasped-hands symbol kinetically during slogans and dancing, and when shouting to supporters, and it appeared on all their paraphernalia, offices, and vehicles, thus ensuring that voters would recognize the symbol come voting day.

The efficacy of convincing large numbers of people to display UDF paraphernalia has to be qualified given that Malawians were well aware of parties' strategies. Some remembered that in 1994, the MCP very energetically distributed its party materials, yet its candidates lost the general election. Others interviewed during Muluzi's presidency explained that they knew that many of the people wearing yellow were not actually UDF supporters, but rather were hoping to be compensated for their displays of commitment. When these critics saw people wearing yellow, it detracted from the UDF's intended message because some interpreted the ubiquity of these symbols as a sign of the UDF's greediness and willingness to do anything to appear as though it enjoyed support. Politicians, performers, and many in the general population were well aware that performers clad in yellow may or may not have been members of the party sponsoring the rally.

Furthermore, the dissemination of party symbols embodied the risk that people would use the symbols subversively to communicate alternate and even derisive messages about the party. In *Subculture: The Meaning of Style*, Dick Hebdige described how members of a subculture appropriate items associated with one context and place them in a different "symbolic ensemble" that works "to erase and subvert their original straight meanings" (1979: 104). People could appropriate the pieces of a party's paraphernalia and place them within a new "symbolic ensemble" or use them in a manner deemed inappropriate, thereby transforming the messages conveyed. This could happen, for example, if a person stole a car while wearing a UDF T-shirt or tore up the T-shirt and used it to haul trash. Some women, for example, who received political cloth did not display the fabric publicly to express their support, but rather used it as bedsheets, where it was out of view. In doing so, they used the cloth not to convey messages intended by the UDF leadership about the party's popularity or legitimacy, but rather reduced the cloth to a useful object hidden within the private realm.[2]

Slogans

A party's visual symbols at rallies intertwine with slogans, creating overlapping layers of signifiers intended to reinforce a party's messages. Politicians often relied on women party members, usually the most covered in party symbols, to also be the loudest respondents to slogans. At the Mzuzu launch, The MC and other speakers often directed their slogans in the direction of the women who dance, who were seated prominently to the fore of the audience space, or at the Mzuzu launch in the center of the performance arena. Slogans were used to focus attention on the podium, to raise emotional levels, and to further disseminate symbols and messages. At the Mzuzu launch, as the rowdy opposition members were being apprehended, the MC attempted to draw attention back to the podium by loudly initiating the popular UDF slogan.

The most popular party slogans in the 1999 campaign were simple and familiar to most people in the country. The slogan used by the MC to mark the commencement of the Mzuzu launch was one of the most popular at UDF rallies:

MC:	*U*	U
AUDIENCE:	*DF*	*DF*
MC:	*UDF*	*UDF*
AUDIENCE:	*Boma lenileni*	The real government
MC:	*Kumpoto*	In the north
AUDIENCE:	*U*	U
MC:	*Pakati*	In the center
AUDIENCE:	*D*	D
MC:	*Kumwera*	In the south
AUDIENCE:	*F*	F
MC:	*Dziko lonse*	The whole country
AUDIENCE:	*UDF*	UDF

This slogan presented an image of national unity that differed from the political reality. Through this slogan, the UDF conveyed the message that the party was not the party of the south as was popularly thought, but in fact a national one. The lead line of another very common UDF slogan was "*Zinthu zatani*?" (What have things done?) with the audience answering "*Zasintha*!" (They have changed!) This single phrase encapsulated references to all the bad things of the Banda regime and all the positive accomplishments of the UDF, and implicitly moved to the forefront the leadership role of Muluzi and his party to the exclusion of others that were also involved in bringing about the change.

A common slogan for AFORD during the 1999 election campaign was as follows:

INITIATOR:	*AFORD*
AUDIENCE:	*Moto, Moto*
INITIATOR:	*Chihana*
AUDIENCE:	*Simbi ya moto*
INITIATOR:	*Ukayigwira?*
AUDIENCE:	*Wapsa*
INITIATOR:	*Ukupsa kangati?*
AUDIENCE	*Katatu Psa, psa, psa!*

INITIATOR:	AFORD
AUDIENCE:	Fire, fire
INITIATOR:	Chihana
AUDIENCE:	A hot iron

INITIATOR:	If you touch it?
AUDIENCE:	You will be burned
INITIATOR:	You will burn how many times?
AUDIENCE:	Burn, burn, burn!

This slogan extolled Chakufwa Chihana, claiming that he was so powerful that anyone who challenged him could not succeed.

Slogans also provided a verbal medium for the repetition of visual symbols displayed on party paraphernalia, further reinforcing relationships between the symbol and the party. In the following example from the March 30, 1999, Chinteche MCP rally described in Chapter 4, a party leader initiated a slogan whose express purpose was to remind people that the rooster would be the symbol for MCP candidates on the ballot:

MC:	*Voti*
AUDIENCE:	*Yang'ana pali tambala*
MC:	*Nawu a Chirwa*
AUDIENCE:	*Nawu a Chirwa*
MC:	*Wawusyaso*
AUDIENCE:	*Wawusyaso chipani. Yang'ana pali tambala*

MC:	Vote
AUDIENCE:	Look where there's a black cock
MC:	Even Mr. Chirwa
AUDIENCE:	Even Mr. Chirwa
MC:	He has uplifted
AUDIENCE:	He has uplifted the party. Look where there's a rooster

Speeches

The relationships among the constituent genres within Malawian political rallies highlighted the social differentiation and political stratification of the participants and that of the political and social environment in Malawi more generally. Speeches were the most restrictive genre, and only those of the highest status and who had been explicitly granted access by political power wielders had the opportunity to address the audience using this genre. Relationships between formal and ideological conventions of this genre were especially strong: Individuals in positions of power stood confidently before the audience and made proclamations that affirmed and legitimized their authority (see Bakhtin 1981: 259).

Often five or more individuals made speeches, culminating in that of the highest-level political figure present, in this case, President Muluzi.

Continuing the model established during the Banda years and widespread throughout the world, the sequence was also an enactment of status gradations within the party, with the lowest-status speaker going first, followed by the next higher person, and so on. It provided opportunities for each speaker to repeat the monologic messages most important to the event. As representatives of the local community, the first speakers in the sequence also voiced the needs of the community to the power wielders present. This sequencing thus allowed for some dialogism, as each speaker had the opportunity to comment upon or respond to things said or performed previously.

Though rally organizers attempted to control the tone of the messages, the speech genre allowed for some agency in that speakers could imply criticism of the party or politician(s) using the generic convention of requests. Speakers who represented communities usually appealed to party leaders for material or development needs, such as schools, wells, hospitals, roads, or fertilizer. These requests were sometimes intended to be or interpreted as diverging from the monologic aura of a rally. Participants—politicians and members of the general audience—sometimes considered them to be direct or indirect criticism. An example of overt criticism might be when a speaker reminded a politician that in past rallies, the politician promised to build the community a well, but they still did not have a clean water supply. Indirect criticism might include a speaker requesting a well without referring to past promises. Members of the community may have heard the politician's promises in the past, and so they could interpret the speaker's request for the well as criticism of the politician's lack of attention to the community's needs.

The Mzuzu launch was less like others I observed in that the ruling party exercised greater control over the messages disseminated in the early speeches. Prominent UDF politicians were selected to give these addresses rather than local officials at the lower echelons of the party as was usually the case. These choices helped to ensure that the overall messages would be supportive.

In his speech, Muluzi alluded to his awareness that he did not enjoy widespread support in the region, and this event was intertextually linked with Muluzi's previous launches in the central and southern regions. Many felt that the decision to leave this region for last reflected his general attitude about the north. Muluzi therefore addressed the ongoing criticism that his government had systematically neglected this region and emphasized his plans for the north, even though these criticisms had not been expressed in the early speeches. Muluzi explained, for example, that only the day before, he had launched his manifesto at Mount Soche in Blantyre, in which he had "made 289 pledges—things that we are going to do to develop the country." Among these pledges, he emphasized that he had finally found funding for a project long promised to the region, the completion of the Karonga-Chitipa Road, which would provide direct transportation to the northernmost district: "I am very pleased to inform you today that I have identified the money from the African Development Bank and also from the Republic of China to construct the road. In fact, the Ambassador of China came to see me yesterday at ten o'clock to tell me, 'I know you are going to the north. Tell the people there that we are releasing the money for the construction work.'"

As in many parts of the world, the audience was aware that making promises was a convention of the genre of political speeches; this awareness combined with their past experiences of Malawian politics impacted their interpretations of Muluzi's pledges. Northerners had long been promised the Karonga-Chitipa Road and had long been disappointed by the government's failure to deliver. Though Muluzi was reelected in 1999, by the time of this writing, the Karonga-Chitipa Road had still not been built, and newspaper headlines continued to address northerners' dissatisfaction (e.g., Ashaz 2008).

Women's Spontaneous Singing and Dancing

Party women participated actively throughout the speeches by encouraging orators with their ululating, clapping, groaning, or shouting. The songs that women sang when interrupting speeches often directly related to what was just said, creating layerings of messages, though usually conforming to the overall monologic tone of promotion. For example, soon after the MC initiated the UDF slogan to refocus the rally after the opposition party's disruption, mentioned earlier, the women seated in the middle of the performance arena burst into a song repeating the narrative that the speaker at the time of the commotion, Manoah Chirwa, was making about his experience with repression during the MCP years, thus bringing the attention back to the subject at hand:

MCP MCP	MCP MCP
Aee aee	Aee aee
MCP	MCP
Amara wanthu	It finished people
A Manoah ndi a Chisiza	Mr. Manoah and Mr. Chisiza
MCP	MCP
Amara wanthu	It finished people
MCP	MCP
Amara wanthu	It finished people
A Chiwanga ndi a Gadama	Mr. Chiwanga and Mr. Gadama
Aee aee	Aee aee
MCP	MCP
Amara wanthu	It finished people

At another moment in the Mzuzu rally, during his speech, Aleke Banda warned the audience that if they voted for Chihana, they were "simply throwing your vote into the water." The women responded with a song critical of Chihana.

Patron-client relations were also encoded in intergeneric exchanges. At the Mzuzu rally, when a UDF politician presented in a speech his or her commitment to developing an area or the work he or she had already done, women interrupted with the development song "Boma Lachitukuko," which characterized the government as being "development conscious" and responsible for instituting such things as free primary education. Meanwhile, Muluzi explicitly stated his commitment to develop only those parts of the country where people had voted for him, evidence of the politicization of development: "Any constituency that votes for an opposition member of Parliament will not benefit from any development assistance from my government. Let us make an agreement here! Everybody knows that UDF is winning this year. So those who vote for an opposition party, no development! You are going to eat opposition politics! Let us tell the truth here!" Shortly after, the women responded with a song proclaiming that they would vote for Bakili, affirming that they should vote for him to receive development.

Tizamvote, ah-ah
Tizambota mavoti
Tizamvota Bakili na waphungu anyake
Eee-ya-ee wawela waka
Aa-ee wawela wakana

We will vote, ah-ah
We will cast our votes
We will vote for Bakili and his leaders [parliamentary candidates]
Eee-ya-ee they will have nothing
Aa-ee they will have nothing

As with speeches, some song texts comprised specific requests from politicians, what some politicians I interviewed referred to as "begging songs." These songs were intended to contribute to the promotion of politicians and the party, yet, because members of the audience were familiar with the generic conventions of praise singing, song texts could also work to undermine the goals of political organizers. The audience knew that singers were organized to show up at rallies and sing songs of praise, and they knew that the convention was for singers to fulfill their generic obligations regardless of the actual qualities of a politician. The interpretive frame for many people receiving the messages was therefore that the content of songs could have little to do with the actual strengths or accomplishments of a politician. Furthermore, expressions of praise could be interpreted in multiple, often contradictory, ways, as is discussed in Chapter 6.

Richard Bauman wrote that "the process of entextualization, by bounding off a stretch of discourse from its co-text, endowing it with cohesive formal properties, and (often, but not necessarily) rendering it internally coherent, serves to objectify it as a discrete textual unit that can be referred to, described, named, displayed, cited, and otherwise treated as an object" (2004: 4; Briggs and Bauman 1992: 73; Barber 1999). As an objectified text, it becomes extractable and recontextualizable each time it is performed. In the case of praise singing, the practice long predates the existence of party politics. During the movement for independence, activists in a sense extracted praise singing from other contexts in which it was practiced, recontextualized it, and made it appropriate for the political arena. Recontextualization then occurs each time praise singing is enacted again, and thus, praise singing at a given rally necessarily references praise singing that has occurred in previous contexts at the same time that it has new meanings specific to the performance context, contributing to intertextual layerings, what Turino called the "semantic snowballing effect" (2000: 176). When a song was sung at an AFORD rally that had been sung the day before at a UDF one, the referential meaning of the song had more to do perhaps with relationships between those in the roles of singers and politicians generally than it did with any inherent qualities of the politicians who were glorified. Praise singing in contemporary Malawi also directly referenced Banda's dictatorship. The continued incorporation of this same genre into the current political culture referenced the oppression of the past. At the same time, that songs criticized opponents in other parties reflected the new multiparty system. Contemporary praise singing also referenced the independence movement, and messages about women's political commitment and pride continued to be central ideological associations of the genre.

That the majority of politicians whose praises were being sung were men and that the majority of the people singing the praises were women revealed an obvious gendered relationship. In Malawi, most women took care of their husbands and families by doing such things as managing households, caring for children, and making sure husbands and children were properly dressed, healthy, and well fed. Men in turn were supposed to provide materially for women and children and were not expected necessarily to take care of them emotionally. Or, as one MCP official explained to me, "with due respect without offending you, you remember that God, in his original plan, according to the Holy Bible, created man, but created woman specially so that the man would be happy" (Dausi, personal communication, May 30, 2000). Within this framework, the dancing of women for men served a similar purpose of taking care of their emotional well-being. By singing for their leader, a man, women helped him feel good about himself and his work. Being made happy in this way, he may do a better job and be more apt to serve the women well. That women also sang for women politicians in the same way does not detract from this argument. The model was based on gender and status differentials. The male politician was in a position to receive emotional bolstering through both his gender and his political position. A woman politician enjoyed similar status through her political position, and some argued that she fulfilled a gendered male role regardless of her biological sex. Former vice president Justin Malewezi expressed this point of view: "It's mostly the position. One might say that in these cases, the women [politicians] are associated males" (personal communication, June 1, 2004).

Entertainment Segment

At the Mzuzu launch, the party organized numerous established groups to perform a wide range of dance forms from the northern region, including malipenga and chiwoda from Nkhata Bay District, chiwenga from Karonga District, vimbuza from Mzimba District, and *ndolo* from Chitipa District. Scheduling performances from across the district contributed to the aura of northern support. The inclusivity of performers also ensured that representatives from throughout the region heard Muluzi speak and returned home with UDF paraphernalia and messages.

The Mzuzu event was unusual because the Tanzanian TOT Band had been hired to promote Muluzi during his 1999 campaign, raising much discussion from Malawians, who questioned his choice of a Tanzanian rather than a Malawian band.[3] The songs they composed became signature songs of the campaign and were performed at UDF functions across the country. The most widespread was "President Muluzi," whose text is given in full above. At the rallies of other UDF candidates, their name was inserted in the song in place of Muluzi's.

One group during the entertainment component comprised seven school-age girls wearing yellow dresses who lined up in front of a similar number of boys wearing black trousers and yellow polo shirts. They stood behind the microphone facing the VIP guests. An adult man accompanied them strumming on an acoustic guitar. The song in English began with the line "We thank you, President Muluzi, for all you have done for us." It then proceeded to liken Muluzi to Jesus Christ:

> The reason for your travel
> Is the care for us
> You sacrifice to care
> For the trouble we should face.

Never in this world
Is another like you, king,
Who teaches us to love
Love like our Lord Jesus Christ
For this we say, God bless.

I have no information about the identity of this group; the MC called them simply "children from Mzuzu." It is possible that the group had some connection to a local church, which could have explained the Christian reference. Regardless, the comparison of Muluzi to Jesus Christ probably referenced the frequent likening of Banda to biblical figures. Likening Muluzi to Jesus Christ elevated him to a status above human judgment, and was especially interesting given that Muluzi is Muslim, evidence of the general lack of religious tension in the country. The similarity between the lines "Never in this world / Is another like you" and the TOT Band's song "There Is No One Comparable" illustrated the type of intertextuality that emerged as individuals drew inspiration from existing songs to create ones appropriate for specific events.

During the entertainment segment, women from each district were scheduled to perform chiwoda-like dances as individual groups. All women organized to perform at this event were dressed especially well. The party's effective distribution of its fabric in the weeks prior to the event allowed women the time to tailor new party uniforms. Several weeks before the launch, as I was doing errands in the town of Nkhata Bay, I met people from Nsanje, the village of Mayi Md. Longwe, who had taken the boat all the way to town to pick up their UDF fabric from party officials in preparation for this event, indicating that the party started the process of distributing fabric well in advance. Women from Rumphi District showcased mbotosha, women from Chitipa and from Karonga danced ndolo, and women from Likoma Island on Lake Malawi performed chiwoda, as did women from other parts of the Nkhata Bay District. All these variants shared the combination of stepping and hip and pelvis movements, the circle formation, and the basic drumming styles at the same time that the step patterns and types of hip movements differed enough that they were distinguishable.

In addition, women who worked for the same professional organizations, specifically teachers and others labeled "civil servants," came together to form dance groups for this event, reminiscent of the Banda years. A group of about 150 teachers dressed in UDF skirts (zitenje) and white blouses danced mbotosha, and their song repeated the line *"Tikupempha maloni"* ("We beg you for loans"). A group of about 200 civil servants also wore white blouses with UDF zitenjes. Unlike the teachers, they did not dance a chiwoda-like dance, but they stood in a large mass behind their song leader swaying back and forth and singing diatonic choral harmonies:

Oh-o a Muluzi
Taonga kwiza kwinu
Oh-o a Muluzi
Mufwase kuno
Ku Mzuzu
Oh-o a zinduna
Koleskani ulongozgi
Wa Muluzi
Mzuzu timphalire
Kukawevye chipatala
Tiwonge Muluzi
Chitukuko chakula
Ta ma civo tikupempha

Oh-o Mr. Muluzi
We appreciate your coming
Oh-o Mr. Muluzi
Feel at home here
In Mzuzu
Oh-o ministers
Safeguard and hold on to the leadership
Mr. Muluzi
We will tell Mzuzu
There was no hospital
We should thank Mr. Muluzi
There has been a lot of development
We civil [servants] we beg

These women probably held a variety of positions under government ministries, such as health, education, and agriculture. No male civil servants performed in this event within similar occupational groupings. Inviting professional women to dance, don party fabric, and sing in support of the president and his party reduced women once again to the level of party cheerleaders at the expense of their expressing individualized political opinions. It is noteworthy, however, that the song texts of both groups referred to their needs within their professional capacities, hospitals and development in the case of the women who sang this song.

Compensation

Politicians' enactment of their roles as current or potential patrons at this event was especially grand. When the politicians flocked into each dancing throng, they gave money to one representative of the group, often the dance leader, who was expected to divide it fairly among its members. The visual image of Muluzi, flanked by other party power wielders, moving with them in demonstrations of the party's abilities to provide, was a performance not only of the party's generosity, but also of Muluzi's role as a patron to the other politicians, who in turn enacted their commitment to provide for their constituents by giving gifts.

Dialogism

Though politicians made great efforts to ensure that the messages promoting the party were disseminated through all communicative channels operating at this rally, alternate and contradictory messages nevertheless seeped out. Rhetoric about the UDF government's commitment to poverty alleviation abounded during the 1999 campaigns. Praise songs, slogans, and speeches were replete with messages about the president's dedication to and success at poverty alleviation, such as the song thanking Muluzi for free fertilizer, maize, cloth, and "all you have done for us." Muluzi declared in his speech, "We have almost 2.7 billion Malawi kwacha [the local currency] that we are using in poverty eradication. We are no longer calling it poverty alleviation. It's eradication!" The dress worn by many of the women singing the praise songs told another story. Because many women had recently received new fabric, their uniforms were in unusually good shape, as compared to its appearance at other events I attended, where women sometimes wore faded or torn party fabric, or none at all. This newness of women's dress contributed to messages about the party's commitment to helping the country's poor. Participants' knowledge about the economic realities in Malawi and the ways in which politicians organize poor women to dance, however, informed their interpretations: Some people with whom I discussed this issue, for example, felt that women's dress at this event amplified the fact that Muluzi's government spent great deals of money on its campaign (i.e., on party fabric) that it could have used toward redressing poverty.

Participants' corporal displays also interacted to signify economic hierarchies. For example, the differences in quality of seating provided to those at different strata was evident during the performances. For example, some women who danced wearing brand-new bright yellow outfits nevertheless had dirt stains on their backsides from having spent hours sitting on the dusty ground prior to their turn to entertain. The elites who descended from their comfortable seating to briefly join the women did not share this problem.

Furthermore, though the organizers exerted great effort to ensure that all women dancers wore the appropriate yellow costume, they did not pay for such things as tailoring, accessories, skin products, or shoes. The occasional worn garment, the poor tailoring, the deteriorating shoes, and the dried-out skin of many were signifiers of poverty. Despite the similarities in general style, elite women's outfits interacted dialogically with those worn by women in the poor majority, indicating class hierarchies and restricted access to political power. Whether women intended to express messages about economic inequities, some Malawians with whom I have discussed this issue interpreted the contrasts between the poorer quality of the sartorial presentations of women dancers with the relative lavishness of those worn by elite women as one more indication of the contradictions between Muluzi's claims to be committed to poverty alleviation and the reality, whereby a large percentage of the population remained visibly poor.

The clothing worn by male politicians contributed to the multitextual mix. Muluzi distinguished himself at the Mzuzu event by wearing a bright yellow-orange button-down shirt rather than a suit, which served to reinforce his relationship to the UDF as well as to offset him visually from the other UDF politicians present. The disparities in wealth between the politicians and women performers were expressed through their expensive dress, amply nourished bodies, moisturized skin, and coiffed hair. The dialogic relationship between the divergent dress styles and quality ultimately referenced the widespread corruption, whereby many politicians during Muluzi's presidency benefited personally from donor aid, rather than using it to alleviate the poverty of the general population (see Chinsinga 2001).

Notes

1. Kelly Askew made a similar point in her analysis of the lively welcome that greeted Tanzanian president Ali Hassan Mwinyi's arrival at the Tanga airport on September 13, 1993 (2002: 4–5).

2. In my attempts to collect pieces of Banda fabric, I was told that after the transition, most women used the cloth as bedsheets. The bedroom was a safe place for these symbols because women could benefit from the functional use of the fabric they had been required to purchase while not risking being criticized for continuing to display the symbols.

3. According to Laura Edmondson, the TOT Band was founded by Tanzania's ruling party, the Chama Cha Mapinduzi, in the 1990s as part of its preparation for the country's first multiparty elections in 1995 (2007: 3; see also Askew 2002: 247). Unfortunately, I do not have any information about why this band supported Muluzi in his reelection bid; I assume that it had something to do with relationships between the two ruling parties at the time.

6

Why Do Women Dance?

Justin Malewezi served as Malawi's vice president from 1994 to 2004 under Bakili Muluzi and then ran for president as an independent candidate in 2004. I was introduced to him by a friend who had worked on his 2004 campaign, and he agreed to a hurried interview on June 1, 2004, shortly after he lost the election. I asked him what contribution he thought women dancers made politically. He answered, "In my own experience, . . . in UDF, in PPM [People's Progressive Movement], and as an independent candidate, we found that women were extremely important for a successful rally. At meetings where there were no women singing and dancing, the meetings were rather—what shall I say—inactive, and you tended to go straight into the speech," which he indicated was less than desirable. The AFORD parliamentarian who requested that he remain anonymous similarly explained that some people come to rallies primarily to be entertained by the dancers; once they are there, he could disseminate his messages (personal communication, May 6, 2000). The MCP regional chairman for the north, Wyson Mkotchi, said:

> And you may notice, though it is not on a wide scale, soon after the dances, some people tend to walk away. They have seen what they wanted to see. As for political speeches, [they think,] "Oh, enough of this! We're here to see the dances and then we'll go." So usually, to bring more people to your meetings, you are going to drum and perform some dances. And then when you are halfway through with the dances, then you can stop and put in a political speech. (Personal communication, March 29, 1999)

AFORD supporter Mayi Nyirenda went so far as to call the dancing "the bait" that drew people to rallies (personal communication, April 9, 1999), which corresponded to the messages on many posters advertising rallies. The phrase *there will be dancing* was often written much larger and positioned more centrally than was the information about the party hosting the event or the presiding politician(s). Most people with whom I have discussed the issue of women's political dancing concur: It is a vital ingredient for a successful rally.

In order for women's political dancing to continue to play this important role, women have to be willing to participate. Since the 1994 transition, women are free to dance or not, and they can choose which party to support. If women refuse to dance, the practice would either cease or politicians would have to find new ways to entice them. Because singing and dancing have long been used by those in subordinate positions in this part of Africa to respond to domination, politicians' use of these genres also embodies the ongoing risk that women might use the very medium intended for promotion to undermine or rebel against politicians' interests.

I therefore now explore some of the reasons why women choose to contribute to the political sphere through performance. I consider multiple and sometimes contradictory motivations for women to participate in addition to ways in which women who dance politically both do and do not challenge the political and economic inequities built into the structures within which they operate. By providing a broad range of possibilities for individuals' responses to subordination in this context, my intention is both to shed light on the specific situation of Malawian women political dancers and to contribute more broadly to scholarly understanding of how people exist with and respond to inequities.

Women, Dancers, and Party Structures

Most women active in their parties since the transition, especially those at the grassroots level, are channeled into political participation through the women's wings of parties. Party structures institutionalize intersections of gender, class, and politics. A party's women's wing is intended to ensure female participation, yet it also creates a gendered division of labor and yields differential access for men and women to political power. The pyramid structure, intended to facilitate mass participation, contributes to economic stratification because those positioned closest to the pinnacle enjoy both greater economic and greater political power. The majority of women active in their parties are channeled into the women's wings, which are ancillary to the main bodies, and most operate in the lowest echelons of the wings, which structurally ensures their marginalization within parties. Furthermore, though politicians recognize the value of political dancing, it is not accorded as high a status as most other political activities, and those who dance have relatively limited access to decision-making opportunities within parties.

The pyramid structures also comprise a framework through which an individual can ostensibly advance from the lowest rungs of a party into its higher echelons, potentially obtaining positions at the very highest levels or even running for elected office. The reality, however, is that most people at the lowest levels remain there and have few opportunities for political mobility. The opportunities are especially limited for many of the women who dance. If someone started as a dancer at the lowest level, she could move into a leadership position within the branch or area level of a women's wing, which would give her leadership at these lower levels. As one moves up the pyramid structure, the numbers of leadership positions decrease. The executive committee of the women's wing of any party might comprise ten to fifteen women, and each of the three regional committees have a similar number. The few women who do make it into these highest levels usually remain for a long time. I met with Mayi Wonga on June 1, 2004 in her home, a small two-room village-style house in Ndirande, a high-density neighborhood in Blantyre. She was probably in her forties and had been left a widow nine years before. She made her living selling beans. When she had enough money for firewood, she sometimes cooked and sold doughnuts. She suffered from rheumatism, which she said made it difficult for her to hold a position within the party because she did not always feel well enough to attend meetings and other events. Every Tuesday, she went to the UDF office, where the women were divided into groups of twenty to practice singing and dancing. After the rehearsals, she explained that UDF officials gave each of the women some money depending on how much was available. When I asked her about opportunities for political mobility, Mayi Wonga explained, "We are too many. Those who started dancing a long time ago are failing to get these positions. The ones who already have these positions are the ones who stay in them." Given the gendered and class subordination built into party structures, it is necessary now to consider why women choose to dance despite these inequities.

Why Do Women Dance?

Many women I interviewed were dedicated party members strongly committed to strengthening and promoting their parties. Many chose to dance because they understood that it was an invaluable way for them to demonstrate support and assist their preferred party and its politicians. By performing in rallies, they contributed to images of the party's popularity, and their performances were important conduits for spreading the party's symbols and messages. Mayi Chimzimbe, twenty-two years old at the time of our interview in the Ndirande neighborhood of Blantyre on June 8, 2004, was one of the very few dancers I encountered who had completed secondary school. She explained that she and other dancers were largely responsible for attracting people to rallies and that they helped the party by increasing the number of voters.

An added benefit for some women was the leadership opportunities it afforded (cf. Johnson-Odim and Strobel 1999: xlix). Although intersections of class and gender relegate most poor women to the lowest echelons of the women's wings, it is important that women from the grassroots fill the positions within lower levels. Aside from women's associations in religious institutions, many of these women have few other opportunities to exercise leadership in other established organizations.[1] Those who were leaders within parties exercised some power and had access to some channels for participation and communication with those at higher levels. Some women also benefited from the chance for political mobility. If a woman proved her skills and dedication as a leader at the branch or area level, she could be promoted to the district level. As a chairman of the women's committee of the Nkhata Bay District, for example, Mayi Chicago was central to the campaigning that took place across the district.

As with *lelemama* dance associations in Mombasa in the first half of the twentieth century, which have been described by Margaret Strobel, the dance realm within Malawi's political sphere also provided women with an "alternative set of status distinctions and rewards" from those available through other frameworks, such as economic, political, religious, and sometimes familial (Strobel 1976: 192). Some women prided themselves on their artistry and enjoyed showcasing their creativity. Party leaders recognized the best performers for their skills as composers, singers, choreographers, and dancers, and often showered them with praise and material gifts. Performing at rallies yielded them opportunities to expand their audiences and gain greater recognition.

Many women also enjoyed the opportunities to perform. The emphasis on dance in the political arena during the Banda years impacted the contexts in which dancing occurs, as I describe in Chapter 8. Because people were required to invest much of their leisure time performing within the political culture, some dancing that previously occurred in nonpolitical contexts subsided or even stopped altogether. Some women now relished the resurgence of dancing within the multiparty system because it provided opportunities to perform what to many were highly valued cultural practices. Dancing at rallies also provided opportunities for people from different parts of the country and different ethnic groups to showcase their dances to one another.

Furthermore, in Malawi, as in many African countries, social norms restrict many women's access to certain performance domains, especially those that require a woman to leave her home and that draw attention from audience members. Moreblessings Chitauro, Caleb Dube, and Liz Gunner, writing about Zimbabwe, explained that women moving freely "as performing artists in to the open space beyond the domestic domain are constantly challenged both by their own menfolk and by the dominant concepts of gender roles" (1994: 111).

This observation is applicable to Malawi as well. Women who choose to perform publicly were often labeled "loose" or prostitutes (Chitauro, Dube, and Gunner 1994: 112; see also Gilman and Fenn 2006). Husbands and family members of Malawian women often restrict women's participation in performance domains. Several members of the Msani chilimika team, for example, were divorced. They explained that they had stopped dancing when they were married because their husbands prohibited it. They had resumed chilimika dancing only after their divorces. The village headman of Msani, Group Village Headman Chilelawana, similarly referred to these attitudes when he explained that he strongly supported his village's chilimika dancers and did not agree with the commonly held opinion that equated them with prostitutes (personal communication, February 12, 1999). Because these ideas were widespread, the political arena provided a socially sanctioned "safe" space within which some women could travel widely and perform for various audiences.

Dancing politically also yielded opportunities for women to take a break from their domestic and agricultural obligations. It provided the chance to travel, see new things, engage in alternate activities, and meet new people. Asked what motivated her to dance for the UDF, Mayi Sapule answered, "Nothing. I just don't want to stay home. Going there [to rallies] is a way to pass the time" (personal communication, June 8, 2004). Similarly, Mayi Welosi explained, "I go to relieve my worries. I go so that I can spend time with and talk to my friends" (personal communication, June 8, 2004).

Performing politically also provided women with avenues for political expression. Mayi Mfuni, who suffered under the repression of the Banda years, was very committed to AFORD and contributed to the party in many ways as the treasurer of the Mzuzu constituency. She explained that she enjoyed attending the weekly rehearsals because dancing allowed her to express her feelings (personal communication, April 9, 1999).

Many women I interviewed understood that their participation resulted in multiple channels of communication operating through such things as their physical presence, movement, song lyrics, slogans, ululation, and costume. They knew too that their singing and dancing could sometimes impact politicians' decisions. In the primaries leading to the 2004 elections, UDF parliamentary candidate Ettinor Koloviko lost in her constituency to the incumbent UDF heavyweight after the voting was suspiciously halted. She explained in an interview on June 17, 2004 that her supporters in the constituency encouraged her not to give up and to run as an independent. She explained that elderly women gave her moral support through their song texts: "We really need you, madam. Please, please, please don't change your mind." Their encouragement contributed to her decision to run as an independent, and she ultimately won a parliamentary seat. Women also used their song texts to express their needs, as in the example of the song by civil servants at Muluzi's Mzuzu launch.

In another example, in June 2000 the rivalry between the two MCP heavyweights came to a head when the party's president, Chakuamba, was suspended from parliament. His rival and MCP vice president at the time, John Tembo, replaced Chakuamba as leader of the opposition. In response, the MCP women of Blantyre organized a rally on July 1, 2000, to which they invited Chakuamba's wife to convey their solidarity with her husband. Similarly, when the AFORD-MCP alliance took the UDF to court to contest the 1999 presidential election results, women supporters of the three parties showed up at the rallies that took place during the hearing to demonstrate their support for their respective parties. When the court ruled in favor of the UDF, yellow-clad women hit the streets in great numbers, singing songs of victory.

Women dancers, politicians, human rights activists, journalists, and members of the general public with whom I have discussed the issue of women's political dancing agreed that one of the biggest incentives for women to dance politically in the current dispensation was the possibility of receiving money, food, and material gifts. Mayi Wonga explained that she started dancing for UDF because "during the time of Kamuzu, we were just dancing; they were not giving us anything. . . . They never gave us money. But in UDF that's where we saw our friends receiving money. So, we also joined them so that we could receive some too" (personal communication, June 1, 2004). When I asked Mayi J. Tembo, an avid chilimika dancer from Nkhwali who also occasionally joined women dancing chiwoda at political rallies, why she danced, she candidly explained that she would dance for politicians of any party because she wanted the money (personal communication, January 10, 1999).

In addition to earning remuneration for individuals or groups of performers, women were also concerned about making a good impression on their representatives in government. Women were aware that parliamentarians were given limited resources to initiate development in their constituencies and that some communities would benefit more than others. Given the politicization of development, women understood that politicians sometimes rewarded those communities within their constituencies from which they had received the most support. It is worth repeating that in his speech in Mzuzu, Muluzi explicitly stated, "Any constituency that votes for an opposition member of Parliament will not benefit from any development assistance from my government." Women were motivated to enthusiastically back their representative in the hopes that their community would be chosen over others.[2] During Muluzi's presidency, women who joined the UDF had greater opportunities than did nonsupporters for obtaining loans from the government to use for capital to start small businesses, creating another financial incentive to join the ruling party.

Resistance

Though the motivations for women to dance are numerous, participants interviewed were also often critical of their poverty, and many expressed that their representatives neglected their needs. Women supporters of all parties complained about the economic downturn under Muluzi, which resulted in a series of massive devaluations and subsequent price hikes. Some articulated that politicians were getting richer while they continued to suffer. They complained about the cost of school fees and lack of adequate medical care. Most expressed that they wished that they and their family members had access to salaried jobs that would enable them to better care for their families and give them financial stability, rather than having to regularly scramble for crumbs. Many decried the small amounts they received in exchange for dancing. the long hours they spent going to and from rallies, and the high cost of transportation. Given these expressions of dissatisfaction, I now consider ways in which women resisted the inequities built into their political participation as performers.

The introduction of compensation by politicians in the post-Banda period, even if not officially designated as such, shifted relationships of power so that women dancers are now offering a service in exchange for some type of compensation, as opposed to the systems of expectation and coercion operating during the Banda years. Because these relationships are not overt, it provides opportunities for negotiations of power. Thomas A. Hale explained that griots in the Mande world are positioned at lower social strata than are those from the noble caste, whose lineages and praises they regularly perform, creating what appears on the surface to be clearly demarcated relationships of power. Yet, that griots can manipulate their word craft to undermine or castigate as well as panegyrize their nobles shifts the location of power, complicating relationships between these two groups, in which the nobles depend on the griots and must compensate and treat them appropriately so as to maximize their chances of receiving the desired praise (Hale 1998: 193–216; Hoffman 1995). Similarly, if politicians hired women to perform, terms of employment would be clearly delineated. Politicians would inform women of the amount of compensation and what was required of them. By agreeing to the terms, women would know that they had to show up at particular times and engage in certain activities in order to receive the agreed-upon amount. Instead, the details of what is expected in the service and compensation are fuzzy, allowing actors in both camps to engage in strategic manipulations to try to maximize their own goals. Politicians, for example, distribute money and objects before and at rallies and promise development projects in order to entice women to contribute the much-needed service. Many women I encountered who danced strategized to maximize their material benefits. Just choosing to dance at a rally could be strategic: A woman voluntarily provided the service, thereby indirectly obligating the politician to reciprocate with a material gift. If the politician did not, she or he risked losing both the dancer's service at subsequent rallies and the dancer's vote.

More and more, women choose to dance because of these possibilities for remuneration. In John Lwanda's characterization of the economic disparities in the country—economic elite and poor majority—he suggested that the poor majority's "predominating imperative is the desire, not to form a mass movement for overthrowing a dominant group, but for each individual or family to escape poverty" (1996: 19). My fieldwork supported this contention. Regardless of whether or not they supported a party, many women I know participated in the rallies that they thought would be the most lucrative. During Muluzi's presidency, UDF rallies drew the largest numbers of women for these reasons. Some women danced for AFORD or MCP, the party they actually supported, as well as the ruling UDF, in order to be compensated by the UDF. Some danced for any rally where they thought money would be distributed, but did not necessarily support a party or even vote come polling day. Given the sensitivity of this issue and people's suspicions about my relationship to party leaders, I did not ask interviewees directly whether they danced for multiple parties in this way; rather, I asked them if they knew of any who did. All answered yes. UDF supporter Mayi Wonga answered, "There are . . . women do indeed go to various parties. Their goal is to receive money from each of the parties whose rallies they go to. But they don't do this openly. They do it secretly." Asked whether women would continue to dance if they did not receive money, she answered, "Some may not because they are used to receiving money" (personal communication, June 1, 2004). Related was the issue of wearing party cloth. A woman who wore the political uniform to a rally increased her opportunities for receiving additional gifts at subsequent rallies because politicians often gifted those who demonstrated the most support.

When women danced for material gain, they manipulated the system to their advantage and subverted politicians' goals of drawing supporters into their parties through material enticements, or buying votes. Yet the material amounts women gained were negligible given their needs. Asked how much she received when she danced at rallies, Mayi Wonga explained that it depended on how many other dancers participated and how much money was distributed. She explained that sometimes she received MK20 (44 U.S. cents at the time), MK17 (37 U.S. cents), or MK7 (16 U.S. cents). She said that the most she had ever received was MK50 (US$1.11) for a rally that was poorly attended so the money did not have to be shared among as many dancers.[3] Her answer resonated with those of other UDF supporters I interviewed. Asked how this money helped her, she answered, "Nothing. That's the way it is. There are so many things that require money. We share it." Asked if the party had provided or reimbursed her for transport, she answered that it had not. A minibus within town at the time cost MK10 to MK15 one way. Paying roundtrip for transport from Mayi Wonga's home to the UDF event cost more than she usually received for one's day's rehearsing. Yet her economic needs were so great that she often chose to walk several miles in the sun so that she could use that little bit of money for some basic need. Sounding tired, she explained that they "just give us a little bit so that we won't be disappointed and that we'll be quiet" (personal communication, June 6, 2004).

Some of the most active political performers expressed criticism of the political arena. Women frequently complained about their poverty or lack of access to political leaders. I interviewed Mayi Welosi, a forty-eight year-old UDF supporter living in Ndirande in Blantyre, at her home on June 3, 2004. As we talked, she carefully spooned glycerin-based skin moisturizer, the least expensive option available, from a large wholesale container into small recycled jars. Several times during our conversation, neighbors interrupted by dropping by to purchase one. When I asked her why she chose the UDF, she began by pointing out the economic disparities between politicians and the general population: "Those who have money—you have seen them, maybe since you have been in Malawi? You can see the difference!" She then elaborated that immediately after the transition, "Things were good. Now things have changed because of those people in high positions," though she clarified that Muluzi was not at fault. She complained that party leaders had lots of money, but often did not follow through on promises they made to those at lower levels. At times, she explained, UDF women had been promised loans to start businesses. Yet, neither she nor her friends had yet to receive such a loan, though they had heard on the radio that other people had:

> That's why I'm saying our leaders are the ones who oppress us. They took us to go for training. When we returned, they said we would receive money. But when the money came, they told us to go to training again and that we had to be interviewed. We went. But then, we realized that it was the people in the offices [high-level party officials] who had received the money. Those of us doing the work of the party did not get anything. (Personal communication, June 3, 2004)

One of the more common ways that women could subvert the goals of political power wielders was by choosing not to participate. Some women who did not perform politically did so out of disinterest or disengagement, choices that I would not categorize as resistance. Others were critical about the practice and so deliberately made the decision not to participate. When I asked some of my friends why they did not go dance, for example, they often laughed and asked me why I thought they should. They frequently scoffed that politicians were merely attempting to buy votes. Not participating was a fairly inactive form of resistance in that it did not challenge the system, but at the same time, it also did not support it. The fewer the number of women who danced, the less politicians could profit from women in these ways. If enough women resisted by refusal, politicians would have to either think of new strategies for attracting people to promote their parties or reconfigure relationships of power and compensation within their parties to make dancing more attractive to potential participants. In my observations and discussions with women from a variety of economic and political standings, I ascertained that most women who resisted by choosing not to dance were not vocal about their decisions, nor did they mobilize other women into a more widespread boycott, and so their opposition to the practice was easily ignored by politicians.

Given the long history of song texts being used for resistance by women and other people in subordinate positions in this region, one might expect that women would have taken advantage of the poetic license often accorded song texts or the potential for coding to challenge the power inequities evident in political parties specifically and the state system more generally. However, I encountered few examples of this practice. When I asked women dancers, politicians, and human rights activists whether such examples exist, most answered no. When I asked UDF parliamentarian Bertha Masiku whether she was ever criticized in song texts during her election campaign, she answered with an emphatic, "No, no, no. There was nothing of the sort" (personal communication, June 16, 2004).

For the most part, dancers and politicians I interviewed explained that song texts were not used to comment on dynamics within the party sponsoring an event. The transformation of praise singing that occurred through processes of traditionalization—from the independence movement, through the Banda regime, and into the current dispensation—from a medium for both elevating and criticizing leaders into one used almost exclusively for their glorification, ultimately reduces poor women's and other marginalized people's possibility for political expression. Outside of contemporary political structures, praise singing often occurs within authoritarian and patriarchal structures. Yet, subordinates have opportunities to express themselves and criticize their leaders. In the current "democratic" system, subordinates, despite claims to the contrary, have for the most part lost these avenues. In the current political dispensation, it is significant that women at the lowest rungs of political hierarchies have direct channels of communication with their leaders via song texts as well as other communicative channels embodied in their performances. Yet, rallies are considered to be sites for promoting a politician and his or her party rather than for criticism. The result is that despite discourse about the importance of popular participation in the public political arena, those in marginalized positions have even fewer opportunities for self-expression than they would in more overtly authoritarian models where poetic license allows for socially sanctioned criticism to be expressed through song texts.

Some types of songs did function in ways that could be considered resistance. Politicians sometimes interpreted the requests for goods or services expressed in lyrics either as criticism that they had not already provided for their constituents' needs or as threats that they might be criticized in the future if they did not meet their constituents' demands. When I asked an AFORD member of Parliament interviewed on May 6, 2000, who requested that he remain anonymous, how he felt when he heard women singing and dancing his praises, he first answered, "Good!" with a big smile. Then he said, "It's flattery, but flattery can provide a challenge." He explained that dancers belonged to disadvantaged groups that were taking advantage of singing at rallies as opportunities to tell him what they expected from their representative in government. As he sat listening to them, he realized that their livelihoods depended on him. As they sang his praises, he wondered, "What if I don't deliver? They are not dancing for naught. It is a sign that they are in search of some deliverance." Similarly, former vice president Malewezi explained,

> They are very clever at it. They rub you the right way and then something comes in. An example for me was that there is generally a belief in Malawi that when you are the leader, your first priority for development is your home. You should do a lot of good things in your home area. I do not subscribe entirely to that. I think that when you are a leader, particularly at the level that I was [vice president], you should look at the whole country. If your home does not qualify for certain things, it doesn't mean that you have to make it qualify. So, in my home area, there had been a problem of certain roads that people wanted. Of course, I think that they are important, but at that time, the women sang a song saying to the effect, "You look after your own, look after your own." And "Everybody looks after their own" or something like that. So, they could speak directly to me through their song. There are also other songs that are more direct, such as "We have schools here, but there are no desks." Or "We have a river here; there is no bridge." And you listen carefully to those songs. You hear them and you respond in your speech. (Personal communication, June 1, 2004)

Trevor Cope made a related point when he explained that praise poetry in the South African context functions "to bring about conformity" in a chief's behavior. People praise a leader for what they think he or she *should* provide for them, ultimately pressuring him or her to do so (1968: 31). The following song was sung in English by a group of female schoolteachers in the northern city of Mzuzu at President Muluzi's launch in the northern region during his campaign for reelection in April 1999:

Kneel down!
See chalk!
We teachers from Mzuzu
Are very proud
Here in the north are proud
We teachers from Mzuzu are asking
We are begging for loans
Muluzi
We teachers are proud of you, Muluzi
Consider us for loans
We are proud

Though in the form of a praise song ("We teachers are proud of you, Muluzi"), this song, similar to the one presented in Chapter 6 that was sung by civil servants, expressed an implied criticism. Its content was a request for loans. A message embedded in the dialogic relationship between "We teachers . . . are very proud" and "We are begging for loans" suggested that the teachers had to put aside their pride to beg. A real commitment from a government to provide these essential services would not require a population having to plead for them. The song line "Here in the north are proud" also might have referenced the frequent criticism that President Muluzi favored his own southern region when it came to development. The song's ambiguity—it was not clear whether the teachers were proud of Muluzi or themselves—allowed for the song to be interpreted as both a song praising Muluzi and a song highlighting regional pride. Embedded was also the message that if President Muluzi did not deliver, the singers might feel that he had not adequately fulfilled his role, and thus it contained a threat of criticism in the future. Notice that the request was directed specifically to the president, pointing to a common perception that the president controlled government coffers and as such was the supreme benefactor.

Song texts did feature much criticism of politicians in opposition to the ones for whom dancers performed, such as the following song critical of the UDF government that was performed at an MCP rally for the chair of the party, Chakuamba, in Phalombe on May 10, 2000.

Ife tikuzuzika, boma likuona, tikuzuzika
Ife tikuzuzika, anthu akuona
Anthu akuona
Tikuzuzika, ee, boma likuona
Ife tikuzuzika boma lili lathu
Akumangika, boma likuona
Boma likuona

We are suffering, the government is watching, we are suffering
We are suffering, people are watching
People are watching
We are suffering, yes, the government is watching
We are suffering though the government is ours
They are being arrested, the government is watching
The government is watching

This song criticized Muluzi's government for standing by while people in the country suffered and were mistreated. These songs cannot be interpreted as resistance because they fell into the larger framework of a political culture in the multiparty era in which parties compete against one another. However, the willingness of supporters of opposition parties in the current dispensation to publicly express criticism of their president and a ruling party indicated that they felt greater empowerment since the transition, and that women understood and enjoyed newfound freedoms. They felt confident that they could criticize the ruling party without fear of retribution.

Rebellion

It is illuminating to consider these ways in which women performers resisted the aims of political power wielders. It is also necessary to consider the extent to which these acts were transformative. Their resistance provided some women with additional opportunities for political expression and material benefits. However, it did little to challenge the structural systems that relegated them to the marginalized and disadvantaged positions in which they lived. Martha Kaplan and John D. Kelly suggested that some scholars present resistance as an aim in and of itself and that some, such as Raymond Williams, "seem embarrassed about serious discussion of revolution or vanguards" (1994: 126). Given that acts of resistance often do little to challenge power structures, perhaps they should not be celebrated as the ultimate end. It is important to explore the existence or possibility of a more systematic rebellion, and when it does not exist, to consider why not.

Some of the acts by women dancers outlined above could be understood to be resistance at the same time that they contributed to sustaining the inequitable political culture. For example, by participating to obtain material gain, regardless of whether or not they voted for the party, women nevertheless contributed to politicians' goals of spreading images of widespread support, attracting people to and energizing rallies, and disseminating a party's symbols. Though a woman might have expressed defiance by performing for more than one party, she still contributed to the perpetuation of the political system as it existed, and thus also to politicians' maintenance of power. She did not challenge the power structures that marginalized many women and more generally people of lower socioeconomic status. And although she manipulated it to her benefit, she nevertheless participated in the system of patronage relationships, contributing to its ossification as a defining characteristic of Malawi's political culture. The potential exists for women to challenge gender inequities within the political world of contemporary Malawi, but women have yet to come together to do that. Women could, for example, use the same party structures through which they are currently organized to dance to coalesce around women's issues. Or, given how important dancing is to politicians, they could use the threat of singing critical songs at rallies or of organizing a dance boycott to pressure party leaders and politicians to consider their marginalization. Or women could impact politics through strategic voting because women comprise over half the eligible voters. Reen Kachere, director of the nongovernmental organization (NGO) Association of Progressive Women, cogently articulated the capacity for women to use dance to effect change: "They are the ones who have power. Just to be together and dance is power. That is power. Togetherness is power. Many, many women working together, that is power. But they misuse the power. If you could take hold of that power and use it, maybe things could change" (personal communication, June 9, 2004). The situation in Malawi resonates with those in other countries in the region. Writing about the women's wings of political parties in Zambia, Zimbabwe, and Botswana, Gisela Geisler (1995) documented that women in these countries have similarly not used the women's wings to effect social change. Making a similar point about the situation in Malawi, Kachere elaborated:

> These women have a good platform to talk to their leaders because they talk to these leaders directly. But what happens is that the messages that they give are not good ones. They are not beneficial to the nation because the messages that they give castigate other politicians. And yet, if they could just transform and use these vehicles to tell the leadership of this country, things would change. To challenge their leadership, "Look here, sir, where are the women in your parliament? Sir, where are women in local governance? Sir, how many women are supporting you and how many men supporting you? And what do you think about us? Sir, what about poverty in our country?" If they could just use this as a channel. Definitely, they would be making strides.

Since the transition, the international community has emphasized gender issues in its development efforts, and numerous NGOs focused on women's concerns are active in the country, making the present a fertile time for women's activism. A lively debate over politicians' use of women dancers did emerge in February 2000 between human rights activists and politicians, all of whom for the most part belong to the country's political and economic elite. Dr. Vera Chirwa, a prominent person in Malawi's history and a lawyer and director of CARER (Centre for Advice, Research, and Education on Rights), a human rights NGO, initiated the debate with a paid advertisement in *The Nation*, the newspaper associated at the time with the UDF:

> We [Malawi CARER] also condemn the induced dancing of women for political leaders. The value of women as human beings is the same value all political leaders have. And the duty of political leadership is, after all, to protect fundamental freedoms, including freedom of conscience. To the contrary, we have observed that our women have been induced to dancing for leaders for purposes of obtaining money. We do realize that Malawi is a poor society and that women are the most vulnerable. But inducements such as monetary handouts will only reduce our society to beggars and ultimately to uphold misery and laziness. Consequently, we do condemn on the strongest terms the tendency of leaders taking advantage of the disadvantaged vulnerable groups in our society. We thus call for a complete and immediate stop to that. (Chirwa, V. 2000)

Chirwa criticized the ruling party's use of women dancers on two grounds: on the one hand, these "unnecessary political rallies" disrupted people's work schedules and activities. On the other hand, she argued that women were being used as political tools, something that the UDF had opposed when campaigning against Banda's government. Her advertisement invoked a rush of responses, from local human rights organizers, politicians, journalists, other members of the general population in Malawi, expatriate human rights activists living in Malawi, and international human rights organizers. Some came out in support of Chirwa, and some concerned citizens and leaders in the UDF defended the practice.

In support of Chirwa, a spokesperson for the NGO Human Rights Consultative Committee (HCRR) was quoted in an article in *The Nation* as saying that "the practice [of women dancing at political rallies] was a violation of women's rights." The spokesperson argued that "such a practice degrades women who could otherwise engage themselves into productive ventures." Catherine Munthali, chairman for the NGO Women's Rights Network, said that "politicians are taking advantage of the ignorance of the poverty-stricken women who dance for monetary rewards." She acknowledged that in the new government, women had a choice of whether or not to dance; however, she said, "'our concern is that these politicians take advantage of the women's poverty and their ignorance' . . . because it is not true that the women dance on their own will but that they are forced by circumstances." She argued that women dance only for money: "If politicians stop dishing out money the women would also stop the dancing." Citing the irony of Muluzi's Poverty Alleviation program as a context within which to consider the generous gifts given to dancers, she said, "If it is a means of alleviating poverty among women, then it is being done in a wrong way. Government should find workable mechanisms to put women out of poverty rather than reducing them into dancing objects." The human rights leaders also referred to the fact that AFORD and UDF came out against this practice during thc transition period. HCRR chairman Rodgers Newa was quoted as saying, "This present government was voted into power on the basis that the human rights record would improve and we are disturbed that human rights violations including that of allowing women to dance for politicians are resurfacing" (Sonani 2000).

The official position of the UDF in response to the above comments appeared in a paid advertisement in *The Nation*, the same newspaper that carried the Chirwa advertisement, on February 18, 2000. Following are some excerpts, which was entitled "Reaction by Concerned Citizens to the Statement by CARER on Political Rallies and Dancing by Women at Such Functions":

> It is total naïveté to suggest that anybody, in a free democratic society today, like ours, would have the right to prescribe to any fellow citizen how they should conduct themselves vis-à-vis political activities. Such an attempt runs counter to the very principal of the fundamental freedoms enshrined right through the fabric of the Republic's present constitution. . . .
>
> Such attempts as advanced by Dr. Vera Chirwa, Executive Director of the Centre for Advice, Research and Education on Rights (CARER) suggest one thing—that the author underestimates the ability of Malawians to think for themselves what is in their best interest at any given point in time. What we fought for from the early 90s, culminating in the attainment of a new democratic dispensation in 1994, is the very principle of restoring genuine freedom and rights for people to think for themselves—moving away, for good, from the GODFATHER image that horrified and haunted Malawians for three decades. Don't Malawians deserve those rights as pillars that re-enforce their dignity? . . .
>
> Indeed, the politics of dishing out money to people in order to gain political mileage should be discouraged. However, no one would advance the thought that campaigns do not call for pecuniary requirements. . . .
>
> Dancing, parading, etc., by anybody, be it women, children or men, is a cultural expression. The author of the statement to which this cor-

> respondence is referring, Dr. Chirwa herself, joins Ingoma Dancers from her home district—Mzimba—at public/national events presided over by the Head of State. . . . There are many occasions where humans demonstrate such expressions.
>
> Such occasions include:
>
> (1) Public or national events which provide an obvious opportunity for people to express their jubilation or happiness and at the same time show-casing their cultural values.
>
> (2) Traditional functions and/or festivities which also enable people to get together and express cultural values.
>
> Giving some gifts, even if they are in the form of cash, is nothing strange in Malawi's culture and tradition. It is normally expected in our tradition that spectators of traditional dances or performances give gifts for outstanding performances . . . the act of awarding such gifts is called *kufupa* in Chichewa and is a mere expression of joy, gratitude and satisfaction.
>
> Perhaps the alarm felt by Dr. Vera Chirwa emanates from the fact that at national events a lump sum of money could be given to groups of women of a given area. This could lead to all kinds of interpretations such as the erroneous reading by Dr Vera Chirwa that the monies so given are an inducement for them to dance for who ever leader has so made the *kufupa*. The truth is far from the erroneous interpretation advanced by CARER's chief. There is no question of taking advantage of the poor and the vulnerable as the Executive Director of CARER asserts. After all, such occasions are too few to make an impact on the magnitude of the poverty that exists in our country.

The advertisement is signed, "Concerned Citizens" (2000).

At a private function for the local food manufacturer RAB Processors on February 26, 2000, President Muluzi responded personally to the criticism railed against him. After giving a prepared speech in English that was relevant to the occasion, Muluzi switched into Chichewa, to address himself directly to the large group of women dressed in their UDF garb seated on the floor between the speech makers and the rows of chairs for the invited audience. His choice of Chichewa communicated his implicit recognition of the class differences that separated himself, the people he came to address, who were sitting on chairs and presumably had more formal schooling and thus understood English, and the women seated on the ground before him, who he assumed, probably correctly, were most likely not to understand English (Matiki 2001). Following is an excerpt from his speech:

> Yes Bakili gives money. I say that whatever little I have, I share with people of the country of Malawi. . . . I am one of the champions on

> issues of human rights. Alright? . . . If there are NGOs, those NGOs have come with Bakili Muluzi and the UDF party and democracy here in Malawi! . . . Someone should not . . . [want] . . . to teach me issues of human rights. . . . Some have an agenda of wanting to weaken women in this country of Malawi. . . . Women, we do respect them very much. . . . But that we should shut their mouths that they don't sing! . . . I don't take money from the government. No. . . . Not even one tambala. Never! . . . Everything that I, whether I take one tambala, whether they dance . . . its my money, not the government's. No. So who are you [referring to Vera Chirwa] to stop me? Who are you? . . . I respect and I listen to what God says that whatever little you can have, share with the poor! . . . These women will continue to sing! We too, men, if we can have our choirs, we will continue to sing. . . . There isn't anyone here to stop our culture. No! Singing is our culture. Giving each other money is our culture. If you copy some stuff from England, that's your problem! . . . Women with this dancing thing! Yes! You, here, can you stop a woman dancing? [Audience: No!] After all, the UDF party does not force a person! No! No! . . . Before, before, the youth leaguers were going on doors, let's go, let's go. Today, are there UDF youth leaguers? [Audience: No, there aren't!] . . . If Bakili has five kwacha, he should take one kwacha and help someone who is needy.

Politicians defending women's dancing did not deny that women sang their praises or that the politicians sometimes compensated them with monetary gifts. They clarified that women did so of their own volition because they wanted to express their happiness with their political representatives. Defenders tended to ignore any comparisons made between the institution of women's dancing during Banda's time and the practices of the current era, scoffing at allegations that they were violating human rights. They were, after all, the very same champions of human rights who brought about the transition to democracy in the first place. Any references to their opposition to women dancing during Banda's time was either ignored or swept away with the explanation that women were no longer forced, the main issue they claimed that they had opposed during the previous regime. They upheld women's dancing as an example of the new political freedom enjoyed by citizens of Malawi: Women were free to select whom to support and to do so in the manner of their choice. More than any other reason given for the defense of the practice was that women danced because it was "our culture" or "the tradition." Defenders used discourse about traditionality to make it not only acceptable, but almost sacred and untouchable. Politicians, starting with Muluzi, also refuted claims that they were emptying government coffers and claimed instead that they were using their personal money to provide gifts to the dancers.

Largely missing in this debate, at least as it was transmitted through the media, were the voices of the women dancers whose causes activists claimed to champion. Nothing in the various newspaper articles on the topic indicated that anyone from either side had bothered to ask the dancers how they felt. Women dancers' contributions came through their continued participation in rallies and in their spontaneous outbursts and in song texts at political events, in which they supported the politicians rather than the activists. Interrupting a speech by Muluzi at the RAB Processors launch, a woman seated among other women clad in a UDF uniform shouted out, "Some people in the name of human rights bring unknown things here? No! After all, who did she [Chirwa] consult?" This dancer discursively positioned Chirwa as an outsider, suggesting that in criticizing the political use of dance, Chirwa was denying her own African and Malawian cultural heritage in favor of European ideals. This woman also suggested that Chirwa initiated all this controversy without having consulted the women who dance.[4] A song sung at the same event blatantly dismissed Chirwa:

Inu, chamuwawayo, mama, chamuwawayo
Iwe, chakuwawawe, mama, chakuwawawe
Iwe, chakuwawawe, Vera [Chirwa], *chakuwawawe*
Aleke katundu wake achoke

You, if he has hurt you, Mom, if he has hurt you
You, if he has hurt you, Mom, if he has hurt you
You, if he has hurt you, Vera [Chirwa], if he has hurt you
She should leave her belongings and get out

My interviews with women dancers about this controversy similarly did not reveal support for the human rights activists. The women I interviewed expressed a range of opinions on the debate. Some explained that unlike during Banda's rule when women's political dancing was exploitative, now women chose whether or not to dance. Others explained that they danced because it was "our culture," not because they were bribed into doing it. An MCP supporter explained in March 2000, "We are used to it. It is our way of respecting." Significantly, most were not even aware of the debate.

It was important that the women who dance did not initiate the debate. Had it emerged from a shared sense of dissatisfaction and collective decision for action among these women, the details of the criticism would probably have been different. While human rights activists considered the practice in relation to larger structural issues of gender inequities within the political sphere, the perspectives of many who dance tended to be more individual and community oriented. Based on my many interactions, I would assume that had they initiated the debate, the women who dance would have more likely requested such things as a more official employment designation so that they would be certain of receiving compensation when they performed and so that they would know exactly what was required of them. They most likely would have requested payment for their transportation and more compensation for their time spent at rehearsals and rallies. UDF supporters might have demanded the loans that were promised to them by Muluzi's government in exchange for their commitment to the party. Their critique would have come from their experiences and needs rather than the more abstract critique of gender and democracy put forth by human rights activists. Nevertheless, it is interesting to consider why women dancers did not take advantage of this moment to voice their own concerns or have not up until now otherwise organized themselves to demand more economic and political opportunities.

Multiple Agencies

While doing this research, I have been consistently interested in identifying ways in which the mostly disadvantaged women who dance use their performances for resistance or rebellion. Though I have certainly found some compelling examples, such as those given previously, I have also discerned that many women to a large degree do what is expected of them within the political context, express limited criticism, and do little to try to improve their opportunities and status within party or state structures. After a great deal of thought, I have come to a conclusion similar to Abu-Lughod's that by searching for examples of resistance, I might ultimately have been "more concerned with finding resistors and explaining resistance than with examining power" (1990: 41). My concern is that if one begins with a quest for resistance, if even for its role in highlighting "the presence and play of power" (Ortner 1995: 175), one may inadvertently overlook the many different ways that people experience and respond to power that may not fit under the rubric of resistance. One danger of questing resistance is that a scholar might neglect to accurately identify the multiple webs of power within which the "resistors" they write about actually exist (Abu-Lughod 1990). Second, investigators may over exaggerate the libratory potential of the resistance they do find, possibly minimizing the nature of the oppression.

Third, Saba Mahmood argued that notions of agency in much feminist scholarship are used synonymously with action: "Agency, in this form of analysis, is understood as the capacity to realize one's own interests against the weight of custom, tradition, transcendental will, or other obstacles (whether individual or collective). Thus the humanist desire for autonomy and self-expression constitute the substrate, the slumbering ember that can spark to flame in the form of an act of resistance when conditions permit" (2001: 206). She rightly critiqued this perspective on a number of grounds, including that the ideas of individual freedom and autonomous will that undergird much feminist thinking about agency are constructs that are historically and culturally specific, and so should not be promoted as the desired response for all subordinated women in all contexts. Much feminist scholarship, she argued, is both analytical and prescriptive: "[F]eminism, therefore, offers both a *diagnosis* of women's status across cultures as well as a *prescription* for changing the situation of women who are understood to be marginal, subordinate, and oppressed" (Mahmood 2001: 207). As an example of this type of feminist perspective, Judith Kegan Gardiner wrote, "[A]ll feminists believe that feminism must be a movement for social change that will improve the lives of women, especially the most oppressed and disadvantaged" (1995: 8). The prescriptions in these cases are all too often some type of action that challenges male domination regardless of the social and historical context in which it occurs. This orientation posits male domination as the overarching power structure that demands to be subverted, and as some feminists with other perspectives argue, it leaves little room for women's actions that may not fit common ideas of resistance, such as "docility" or "passivity," to be understood as products of agency (Mahmood 2001: 210).

My own interrogation of these issues emerges from years of presenting on Malawian women's political dancing at academic meetings and submitting manuscripts for publication: I have been frequently challenged for not presenting many examples of resistance by the women who dance politically. I find this assumption that people who are in especially disenfranchised positions *should* be constantly vigilant both of their oppression and of opportunities to act, and *should* always be responding with action, to be problematic because it defines what an appropriate response to domination should be. It also presupposes how the individual *should* interpret and prioritize her positioning within the various webs of relationships within which she finds herself. This emphasis can also evade differences between an individual's immediate and long-term goals. This perspective creates a double standard of what is expected of "subalterns" that some of those writing about "them" do not meet in their own lives. Some, for example, who function in university environments, myself included, put great energy into fulfilling their administrations' requirements so that they can be successfully promoted. They might grumble among themselves when they are displeased, but I must admit that I see relatively few responses that I would categorize as resistance, and even fewer as rebellion.

Agent and *agency* have been used to refer to a range of qualities from "the capacity of social beings to interpret and morally evaluate their situation and to formulate projects and try to enact them" (Ortner 1995: 185) to a more active designation of "someone who is contemplating an action, has already acted, or is presently acting" (Bartky 1995: 178; cf. Gardiner 1995). Similar to resistance, the latter definition equates agency with action and is problematic because it presumes what an appropriate response of an agent should be to specific contexts of domination (cf. Kaplan and Kelly 1994: 125). My use of *agency* aligns with Sherry B. Ortner's definition and is based in an understanding that any given person operates within a unique web constituted by such things as her personality, needs, abilities, desires, and multiple social relationships, all of which can inform each decision that she makes. Each agent is therefore going to have a different and fluid perception of her social world, and her agency is exhibited through the way she makes choices either to act or not to act at any given moment.

Any individual operating within political parties in Malawi, whether at the level of president or at the lowest echelons of a party, does not exist in a binary relationship of power—ruler and ruled—but rather is embedded in webs of power tied to her or his economic, social, familial, political, and religious life, all of which impact her or his decisions at any given moment (Foucault 1990 [1978]: 94; see also Ortner 1995: 176–77). Considering women's positioning and response to this stratification within the political realm demands the acknowledgment that a woman's decisions within this arena are necessarily tied to other aspects of her life, and that her positioning within this realm does not necessarily resonate with how she negotiates power in other domains. The same woman, for example, might acquiesce to political power wielders at the same time that she challenges other people in positions of authority in her life. Also important is that "agency cannot be apprehended outside the realm of possibilities—material or otherwise—available to individuals or communities in the larger society" (Alidou 2005: 4). The heading to this section, "Multiple Agencies," refers to this idea that people respond in various ways at different times to the webs of power in which they operate.

As illustration, I outline here some of the webs of power within which Mayi V. Mwale operated. During the time of the 1999 campaigns, Mayi V. Mwale, who was in her early twenties, lived with her husband and two-year-old son in the extended Ngwira family's hamlet where we lived. Her mother, who lived in a nearby village, was an avid UDF supporter, and Mayi V. Mwale occasionally danced at UDF rallies. In her life with the Ngwiras, she enjoyed a certain power over her son, and the social structure in which she lived ensured her well-being to a certain extent. Yet, her husband dominated some aspects of her life; for example, she had little influence over his economic pursuits or how he distributed the money he earned. Though his income was considerably greater than that of many other men I knew, he regularly spent his money on himself rather than providing such basic needs as food and clothing for his wife and son. I frequently encountered him in town eating at restaurants on days when his family was home literally without food. Mayi V. Mwale was in the dominant position over her son and felt responsible for his well-being even if the cultural expectation was that her husband should provide for any needs that required money, especially since he earned enough to do so. Her economic power was limited because normative gender ideas positioned her in agricultural and domestic spheres, and her husband restricted her from working outside the home. She therefore occasionally chose to join her mother to dance for the UDF in the hopes of receiving some remuneration. The current multiparty situation provided her access to some economic power that she would otherwise not have had.

Mayi V. Mwale was an agent who was acutely aware of her situation and her marginalization within the many webs within which she lived. She actively assessed the resources that were available to her and made decisions about how to act or not act. Her decision to dance politically could be read as resistance to her husband's dominance over the family's finances because it provided her with some means of obtaining money on her own. It also could be read as resistance to social norms that obligated her to activities around the home: She took advantage of this socially sanctioned opportunity to travel, interact with others, and become known within the political realm. She did not, however, resist the power inequities built into the political arena that largely limited her political participation to singing and dancing. Did she choose to compose a song text that criticized the UDF for their lack of real programs to alleviate her poverty? No. Did she incorporate veiled criticism of the UDF into her song texts? No. Did she try to subvert the party structures that channeled her into the lowest rung of their hierarchies? No. Instead she focused her attention on what was *her* priority at the time, which was to feed her child and herself, even if only in the short term.

Here it is important to realize that the successful implementation of power structures is often contingent on subordinates perceiving some advantage in accepting or even contributing to the system (Williams 1977: 115–16). Ortner made the crucial point that "in a relationship of power, the dominant often has something to offer, and sometimes a great deal (though always of course at the price of continuing in power). The subordinate thus has many grounds for ambivalence about resisting the relationship" (1995: 175; see also White 1989: 52). It is clear from my outline of women's motivations to dance, my examples of resistance, and this short narrative about Mayi V. Mwale that many women perceived some benefits to the practice, and so contributed to the system in order to maintain these advantages, which was part of the reason that many women did not choose to resist the inequities built into the practice of women's political dancing.

It was also important that most participants, regardless of their political leanings, understood the nature of political rallies: They were intended to be sites for the promotion of political parties, not for undermining them. As Sally Falk Moore suggested, expressions of public unanimity sometimes occur when "the public occasion is understood not to be the proper forum for the expression of serious stubborn conflict" (1977: 152). An AFORD politician explained during an interview in May 2000, "The whole issue of the entertainment and speeches at rallies is about promotion. . . . They try to excel over the views of others. You advance your views and then hope that others will listen and accept you. You can't allow a chance for those who are opponents to voice their views at meetings [rallies]." Most individuals committed to a party would not consider a rally to be the appropriate venue for criticizing it. Rather than emphasizing the inequities inherent to their positions, their energies at rallies were directed toward promoting it. Even those who were critical understood that challenging the party in this context would be marked and could draw negative attention. Correspondingly, when asked whether women ever use rallies as opportunities to express criticism of their parties, MCP official Dausi explained to me on May 30, 2000, that rallies were not the appropriate place, but that the business meetings of the women's committees provided appropriate occasions for women to voice their concerns to party leaders. It should be noted, however, from what I have gathered from my observations and in my interviews, these meetings usually did not give women much opportunity to be heard by political elites. AFORD member Mayi Mtayamanja, who was the vice chair of women at the district level in Blantyre at the time of our conversation on June 1, 2004, explained that one had to be "close to the boss" in order to have one's complaint heard. She explained that even if she were to write a letter and send it through the party hierarchy, she was sure that in the process, it would be intercepted and would never get to its destination.

The relationship between an individual and a collective is also at the heart of much scholarship on agency, where the individual has often been privileged over the collective. Here I return to Mahmood's cautioning that ideas revolving around freedom and autonomous will are historical and cultural constructs (2001). Writing specifically about Kenyan women, though her discussion is generalizable to many African contexts, Patricia Stamp problematized scholarly definitions of agency because they emphasized "western concepts of the individual and rational choice." Most African cultural systems, by contrast, are rooted in very different conceptions of social relations. She wrote, "[I]n this context rights does not mean the right of an individual to exercise untrammeled personal liberty, but the inalienable right of each individual to contribute autonomously and authoritatively to the collective good" (1995: 71). Here I agree with Charles Piot, who wrote, "Westerners appear to me far less individualistic and self-authoring than our ideology and our theories suggest. I would thus challenge orientalism's polarized and hierarchical conceptions not by showing how individualistic Others are—one of the strategies of orientalism's critics—but instead by pointing out how non-individualistic (non-"Western") Westerners are" (1999: 20). The decisions of many people in all parts of the world are at least partly driven by their concerns for the multiple collectives central to their lives, in addition to their individual priorities. Women engaged in Malawian political dancing often articulated their commitment to contributing to a collective, whether that was a political party or family, rather than to challenge these structures to improve their individual status.

The performances themselves were also collective endeavors. In his work on Igede songs and poetry, Ode Ogede explained that individual poets compose and manipulate texts in order to respond to Nigerian political realities (1997: 67–101). The situation differed for Malawian female political dancers because they performed as a group. One person might have wanted to voice criticism through a song; however, for her to do so, the whole group would have had to cooperate. During Banda's time, it would have been difficult for members of a group to publicly oppose the president, given concerns about the potential repercussions. In the contemporary scene, because most women party members who dance perceived that their role was to contribute and help their parties, it would have been difficult for one woman to convince a group with which she danced to criticize the party, as it would have reflected negatively on all of them. Going against the collective would have also negatively impacted not only the individual's but also the group's prospect for benefiting materially.

Many women also participated relatively uncritically because dancing at political functions has long been part of the social and cultural fabric in the country. Because many valued the practice as tradition, they felt some responsibility to participate and sustain cultural expectations. Though scholarly writing tends to emphasize historical transitions delineated as phases, the lives of most people in any context may not be so disrupted by political change, even when the shifts are emphasized in dominant historical narratives. Many people interpret the political realm through a filter complicated by many different factors, from their own personal experience to a range of historical and social knowledge that shape both perception and perspective (Englund 1996: 109). Such things as wars and severe repression that acutely impact people's day-to-day lives often feature significantly in the construction of their personal histories. Other changes, such as shifts in leadership, may affect some people relatively little. For example, I spent the first nine years of my life living under the Mobutu dictatorship in the Democratic Republic of the Congo (1969–1978). My family certainly was impacted by war, curfews, food and gas shortages, and political repression. What remains most significant to us, however, are not these political realities, but rather our friends, our daily activities, the landscape, the food, the music, and so on. Correspondingly, people in Malawi were differently impacted by the political transformations associated with colonialism, independence, and the transition to multipartyism depending on where they lived, their ethnicity, their religion, their level of formal schooling, their interests, and so on.

In my conversations with Malawians, as with people elsewhere about their lives, they tended to emphasize continuities rather than fractures. When asked when they started dancing politically, most women interviewed referenced their memories in relation to when they married, when they moved to a new location, or when certain of their children were born. They tended to define their lives with reference to familial and community histories rather than those of political entities. Bear in mind that most women who dance belonged to the grassroots and many either lived at the time or had spent most of their lives in rural areas distant from political centers. Though the repression of the colonial period and the Banda years certainly impacted them, they also to a great extent continued living their lives in much the same way. Many lived in the same style of houses in the same communities cultivating the same kinds of food and socializing in similar ways throughout the various phases. Those women who framed their dancing histories in political terms tended to be political activists for whom the political domain featured prominently in their personal experience and hierarchy of priorities. Recognizing that people live whole lives rather than lives chopped into historical phases highlights why some women may not necessarily have focused on the differences that distinguished dancing within various political systems, but may have instead focused on the continuities. People in the region have always danced at public functions. Within local customs, community leaders or anyone organizing an event often invites performers to participate. So when women were invited to dance at rallies, it conformed to some people's expectations of what should happen in their lives, and so many participated. Thus, though Mayi Md. Longwe had long been an avid MCP supporter, when asked if she would dance for the UDF president if invited to do so, she answered yes (personal communication, February 17, 1999).

Many in Malawi also considered the current situation to be an improvement over the Banda regime. Though they may have been aware that politicians were using women's dancing strategically, party functionaries were no longer forcing women to dance. AFORD supporter Mayi Mfuni, interviewed on April 9, 1999, for example, explained that she enjoyed dancing at political rallies in the contemporary scene very much. The difference between Banda's time and now was that she was now free to dance or not. She explained that if it was not convenient, if she did not feel like it, or if she was sick, she just did not. In contrast to the heavy repression of the Banda years, the gender inequities in the current system did not seem to be a very significant problem for some, and for many, they were not worth fighting against.

Furthermore, many people (in any location in the world) live their lives focused on the details of their day-to-day existences without necessarily constantly questioning the powers that be. Here it is important to consider again the webs of power within which a person lives. A characteristic of Gramsci's notion of hegemony is that people are born into certain sociopolitical environments and they learn how to behave within these systems from their childhood into adulthood. Many, regardless of the particularities of their situations, take these systems of power as givens (whether they agree with them or not), and so live within them without diverting their energies to manipulate or subvert them (Femia 1981: 24; Simon 1982: 21; Williams 1977). At election time in my country, I thus dutifully fill out my ballot rather than protesting the delegate system, which I find problematic.

People are also often engaged with meeting their immediate goals of day-to-day living, such as feeding their families, raising their children, negotiating their familial and social relationships, visiting with friends, pursuing economic endeavors, and participating in spiritual activities. For many women in Malawi, these dimensions of their lives were more immediate and were of greater concern than were those relating to how a political party or country is run. Mayi V. Mwale and the other women associated with the Ngwira family were very engaged with and concerned with the dynamics in their families and communities, though they paid little attention to what was happening on the political front. They probably also felt that they had greater control—hence more power—over these facets of their lives, and so may have had more motivation to attend to them than to those networks of power that seemed out of reach.

People may choose not to challenge an inequitable system because of feelings of disengagement, disempowerment, or resignation. Gretchen Bauer and Scott D. Taylor explained that since the transition to a multiparty system of government, most Malawians have become disillusioned with the "rivalry, factionalism, shifting allegiances, changing coalitions, and complete U-turns by party leaders." As a result, many Malawians have "little trust and confidence in the country's political parties" (2005: 34). Feelings of disillusionment and distrust can lead to disengagement and ultimately resignation.

The history of repression during the Banda years greatly impacted the political playing field in Malawi, contributing to a fairly weak civil society and limited antigovernment activism. Though churches played a vital role in the transition to the multiparty system of government and continue to carefully monitor the government's and politicians' actions, other sectors of civil society are not as strong (Von Doepp 1998). Bauer and Taylor explained that in many southern African countries, "youth and or student organizations have been an important sector in an emerging civil society" (2005: 38) In Malawi, university students and youth have been involved in some activism. However, the history of youth associations with repressive arms of the Banda government, the Malawi Young Pioneers and League of Malawi Youth, established a pattern of political bodies appropriating youth to serve the purposes of the party, often to stifle dissent and engage in violence and intimidation. The youth wing of the UDF, for example, has been implicated in acts of violence against political opponents (Englund 2002a: 23). In a similar way, the heritage of women's positioning within the Banda years established a culture that persists into the present that defines women as promoters, not contesters, within the political domain.

Certain social and political environments also constitute cultures of resistance or nonresistance (cf. Abu-Lughod 1990: 47). If one lives in a situation in which people generally accept the various powers that be and exist without questioning them too much, then an individual who is displeased with her or his situation might not react because it does not seem like a possible or acceptable thing to do. Conversely, an individual living within a cultural climate in which people are constantly discussing how they feel about power inequities and frequently act in response to them will probably be more likely to respond with action. The general cultural atmosphere for many people in Malawi since the transition was one in which authority was seen as a given, at least partly the result of the long repression under Banda. Some outlets existed for individuals to express themselves and resist. However, on a larger scale, resistance against political elites was not a central feature in the lives of many.

Some environments are more explicitly characterized by resistance to resistance. People may choose to avoid the possibility of being reprimanded or ostracized by their peers or authorities, and challenging authoritative entities can sometimes be dangerous and result in severe repercussions. In the case of Banda's Malawi, a song text interpreted by a party official as coded criticism against the government could result in the composer being labeled a dissident and sometimes being imprisoned or suffering even more severe outcomes. Though the consequences would not be as severe in the current political system, a woman singing coded criticism of a politician from her own party could be reprimanded publicly or even rejected from the party. A woman who chose not to express dissent in these situations made informed choices that minimized the potential for negative repercussions and maximized the potential for gain. Kathleen Fallon made a similar case for women in Ghana when she wrote, "[D]ue to threats created under authoritarian regimes, women may not view newly gained political rights as a safe means to secure rights for women" (2003: 526).

Crucial to understanding the political perspectives of many Malawians is the recognition that political freedoms afforded since the transition to a multiparty system of government are relatively new. All Malawian adults who were living in the country during Banda's rule experienced severe political repression firsthand, and those born after have heard plenty of stories. Though the post-Banda governments have declared their commitment to political freedom, no one knows what the future will hold. The current government could increase its control over the population, or a new dictatorial government could take over.[5] Some whom I interviewed indicated that they were careful about whom they publicly criticized because of concerns about how they might be labeled in the future. These fears are warranted given some instances of journalists being arrested during both Muluzi's and Mutharika's tenures.

An individual may also be motivated by feelings of resignation: She or he may feel that there is no feasible alternative to the system of power in which she or he exists, even if that one is problematic. Some at the time of my research expressed that they did not feel that a viable option to the current administration existed. Similarly, based on research on peasant response to the tenancy system in Central Luzon, Brian Fegan suggested that lack of resistance can be attributed sometimes to "pragmatic acceptance of the imperfect world at hand, within which each man must do the best he can for himself and his family" (1986: 92). A feeling that the situation cannot be improved can freeze an individual into inaction. As Kaplan and Kelly explained, "[T]he extreme alternative to the merely resisting, hegemonized, and fragmented subaltern is not the organic intellectual but the alienated one, self-aware and critical to the point of incapacity" (1994: 127).

In his analysis of the corruption and abuse surrounding a 1996 by-election in the high-density neighborhood of Ndirande in Blantyre, Harri Englund attributed the small voter turnout not to apathy, but to anger and cynicism. "Greed and cynicism, therefore, would be seen as the *only* parameters of political practice, if the discourse of moral partnership were not also understood as a forceful way of representing relatedness between leaders and their subjects" (2002b: 182). I noticed a significant increase in such sentiments during my 2004 research visit. In 1998–2000, most women interviewed portrayed themselves to me as satisfied party supporters, often enthusiastically so. By 2004, a number, most notably UDF supporters, expressed that their needs were not being met, and that they felt that they had little choice but to accept the situation. These explanations suggested a level of political consciousness combined with feelings of disempowerment. In our interview on June 1, 2004 UDF dancer Mayi Wonga explained, "We do not receive money from the party all the time. We can't depend on the party. We just live with our problems."

Women Dancers and Political Discourse

Women dancers' lack of support for Chirwa and the other activists criticizing the institution of women's political dancing also raised questions about their engagement with political discourse more broadly. To what degree did women at the grassroots level understand the political system and their roles within it, and to what degree did they feel that they had the capability to speak out or challenge the system? Women interviewed exhibited a wide range of degrees of understanding and engagement with political realities.

All the women I interviewed understood the defining characteristic of a multiparty system of government: More than one party existed and people had a choice of which party to support. All also understood that they had a choice of whether or not to dance, and for which party to dance. Most also expressed strong feelings of attachment to and desire to be active in their parties. MCP supporter Mayi M. Mwale described her feelings about the problems her party was undergoing in 2000: "I just believe that as the party is coming to an end, so too is my life" (personal communication, May 16, 2000). When I asked AFORD member Mayi Mtayamanja what benefits she received from her contributions to her party, she explained that she received no benefits because AFORD was not in power. She elaborated that AFORD will never win "because people vote along regional lines. And, since there are fewer people in the north, they cannot win" (personal communication, June 1, 2004). She clearly understood the political playing field.

However, many women expressed limited understanding of what democracy meant outside of the immediate context of their experience and the information provided for them by politicians. Their perceptions resonated with those of other women and men in similar socioeconomic strata in the country. *The Nation* reporter George Ntonya, for example, interviewed people "at the grassroots level" and determined that many attributed ownership of political parties to their founders and chairs rather than to their general membership (2004b). Most interviewees demonstrated little understanding of their rights within the system and the possibilities that existed for them to attain a stronger political voice.

Dancers' explanations for why they chose to support a particular party indicated that their perceptions were similar to those of others in the general population. The party affiliation of women interviewed followed similar regional patterns, suggesting that as a group they were no more or less conscious than were other members of the population.[6] The explanations of some whose alliances did not follow regional lines related to their families' political allegiances rather than their own political perspectives. Some said that they had followed in their parents' footsteps, such as Mayi M. Mwale, who explained, "My parents, when we were growing up, they worked for Kamuzu. So when I grew up, I could not do otherwise, but help the same party, the MCP" (personal communication, May 16, 2000). I asked a UDF supporter living in Blantyre whose original home was in the Nkhata Bay District in the northern region why she did not support AFORD, the party associated with the north. She explained that she supported UDF because she was related to the late Katenga Kaunda, a prominent UDF politician (Mayi Banda, personal communication, April 25, 2000).

Most were not critical of the intersections among gender, political power, and economics. Some explained that most women in their parties danced while men were given leadership positions. Few expressed these problems in gendered terms, questioning why they were relegated to the lowest rungs of political parties, or why the government did not effectively address their needs as women. When asked why she continued to dance for the party, Mayi Welosi, whose criticism of the party was very articulate, answered, "I just like the party. Nothing to do with the money. It's like being in a marriage relationship" (personal communication, June 3, 2004). Her comparison of political relationships to marriage was significant given that most marriage relationships in Malawi are patriarchal (even within matrilineal systems).

Many explained their choice to me by listing a party's strengths followed by the other parties' weaknesses. Both lists often consisted of the same things almost verbatim that the parties were disseminating at the time of the interviews. Mayi Rojasi, for example, explained that she supported the UDF "because it is a good party. It is development conscious, not cruel. It doesn't kill and it is development conscious" (Group Interview with Members of a UDF Action Group, May 2, 2000; see Appendix B). Her answer was taken directly from the slogan that UDF supporters continually repeated at their rallies and raises the question of whether she had thought about the issue beyond what the party disseminated:

> *Dr. Bakili, Bakili Muluzi, pulezidenti wopanda nkhanza, wosapha, wachitukuko, woyenda m'maliro, kuntunda, wowinawina, komanso ali wosawumira eee!*
>
> Dr. Bakili, Bakili Muluzi, president who is not cruel, he does not kill, development conscious, one who visits funerals, untouchable—very high prestige, the victor come what may, and also who is very generous.

MCP supporters often expressed nostalgia for the past, during Banda's rule, when things were good, and they were happier. They tended to emphasize that there was less crime and more respect for elders during the previous regime, and people dressed well, referring to the former dress code. Mayi M. Mwale remembered his rule as "a time of freedom. We the people were free at that time." During Banda's rule, "we were a cooperative people, we were a united people, there was no tribalism. We didn't even have the issue that so and so is from this region" (personal communication, May 16, 2000). She referred to the regionalism associated with the multiparty system and contrasted it to the one-party state, which emphasized national unity.[7]

When asked about the repression under the Banda regime, MCP women interviewed in 2000 usually denied that these things happened or blamed what repression did happen on politicians who had been in the MCP during Banda's rule and who were at the time of the interviews leaders in the ruling UDF, notably such figures as Muluzi and Aleke Banda. As one MCP supporter in Blantyre who requested anonymity explained, "[T]hose things, those things, Muluzi and his people were the ones who were killing" (personal communication, May 16, 2000). Supporters of the MCP leader, Chakuamba, in 2000 pointed out that he was in prison for thirteen years during Banda's rule so could not have been responsible for any of the atrocities. Another MCP member explained that "it could not have been Chakuamba because he was arrested. He went to prison. It was Bakili [Muluzi] doing all of this" (Group Interview with MCP Women, May 16, 2000; see Appendix B). That Chakuamba's imprisonment was part of the widespread repression during Banda's rule was never mentioned. Nor did anyone bring up the irony of his leading the very party that had previously imprisoned him. MCP leader John Tembo, who many in Malawi felt was responsible for much of the repression during the Banda years, was largely omitted from women's explanations.

UDF and AFORD women, in contrast, talked a great deal about the repression during the previous regime. UDF women explained that Muluzi was different from Banda. They called Muluzi kind and generous, adjectives found in Muluzi slogans. They remembered that in the past under Banda, they had to carry party cards and were sometimes harassed by Malawi Young Pioneers. They were not free to speak their minds and they were forced to attend and participate in rallies. They sometimes recounted specific incidents in their own lives where they were badly treated by the party. Mayi Smoko came from Bvumbwe in the Thyolo District, and she lived in the high-density neighborhood of Chilobwe in Blantyre. She earned her living doing small-scale commerce, selling doughnuts on the street. Asked why she joined the UDF, she answered,

> I chose UDF because the Congress [MCP] tortured me a little. They forced us to buy party cloths. If you bought the cloth, you were not allowed to wear it anywhere besides at rallies. If you put it on and went to the market and were caught? Like in my case, I once put it on when I was going to the hospital. They caught me, and I spent the whole day at the area office. And they smeared mud all over my body. We filled two pails with mud. Women youth leaguers came and started smearing our bodies with mud. All this because we wore the party cloth. They said that it did not bear the portrait of our husbands. It features the portrait of the president. So why did you wear them, where is the party rally? . . . So when the UDF came, I chose to support UDF, because they give out party cloth and you can wear it anywhere without being punished cruelly. That is why I love the UDF party.

Mayi Welosi similarly attributed her party preference to her family's experience of repression during Banda's rule, when her uncle was a political prisoner for many years (personal communication, June 8, 2004). Many praised the UDF for giving them freedom of movement, freedom of association, and the choice of whether to dance or not. They expressed gratefulness for the cloth, monetary gifts, loan opportunities, free primary education, and development offered by the Muluzi government. Some pointed to me and explained that in the past I would not have been allowed to meet and chat with them so freely.

AFORD supporters emphasized the courage of Chihana during the early 1990s when he bravely entered the country and openly challenged the MCP government. For example, Mayi Mtayamanja, the district vice chairwoman for AFORD in Blantyre mentioned previously, saw Chihana's bravery firsthand and then joined the party. AFORD members remembered how Banda persecuted northerners, making it difficult for them to get education and employment. When asked how they felt about their party's alliance with the MCP, some expressed that they were uncomfortable with it and felt unsure about voting for the MCP presidential candidate because of their concerns about what would happen if the MCP returned to power. Others supported the alliance, explaining that it was the only way to defeat Muluzi. They emphasized the devaluation of the currency and Muluzi's failure to fulfill development promises as signs of Muluzi's weakness, and said that it was imperative that he be replaced. Others explained that the alliance united the country and was an important step in the struggle against regionalism, all sentiments that appeared in the party rhetoric espoused at AFORD rallies.

In the interviews I conducted in 1999 and 2000, few admitted that they had joined a party because of the monetary benefits, though it was an underlying theme. By 2004, the women I interviewed were more open. Note that many actors in the higher echelons of party structures similarly selected their allegiance based on monetary benefits, as was clear from the ongoing allegations pervasive in newspapers about politicians being "bought" by party heavyweights.

These explanations highlighted the webs of social relations in which all actors operated. Some articulated clear reasons for their support, recounted personal experiences that shaped their views, and gave evidence of benefits they had gained from the party they supported. Many of their reasons were also formulaic. Many women in the same party had approximately the same reasons, which incidentally were similar to what the party leadership was putting forth. I should note here that if I were to interview supporters of political parties in any country, I would most likely find similar patterns. Some people are likely to be very engaged with details of a party's platform, policies, and actions. Others know little aside from a few details that either interest them the most or are most prominent in political discourse. Others support the party that their parents or partners or friends or teachers or religious leaders or neighbors do.

The examples of resistance described earlier demonstrate that women dancers understood what had become perhaps the most fundamental characteristic of the multiparty system: the patron-client relationships that existed among all levels within the party hierarchy. When women played up their client status to maximize the material benefits for themselves, their families, or their communities, they exhibited a keen understanding of what had become the political culture. They understood that politics had become largely about convincing the "haves" to provide for them. That they were at the lowest rungs and received small amounts did not lessen their acute awareness of the situation, their positioning within it, and what they had to do maximize their benefit within it. Politics was largely about money and the distribution of goods. If the political reality was that wealth was centralized in a small minority that comprised, among others, politicians, and that politicians distributed some money to those who performed, then women were strategic when they went along with the system for personal gain. Their participation simultaneously contributed to the perpetuation of a system that ossified their marginalization and ultimately dissuaded women from coordinated efforts to improve their positioning within political and economic systems. In Chapter 7 I consider how the status of these women who dance relates to Malawian women's access to the political sphere more generally.

Notes

1. A majority of the women I interviewed who held leadership positions in the women's wings of parties held similar positions within women's organizations in their churches (Henderson Forthcoming). See Henderson and Gilman 2004 for a discussion of relationships between women's participation in Malawian political parties and the Church of Central Africa Presbyterian Blantyre Synod.

2. Following the 2004 elections, President Mutharika declared his commitment to attacking the rampant corruption, including the preferential treatment of supporters for development efforts. However, when he launched his new party in February 2005, he too allegedly wooed politicians into his party with monetary gifts and promises of loans to boost their constituencies (Semu-Banda 2005). Shortly after his presidency started, his opponents criticized him for unevenly distributing development. During his presidential campaign, he allegedly promised to distribute maize mills to all MPs. An article in *The Nation* on September 17, 2004, quoted MCP MPs who complained that no MCP MP had received the promised maize mills, while their UDF counterparts had (Liwanda 2004).

3. The value of the currency was constantly changing, making it difficult to estimate the dollar amount at any given moment. When I began this research in 1995, one U.S. dollar was worth about seven Malawian kwacha. In December 2005 one U.S. dollar was worth about 125 Malawian kwacha, and in October 2008, one U.S. dollar was worth 142 Malawian kwacha.

4. For a detailed description and analysis of this debate, see Gilman 2001a.

5. Fallon made a similar point that in Ghana, women's experience of repression under the leadership of Flight Lieutenant Jerry J. Rawlings "may prevent women from viewing the state as a means to create change" (2004: 77).

6. The political turbulence that has been emerging since the campaigning for the 2004 elections has complicated the political arera, especially parties' regionalism. As new parties emerge and politicians' allegiances continually shift, some people's support follows individuals; others' follows parties; and others' is based on issues or the persuasiveness of individual politicians regardless of their regional identity.

7. Though some claim that there was greater national unity during Banda's rule, many other Malawians and experts on Malawian politics blame Banda's government for the current divisions, contending that though he propagated rhetoric about national unity, he favored his home central region and treated those from the northern and southern regions poorly. See Chirwa 1998: 57–64; Dzimbiri 1998: 98; Lwanda 1993: 172; Kishindo 1998; Vail and White 1989.

7

Gendering Democracy

I returned to Blantyre on May 13, 2004, and was immediately immersed in the buzz surrounding the third multiparty elections, scheduled for May 20. As my husband, toddler daughter, and I traveled from the airport to our hosts' house, the taxi driver talked of nothing else. Women in yellow were everywhere, and headlines about women politicians and election irregularities shouted from newspapers sold by vendors across the city. On this trip, I was interested in meeting with women political performers to trace how their roles were continuing to emerge and to discuss their perspectives on the 2004 campaigns. I also was interested in learning more about the efforts made by human rights organizations and political figures to promote women candidates in these elections. I spent my first weeks meeting with the directors of some of the organizations who had been involved in strategizing with women politicians to increase their chances of winning. As things quieted down after the elections, I also arranged to interview women who had run successful campaigns and had recently been elected to Parliament. I learned that women supporters gathered to sing and dance at rallies for women politicians, draped in the same style of political uniform as was used in other rallies I have described, but this time in distinctive pink fabric that was designed to promote women candidates across party lines. I met with Reen Kachere, director of the NGO Association of Progressive Women, which was actively involved in promoting women politicians, in her home district of Mwanza, not too far from Blantyre, on June 9, 2004. She introduced me to about ten women in her community who had mobilized around women candidates, and together they sang the following song, which became popular at the rallies of many women politicians:

Inu amayi, tinyamule boma
Inu mayi, tinyamule boma
Nyamu, nyamu, tinyamule

You, my fellow women, let us carry the government
You, my fellow women, let us carry the government
Carry, carry, let us carry

Interested by the juxtaposition of the descriptions I heard of performances at these rallies by women associated with two distinct and ideologically laden political poles—parliamentary candidate and praise performer—I took advantage of the opportunity to investigate relationships between the institution of women political performers and the status of women in politics more broadly. I was curious about whether women supporters filled the same roles for women politicians as they did for men, how women politicians viewed the controversy surrounding politicians' use of women dancers, and whether the efforts made to improve gender parity within decision-making bodies would open up opportunities for women who had been actively involved in their parties as performers.

2004 Elections

During his second term as president, Muluzi tried to change the constitution to allow him to stand for a third term. When that failed, he handpicked economist Bingu Mutharika, who had run against him in 1999 under the United Party, to be the UDF candidate, without consulting many UDF heavyweights. The controversy surrounding Muluzi's efforts for a third term coupled with the process through which the UDF candidate was selected fueled much conflict within the UDF, resulting in a number of top-ranking members splintering off to form their own parties (Englund 2004). Additionally, the conflict within the MCP eventually ended with Chakuamba leaving his rival John Tembo to be the 2004 presidential candidate for the MCP. Chakuamba subsequently formed the Republican Party and ran as the presidential candidate for the Mgwirizano (unity) Coalition, which comprised members of a number of smaller parties, mostly formed by leaders who had broken away from the UDF prior to the 2004 elections. A number of disenfranchised former UDF members, including a number of women politicians, left the party during the campaign period to run as independents (Morrow 2006).

These changes greatly complicated the political field. With so many parties, each vied to attract women to perform at their rallies. Because of the UDF's resources and well-organized structure, its rallies featured women dancers most prominently, though women dancers continued to be ubiquitous at the rallies for all parties and for independent candidates.

With great support from Muluzi and the UDF, Mutharika won the elections, though international and local observers noted widespread irregularities, and many in the country rejected the results (Maroleng 2004). In the months following these elections, conflicts erupted between President Mutharika and Muluzi (now the chairman of the UDF) after it became clear that Mutharika was not following Muluzi's directives. In February 2005, Mutharika announced that he was leaving the UDF party, and soon after he formed a new party called the Democratic Progressive Party (DPP). Numbers of former UDF politicians and those from some of the smaller parties then joined the DPP; some have since left the DPP to return to their former parties, develop new alliances, or form other parties.

The 30 Percent Target for Women in Political and Decision-Making Structures

The Fourth UN World Conference on Women, in Beijing in 1995, precipitated efforts across the world to establish quota systems to accelerate increased female representation in decision-making bodies, as evidenced by the signing of the Declaration on Gender and Development by members of the Southern African Development Community (SADC) (Dahlerup 2006: 3; Tripp et al. 2006: 113).[1] This document articulated a commitment to "[e]nsuring the equal representation of women and men in the decision making of Member States and SADC structures at all levels, and the achievement of at least thirty percent target of women in political and decision making structures by year 2005."[2] President Muluzi's signing of this document was a good-faith commitment to achieve this goal. Leading up to the 2004 elections, only 9 percent of parliamentarians were women, necessitating a large-scale effort to achieve the target. However, a policy of affirmative action was not instituted at the state level, for example, in the reservation of a certain number of parliamentary seats for women, nor did political parties establish systems that would guarantee that women political hopefuls would emerge as parties' candidates in primary elections. The attainability of this target therefore depended largely on voluntary compliance by political power wielders in combination with the initiative and efforts of women politicians (cf. Tripp et al. 2006).

The encroaching deadline was on the minds of political leaders in the 2004 campaigns, as they were faced with a tight timeline to achieve the 30 percent goal by 2005.[3] Improving gender equity within the political sphere became part of the platform of all political parties as they prepared for the elections. All party manifestos included sections on the status of women in society and politics followed by strong statements about the party's commitment to improve gender parity. The 2004 UDF manifesto critically addressed the low levels of female representation: "91.5 percent of all management positions are occupied by men. There are only 17 female members of Parliament compared to 183 men and 4 female cabinet ministers compared to 42 men. As such, most decisions are male biased and perpetuate gender disparities" (2004: 79). The UDF also pledged, among other things, to:

- Improve women's access to education and training to ensure their full participation in decision making and leadership.
- Introduce gender based affirmative action in the appointment of individuals to public, political, and leadership positions.
- Strive to attain the SADC requirement of 30 percent women in Parliament. (The United Democratic Front 2004, 80)

The MCP manifesto stated that "to reverse and improve the status of women the MCP administration will," among other things, "[e]ncourage women to participate in presidential, parliamentary and local government elections in order for them to fully participate in the governance process. This would ensure that gender insensitive policies, programmes and laws do not find their way in this nation" (Malawi Congress Party 2004, 70). The National Democratic Alliance manifesto stated that it "[w]ill ensure that the marginalized within our society are well represented in parliament through a fair representation system. Our government will see to it that this group which includes women, people with disabilities and others have a fair participation in the law making process in the country" (National Democratic Alliance 2004, 70).

The language in these documents indicated party leaders' awareness that women were marginalized within the political arena. Much of the rhetoric was directed to the population of women represented by dancers, those who belong to the country's poor majority who have limited opportunities to participate in decision-making bodies. Given that many women who dance politically were already active in their parties, and that many served in leadership capacities within the women's wings, I was interested in examining whether this emphasis on improving women's access to decision-making positions would impact the opportunities available to and status of the women who dance.

Performing Praise for Women Politicians

Following trends across the continent, civil society organizations in Malawi were active in paving the way for the SADC declaration in the first place, and once established, they were a critical force in strategizing how to achieve the 30 percent target (Bauer and Britton 2006: 8; Tripp et al. 2006: 113). In preparation for the 2004 campaigns, Malawian human and women's rights NGOs, including Malawi Watch, PaceNet, Women's Voice, the Association of Progressive Women, and the Civil Liberties Committee, formed a nonpartisan coalition called the Gender Electoral Support Network (GESN). With funding from various international donor agencies, the GESN worked with women interested in pursuing office, organized training sessions and helped to provide them with the resources necessary to run their campaigns. Emboldened and supported by the GESN, many women who had not previously been active in politics ran for office.

The directors of the organizations involved understood the value of having women dance at rallies. A section of their training workshops was devoted to developing strategies for organizing women supporters to perform. This was especially interesting given that some of these organizations were the same ones that had joined Vera Chirwa in 2000 to criticize politicians' use of dancers. When I asked whether women danced at the rallies of female candidates during an interview on May 31, 2004 with Billy Banda, the executive director of Malawi Watch, he answered yes, "politics and dancing in Malawi is one and the same." Kachere emphasized that she supports women dancing politically. What she finds problematic is when politicians use women performers as conduits to castigate competitors or when women receive only "one cent" from the sponsoring politician. She clarified that if politicians wanted "women to decorate their functions, then they [the women] must be paid," by which she meant a reasonable amount of money for the time and effort expended (personal communication, June 9, 2004). She applauded women using performance for political expression, especially in the recent campaigns, when some songs highlighted the importance of electing women to office:

> Women can come and sing songs [at rallies]. But in those songs, there are messages. Some of the dances that women do are gender sensitive, they pass messages to the leadership of this country, that they should give women a chance. The songs—some of the songs do say, "Women wake up! It's time to wake up. Don't just sleep. Wake up and take the sword. Come on, battle, fight." (Personal communication, June 9, 2004)

Some of the songs sung at these rallies were composed by workshop participants during the training session, such as "Inu amayi, tinyamule boma" (You, my fellow women, let us carry the government); others were composed by constituents for individual candidates. These songs were strategically directed at legitimizing women politicians in individual constituencies, but also at spreading messages promoting women politicians throughout the country. As with the songs developed by women activists in the movement for independence and the transition, they were composed in the spirit of rebellion as a strategy to challenge the dominance of men in politics.

I interviewed three successful women politicians who participated in the GESN training to explore the degree to which women supporters danced at their rallies and if so to elucidate what function they felt the performances had played. Each of the women explained that dancing by women and to a lesser extent men played an important role in her campaign efforts. In conversations with some human rights activists and others, I had frequently heard that women were far less likely to dance for women politicians than for men. The female politicians I interviewed expressed that they had no problem motivating women to dance. Patricia Kaliati was thirty-seven years old when she made time to meet with me in Blantyre on June 21, 2004, at a downtown coffee shop. She had just won her second election on the UDF ticket and had recently been named deputy minister of local government. I mentioned that I had been told that women were less likely to dance for women politicians. She answered that it varied from constituency to constituency, but that in hers women were motivated to participate for two reasons: The first was to "entertain the member of parliament," and the second was the women's knowledge that Kaliati would "have a bag of salt to give them that they could use when they returned home."

When I asked women politicians how they coordinated their female supporters to dance, they explained that the leadership in a community where a rally was taking place took care of the logistics. Bertha Masiku, a Blantyre-based businesswoman who had just won a parliamentary seat on the UDF ticket, explained in an interview on June 16, 2004, that she would send a team to the rally space about one hour before it was scheduled to begin. They would blast a popular UDF song called "Yellow, yellow" from a public address system to spread the message that "Bertha is coming to hold a public rally." The music would attract people so that by the time she arrived, "I would find them dancing, and I would join them." She explained that men from an established dance group also sometimes danced for her, usually performing a traditional dance from her community. Ettinor Koloviko, who won a seat also within greater Blantyre, first ran under the UDF banner but due to problems during the primaries won the election as an independent. She relied on her constituency committee though she also explained that the women who cheered and sang did not have to be organized; women who attended rallies participated in these ways on their own. Her description of her rallies indicated that they followed the same formulaic pattern of others I had attended:

> When I arrived, they would meet me from half a kilometer away. Young men and young women dancing for me, praising me, and so forth, up to the venue of the mass rally. And then, I would first of all watch the dances, special songs, poems, choirs, then dancing itself;

> they would dance and dance all in praise of me. Then after that, speeches. My secretary would speak, campaign for me. My chairman would also speak, campaign for me. And then afterward, he would call me to speak, to address the people. Then, I would address the people, tell them my manifesto, and that I would be there for them. I would give them what they haven't had for a long time, development that they were missing in their areas. (Personal communication, June 17, 2004)

The three women emphasized the important roles played by political performers. Kaliati described how she gauged the number of people present and the level of their enthusiasm to determine whether she needed to rethink her strategies. If there were lots of people at her rallies and the women were dancing and singing enthusiastically, she felt confident that she enjoyed support. If, however, she went to rally and found that "people are not cheering for you, then you say, 'What's happening? What is wrong?'" And, she would ask herself, "What do I need to be doing (personal communication, June 21, 2004)?" Koloviko felt energized, especially after the problems during the primaries, when elderly women sang songs asking her not to change her mind about running. She elaborated that through their presence and performing, the women "gave us support, moral support" (personal communication, June 17, 2004).

Women's political dancing also provided opportunities for politicians to display their gender and cultural solidarity with women. By joining the women, they demonstrated their shared cultural knowledge in addition to their shared gendered identity. Drawing women into participation at their rallies through performance was a strategy to establish bonds. As did male politicians, women politicians hoped that the experience of participating as embodied supporters would help the women feel some identification with the politician, and then vote for her. They also recognized that women dancers attracted people to rallies and helped disseminate important messages through their physical presence, energized movements, and song texts.

The GESN also used money from the Canadian International Development Agency to compete with the widespread distribution of party paraphernalia by the other parties, especially the ruling UDF. They designed cloth and T-shirts promoting female candidates (Billy Banda, personal communication, May 31, 2004). Unlike the cloth used by most politicians, which indicated party affiliation, the cloth distributed by GESN participants was nonpartisan and urged people to vote for women candidates. This fabric expressed a symbolic break with the trajectory of using cloth to reify and legitimate a party, and it was radical in its urging of people to vote along gender rather than party lines. At the center of the pink fabric is a circle with the image of a woman standing on a raised podium speaking behind a microphone to a crowd of men and women seated on the ground in front and to either side of her. Surrounding the image within the circle are the Chichewa words *Voterani aphungu azimayi* (Vote for women politicians). Smaller circles lined the edges of the cloth with symbols and acronyms of PaceNet and the Canadian International Development Agency, the agencies that had designed and financed the cloth. Underneath these circles was a border design that included repeated squares with three women (presumably politicians) giving speeches connected by the phrase repeating the mandate to vote for women, as shown in Fig. 7.1. Each participating candidate received some of this fabric and T-shirts to distribute to women in her constituency, many of whom subsequently wore the cloth when performing at rallies.

The Campaigns

The campaigning by women working with the GESN did much to promote the idea that women were capable leaders and worthy of holding elected office. Unlike in European and North American countries, where feminists' emphasis has often been on denying gender differences, the GESN and participating women political candidates focused on common perceptions in Malawi about inherent gender differences. Candidates highlighted their maternal qualities as mothers, caregivers, and community leaders (cf. Tripp 2001).[4] Koloviko recalled, "I was also sensitizing the women so that they should know that we are just the same as men. We can do even better because we are more caring" (personal communication, June 17, 2004). According to Kaliati, "Ladies are more development conscious than are men. We really think of developing the areas. Women think of looking after the voters, being mothers, being sisters, you know? So, men are there, yes, they can develop the area. But they can even think of other things as well." Later, she added, "I even told them that a woman is in charge of the house. We women know that we are missing flour in our house, we are missing relish in this house. It is women. So, I will know your problems in this constituency. . . . Because in each constituency, if you want to have development in your constituency, you need to have ladies" (personal communication, June 21, 2004).

The overriding message was that, yes, women are different from men. Men have had their chance to rule the country, and look at all the problems. Let us give women a chance to see if they can do things differently and better. These maternalistic ideas were reinforced repeatedly throughout the rallies of women politicians, both in their speeches and in song texts, such as the following one sung to me by Kachere and other members of the Association of Progressive Women:

Figure 7.1 Fabric promoting women politicians distributed during the 2004 election campaigns. *(From the author's collection.)*

Mtima wanu amayi	A woman's heart
Mtima wanu amayi	A woman's heart
Ndi mthunzi wamkulu inde	Provides shelter
Tiyeni tikambe, inde	Let us all take refuge
Kwa amayiwa	With women
Inde tikambe inde-e-e-e inde	Yes, let us all take refuge, yes

Despite the strong statements in party manifestos and the systematic efforts of activists and women politicians, the commitment of most political actors to improve gender parity within the political sphere in the 2004 campaigns was questionable. The directors of the NGOs involved in the GESN and the women candidates I interviewed agreed. They complained that the success of women political hopefuls was largely dependent on their relationships to male party leaders coupled with the attitudes and reactions of the male politicians against whom they competed.[5]

All complained that the commitment of politicians, especially in Muluzi's UDF, to the 30 percent target was largely rhetorical and about paper signing rather than action. Anne Marie Goetz and Shireen Hassim asserted that "often states make commitments to advance women's rights without the means of doing so, perhaps keen to receive the plaudits associated with demonstrating gender sensitivity, yet secure in the knowledge that the domestic women's constituency is too weak to hold it to account" (2003: 6, see also Tripp et al. 2006: 126). The Malawi government's dependence on international political and economic support necessitated high-profile demonstrations of dedication to improving gender equity; these public declarations often did not materialize in action. In the campaign leading to the elections, stories abounded about female candidates being physically and psychologically harassed by their opponents and of irregularities in party primaries, a pattern documented in other southern African countries by Gisela Geisler (2004: 173–205). Male candidates sometimes suffered similar types of abuse (see, e.g., Englund 2002b); however, it was not because they were men per se, and the nature of the abuse was not gendered.

Many people I interviewed, including women parliamentarians, explained that women candidates were disadvantaged because of commonly held ideas about gender and leadership that posit men as natural leaders. Masiku related that people in her constituency told her, "I wouldn't vote for a woman. A woman's place is in the kitchen" (personal communication, June 16, 2004). Similar ideas were often at the core of the justification for the lower status of women dancers. Some feel that women dancers are fulfilling their roles as the supporters of men when they promote their male politicians through dance. A woman transgresses societal expectations when she steps out of prescribed roles and strives for a leadership position. This ideology makes it difficult for a woman at any economic level to obtain the support necessary to pursue a successful political career. Throw into the mix widespread poverty, and it becomes an issue of women and men competing for employment. Being a parliamentarian is a job, and a well-paying one at that. Given the prominent idea that men are supposed to provide monetarily for their families and are expected to hold higher-status and higher-paying jobs than women, many men resent competition from women, and do much to discredit female opponents (Kachere, personal communication, June 9, 2004).

As has been documented in other African countries, some male politicians and their supporters castigated women opponents in sexual terms, using sexually charged epithets, such as "bitch" and "whore" (cf. Staudt 1986: 207–8; see also Geisler 2004: 174–75). Masiku told me that she was called a whore, and people spread rumors that she was promiscuous because she was not married (personal communication, June 16, 2004). Meanwhile, UDF candidate Koloviko was called a whore even though she had been married to the same man for years. A number of primaries where strong female candidates were on the ballot were called off, and the male opponent was appointed by the party to be the candidate. After winning the primary in her constituency, AFORD leaders replaced the winning female candidate, Dorcas Malopa Gondwe, with Yeremiah Chihana, the nephew of the then party chairman, the late Chakufwa Chihana. Yeremiah Chihana subsequently won the seat in the general elections (Msiska 2004). Other stories emerged about primaries that were nullified by a party after female candidates won. In other situations, ineligible voters were allegedly brought in to vote for the male candidate. After he lost to Marjorie Ngaunje in the Ntcheu Bwanje South Constituency, UDF secretary-general Kennedy Makwangwala won in a rerun election. In an article in the *Chronicle* newspaper, Makwangwala was quoted as saying, "I am not shaken in any way that there is a woman aspiring candidate in my constituency and there is no way she is going to win the primaries. If these women want to have seats they should just ask the president for special seats because there is no way we can give them a chance" (Nyirongo 2004). His answer exemplified the frequent lack of commitment by party heavyweights to support or even respect women politicians. It was also indicative of the patronage culture of politics: Makwangwala recommended that rather than running in elections and winning seats through competitions, women should beg for political offices as handouts from the president.

Physical violence was sometimes threatened or inflicted upon female candidates and their supporters. Makwangwala, for example, faced charges after the 2004 elections for allegedly destroying Ngaunje's vehicles during the primaries (Makossah 2004). Koloviko's campaign chairman was physically assaulted, and she herself was threatened with violence (personal communication, June 17, 2004). Shortly after the results of the elections had been announced, I met with journalist Pilirani Semu-Banda, on May 27, 2004. I was pleased to finally meet her after having read so many of her articles on gender and politics in *The Nation* newspaper. She told me that the UDF had used its female membership to disrupt the campaigns of independent candidates by sending women to conduct rallies at the same time as those of independents. She explained that the UDF sent these women, who would dance and sing, "to castigate them [women candidates], to insult them, to abuse them." She elaborated that the UDF supporters sometimes criticized the women politicians on gendered terms. She described the campaign of one female UDF candidate in the Phalombe District. After the candidate won the primaries, the UDF disregarded the results and chose to field the male candidate who had lost instead. The woman then ran for the same seat as an independent. Semu-Banda explained that UDF women were sent to her constituency just to express the message, which they did through their song texts, that "she's our fellow woman, but we don't think she's really good for you." This example raised the issue of agency and who was behind the messages expressed through the song texts: Semu-Banda's explanation implied that the women were not acting on their own initiative, but rather served as political tools for the male politicians. It was possible that she was wrong and that the women took the initiative on their own to castigate these candidates. However, in my interviews with UDF women who danced following the 2004 elections, it became evident to me that many women had become used to performing at various events when they were called to do so, and that they were not always directly engaged with or even informed about what was happening, as articulated by UDF supporter Mayi Welosi:

> We are just recruited and told to go to such and such a place where the *bwanas* [important men] are coming, but we don't know what the *bwanas* are coming for. We don't know what they call us for. We just do what they tell us to do. If they say, "Do this," we do this. They say, "Go to Limbe," we go there and listen to what they have to say. (Personal communication, June 8, 2004)

Given Mayi Welosi's experiences and from my conversations with other dancers active in the 2004 elections, I surmised that UDF heavyweights sometimes organized women to travel to constituencies far from their homes to disrupt rallies. It was therefore plausible that the women who tried to break up this Phalombe event might not have known the competing candidates nor had any grievances against the woman running, whom they castigated.

Fourteen percent of the candidates who won parliamentary seats in 2004 were women, increasing the number of female parliamentarians from 17 to 27. GESN activists I interviewed expressed that they were pleased by their successes, but also disappointed by the country's failure to meet the 30 percent goal and by the lack of real commitment of party leaders, especially Muluzi.

Shortly after the elections, in the hopes of coming closer to the 30 percent target, the members of the GESN provided a list of eligible women for consideration to the newly elected President Mutharika as he was putting together his cabinet. Once again, they were disappointed. Of the twenty-one appointees, three were women. Women fared better in the second-in-command positions of deputy ministers. Of the eight, two were women. On August 6, 2004, President Mutharika released a list of thirty-seven principle secretaries, of which seven were women, a result that, according to journalist Chapalapata McDonald, cast "doubts on Mutharika's pledge to increase women's participation in decision making positions to fifty percent, instead of the SADC target" (2004). McDonald referred to Mutharika's campaign pledge to surpass the 30 percent goal and strive for the more equitable goal of 50 percent. Subsequent cabinet reshufflings have not significantly increased female representation.

The contrast between party leaders' articulated commitment to improving gender parity as documented in their manifestos and their resistance to supporting women politicians indicated discrepancies between discourse and action. That these strongmen did not support women in similar economic strata to themselves at the highest echelons of the parties suggested that many would also not support efforts to improve the status of women at the lowest rungs of political hierarchies, such as those who dance, marginalized because of class and gender.

In at least one interview, human rights activists asked me in my capacity as a researcher from the United States for advice on how to strategize to achieve the 30 percent goal. I had to laugh. Though the United States was a dominant force in the international community that pressured countries, such as Malawi, to improve gender equity, it did not itself have a quota system or even a coherent strategy for improving gender parity. The linking of democracy to the empowerment of women "is more a focus in *post-conflict countries* and in countries that are in a process of *transition to democracy* than in old democracies." Countries such as my own "tend to consider democracy to be fully established once and for all—even before women have any right to participate." Whether or not women participated, though they constituted slightly more than 50 percent of the country's citizens, has often not figured into measures of popular participation (Dahlerup 2006: 17). The Web site Women in National Parliaments (http://www.ipu.org/wmn-e/classif.htm) indicated in May 2007 that the United States ranked sixty-eighth: 16.3 percent of its parliamentary seats were held by women. Malawi was not far behind, ranking seventy-ninth with 13.6 percent. At the top of the list was Rwanda, with 48.8 percent, followed by Sweden, at 47.3 percent. Ifi Amadiume, in her poignant critique of Western feminists' scholarship on social conditions in African contexts, wrote, "[W]estern women have proved, by their inability to consolidate their own women's movement, that they are in no position to tell Third World women what is good for them" (1987: 9). I concur and suggest that my country does not have much ground to stand upon in its criticism of Malawi's and other countries' failures to commit to improving gender parity. My critique of the political situation in Malawi comes not from my sense of superiority as a Westerner, but from my interest in social justice; I am just as critical of my own government.

Gender, Class, and the GESN

Aili Mari Tripp (2001) contended that women's associations in Africa have been effective in disentangling their activities from state-linked clientelism through nonpartisan activities that bridge existing social divides based in ethnicity, religion, and clan (see also Tripp 1996: 285–89). The GESN's efforts to bring together human rights activists and politicians regardless of political affiliation to work together in the 2004 elections and their continued plans for the future were very positive moves in this direction and challenged the centrality of political parties as the main actors in the electoral process. The NGOs worked outside of state and party patronage networks; they did not vie for resources from the state president or other party power wielders. In addition to strategizing with women to strengthen their campaigns, the GESN devoted great energy to civic education. They met with communities throughout the country, educating them about the value of seriously considering women candidates, especially important for those who felt that women were not capable of leadership. Their work was unquestionably extremely important and effective, as indicated by the success of many women candidates whom they supported.

At the same time, it is important to consider the webs of power within which the GESN operated. Here I return to a point made by Abu-Lughod, who explained that when resisting against one group of people, resisters can unwittingly enmesh "themselves in an extraordinarily complex set of new power relations" (1990: 52). If women banding across political lines to promote women in politics do not simultaneously interrogate the hierarchies built into their movement, these inequities will most likely persist after their immediate goals are met. Women politicians who capitalized on the symbolic value of shared gender identity, for example, by wearing similar styles of dress, by joining in the dancing, and through maternalistic discourse, emphasized gender identity over class, thereby largely sidestepping the economic gulf that divided them from the types of women who dance. The disparate performative roles of dancer and politician at their rallies enacted the same economic divides between politicians and their constituents as those of male politicians, where gender was not an explicit theme.

Similarly, women politicians understood that much politicking in Malawi was about patronage and that to run a successful campaign, they had to market themselves as benefactors for their communities. The women politicians I interviewed emphasized repeatedly that they had to provide for their constituents—both material gifts and development projects—even before elected to prove their commitment to provide these benefits after the election. They were aware, for example, as in the earlier quote from Koloviko, that many women danced at their rallies in the hopes of receiving gifts and of having their communities selected for development initiatives. Using resources from their parties, donor agencies, private sponsors, and their own savings accounts, women candidates therefore spent a great deal of money distributing money and goods to their prospective constituents as well as initiating development projects (cf. Tripp 2001). Failing to do so would probably have cost them the election.

Each of the women politicians also emphasized their responsibilities as women to provide specifically for the women in their constituencies (cf. Fallon 2004: 82–83). These women comprised a significant bloc of their voters, and politicians expressed concern about their well-being. In explaining what they would do for these women as well as the rest of their constsituents, many described fulfilling the roles of patrons, as did their male counterparts. Masiku explained,

> I wanted to meet all the chiefs, the church elders, and some of the people who were holding political positions, to sit together and set up committees where we could look at each area. Because I have divided the constituency into zones, all right, so in those zones, what are the most important things that we should look in to. If I can find some well-wishers, if I could find them quickly, if they would be able to, if they could assist to put up maybe one or two blocks at school. Why not do it? I don't see myself drawing any more money from my pocket now because I am dry, but I will now have to go shopping for people who can assist, come up with project proposals. And maybe, speak to people like you. You may come across somebody who would be willing to assist children here in Africa. (Personal communication, June 16, 2004)

The pressure on politicians to provide for individuals whom they represented often extended far beyond what was appropriate or feasible for one individual to accomplish. Female politicians (as did men) complained about the financial pressures of campaigns. Kaliati explained:

> You know, Lisa, it's a problem. Yes, in other constituencies, we can give them school blocks, bore holes, and the like. And they will be saying, "She didn't do anything. We were not even able to give them what they want." Like in my constituency, I'm experiencing a lot of problems. The little that I have from my allowances, it's what I give out, constructing bridges, transporting people to the hospital. We

> have these problems where one person comes and says, "My wife is in the hospital, so I need that card for the maternity attendants." Or "My wife is at the hospital; she is having a baby. I do not have a cloth for that baby." I have to help them (Personal communication, June 21, 2004).

Kaliati hoped for more voter education:

> That's why I'm saying that the NGOs need to go down in the local communities telling people the role of a member of Parliament. The role of member of Parliament is to bring all those basic amenities to the people: good water, communications systems, schools, hospitals, those things. The member of Parliament is supposed to give those. The other things are just minor. It shouldn't be that, they shouldn't take it for granted that a member of Parliament is supposed to provide those things. Because a member of Parliament is having her own house as well. She is having her problems as well. If you are employed, you need to look to your problems when you are paid. It doesn't mean that when you are paid, you need to give to the whole village. So, it's better that the NGOs are supposed to go to provide civic education to the people on the role of a member of Parliament. Because of this, that is why we have problems. We need to have resources in terms of cash and materials to give to people. . . . For me, because they don't know what the role of a member of Parliament is, they think that if you are a member of Parliament, it's the same as the husband in a house. (Personal communication, June 21, 2004)

These quotes illustrate politicians' conflicting feelings about problems associated with the patronage system and their feelings that they were obligated to participate in order for them to succeed.

Significantly, those I interviewed made a point of distinguishing themselves from politicians whom they perceived as *just* giving money or other gifts in their attempts to buy votes. Instead, they presented themselves as having a *real* commitment to improving the lives of their constituents by giving needed items to especially poor individuals and by initiating development. This emphasis on helping constituents was also prevalent in male politicians' discourse about their relationships with the people they represented. An important distinction here is that women politicians differentiated themselves from males by emphasizing a gendered difference that highlighted their commitment to caretaking and the community, which they identify as a gendered orientation of women, what I term *maternalism*.[6]

It was crucial that women politicians participated in the existing political culture in order to succeed and to narrow the gender disparity in decision-making bodies. However, the gifting and initiation of development projects by women candidates during their campaigns inevitably contributed to the politicization of development so well entrenched during Muluzi's presidency. Their gifting, within maternalistic discourse, was a gendered articulation of what was largely consonant with and ultimately reproduced the patronage model of politicking; perhaps it could be called *matronage*. Here, again, my critique is not of the individual women, each of whom operated within the political culture as it existed in the same way that I operate within the various social hierarchies in which I find myself. Rather, my intention is to elucidate that when people operate within existing structures, which is what most of us do in much of our lives, we contribute to sustaining inequitable systems even when we are critical or our actions simultaneously have positive outcomes.

Immediately following the 2004 elections, members of the NGOs I interviewed were strategizing how to increase the percentage of female candidates in the next elections, to be held in 2009. Many were optimistic that they would achieve their goal if they started immediately and devoted the next five years to the project. Included in their strategies was increasing the pool of potential female candidates through civic education and training. Malawi Watch director Billy Banda explained that they planned to target young women pursuing college degrees or even those who were still in secondary school to discuss about the prospect of pursuing a career in politics. He explained that most women do not consider politics when they think of possible career paths. Other strategies included developing a curriculum to begin training prospective politicians as soon as possible. These strategies are important strategies for developing a larger pool of women interested in running for office and ready to do so; they would also, however, target women who belong to the economic elite. The girls and women they would identify in secondary schools or colleges would mostly be from richer families who had been able to provide educational opportunities for their daughters.

I asked directors of NGOs whether they had any plans to target female community leaders at the grassroots level and used the specific examples of women dancers already active in their parties. There were plenty of women—individuals such as Mayi Kondowe—who were already leaders in their communities, including some who were leaders within the women's wings of their parties at the lower levels, who demonstrated strong leadership capabilities, but did not have the necessary English-language skills, financial resources, and political empowerment to run for office. Many of these women were highly motivated and some would have appreciated the opportunity to receive language and political training so that they could move into more power-wielding positions. Here, my thinking resonates with that of Drude Dahlerup, who rejected "accusations that women's low representation is primarily caused by women's lack of resources." Rather, she argued that "the real problem is that women's experiences are not recognized and, after all, the counter-argument goes, being a politician is about *representing*, not a matter of university education" (2006: 14).

Most human rights activists I interviewed expressed that they had not considered extending the pool in this way. Women interviewed at the grassroots level similarly seemed to accept that their chances for political mobility were limited. May Chimzimbe, for example, a twenty-two-year-old UDF supporter who had more formal schooling than most other dancers I interviewed, having completed secondary school, expressed that she would like to pursue a leadership position in the party. When I asked if she would be interested in being a member of Parliament, she laughed and quickly said no. I then asked, "Do you think that the party would help you if you wanted to be in a high-level position, such as in the executive or an MP?" She again answered no (personal communication, June 8, 2006). I inferred from our conversation that she perceived running for political office to be completely out of the range of possibility for her. This lack of attention to women at the grassroots level may be attributable to NGOs' focus on increasing female representation in government rather than lobbying for more gender equity within political party structures, something that has been consistently out of the purview of NGO activities (Geisler 1995: 577).

Emma Kaliya, the chairperson of the Gender Coordination Network, acting program coordinator of Malawian Human Rights Commission, and coordinator of Network Against Gender-Based Violence, agreed and explained that with real development that enabled women to have meaningful economic roles, women would become empowered and better positioned to participate at higher levels within the political sphere. Asked about NGOs' strategies to do such things as provide training in English to women at the grassroots level who demonstrated leadership potential, Kaliya pointed out that adult literacy programs already existed and could be better utilized. Time will tell what strategies the NGOs decide to use and what turns out to be effective.[7]

The Women Who Dance

Unfortunately, the timing of this trip precluded my attending the rallies of these women politicians, and they were all much too busy in their first weeks in office to facilitate my meeting with women in their constituencies who danced for them. I did spend time in the high-density neighborhood of Ndirande meeting with women who had been active performing at political rallies in the 2004 campaigns, though they did not perform specifically for women candidates. I included many of their perspectives in the previous chapter's discussion. Most were UDF supporters, and the candidates in their constituency were all men. Many of them had spent a great deal of time and effort traveling far and wide in and around Blantyre to dance and sing during the campaign period. I was struck by some differences between the women I met during this trip and the women with whom I had spent time in Zingwangwa during my previous stay. In 2000, when I asked women why they danced, most emphasized their commitment to the party. By 2004, the association of dancing with remuneration was much more explicit. Many told me about what little bits they had gained materially, and all complained that it was not enough. These women were gauging the new president, trying to determine his attitude toward women dancers.

Immediately after his election, Mutharika claimed that he would discontinue the culture of distributing handouts established by his predecessor. In the weeks after he won the presidency, the UDF hosted an event at the state house to celebrate the victory and to thank supporters for their votes. Hundreds of women registered at the district office in Blantyre had spent the whole day walking great distances to the event to dance their support. According to UDF dancers I interviewed shortly after this event, many had returned to the UDF office a few days later, again walking the whole way, to receive their payment. They were disappointed to learn that the new president had neglected to leave money for them.

My work obligations required that I return to the United States at the end of the summer. Once back home, I read online versions of Malawian newspapers on a daily basis. In the year since he was elected, reports of the president giving monetary gifts to women dancers welcoming him from international trips emerged in the media, suggesting a continuation of these aspects of the political culture (e.g., Ntonya 2004a).

Chaos reigned on the political front in the years following the 2004 elections. Impeachment procedures against Mutharika had begun, Mutharika's government had arrested politicians for castigating him, and a number of the highest-ranking politicians were battling for the leading seat in the country. Though a number of women continued to hold very powerful positions, the insidiousness of the political turmoil sapped the resources (physical, emotional, and material) of politicians, leaving little energy for attention to such things as gender and economic inequities.

Women dancers continued to be central to this messy politicking, fulfilling important roles of party promoters, disseminators of symbols, symbolic actors, and cunning strategists. Women dancers continued to participate at various party events. In a newspaper article about the resignation from the DPP of its former secretary-general, Ken Zikhale Ng'oma, the author made sure to mention that in a highly symbolic gesture, "Ng'oma on Wednesday night disposed of DPP paraphernalia such as T-shirts and cloths to his followers." A female recipient interviewed said that she received more than sixty meters of cloth, which Ng'oma told recipients they could use as bedsheets since he was no longer a member of the party (Liwanda 2005). Ng'oma's distribution of these goods was interesting because, on the one hand, he disseminated the symbols of the party that he no longer supported, increasing the potential for their display. On the other hand, he symbolically undermined the party by distributing its cloth to its former supporters, now opponents, and sanctioning them to subversively use them for their functional rather than symbolic purpose. Women's roles as the public recipients within this symbolic exchange and the disseminators of his discourse were crucial to the success of Ng'oma's political action.

Material incentives continued to be a driving force in women's participation at political rallies, and politicians perpetuated these expectations by attempting to draw dancers to their rallies with handouts. A story in *The Nation* on October 10, 2005, related an incident in which women attending a DPP rally in a by-election physically fought each other over the parceling out of the MK10,000 that DPP candidate Goodall Gondwe made available to them, suggesting that more and more, women's overt reasons for dancing were material rather than political (Chisenga 2005). However, the amount of material remuneration continued to be grossly inadequate for the actual reduction of individual women's poverty.

Shortly after President Mutharika resigned from the UDF party in February 2005 to form his new party the DPP, UDF member and Malawi's vice president, Cassim Chilumpha, was the guest of honor at the launch of the Chia Watershed Management Project in his district of Nkhotakota. An article in *The Nation* reported that while he answered questions from the press about whether he would continue to be a member of the UDF or follow Mutharika in the formation of a new party, UDF women sang songs extolling the UDF's position as the ruling party (Ntonya 2005). Their songs suggested that they did not understand that with Mutharika's resignation from the party, UDF was no longer the "ruling party," and so their lyrics were not appropriate. Some stories also emerged of women dancers being targeted in the conflict between parties. *The Nation*, for example, reported on December 7, 2004, that UDF supporters had been arrested for "allegedly beating up the party's women who wanted to welcome president Bingu wa Mutharika at Kamuzu International Airport" (Langa 2004). UDF dancers were presumed to be supporters of Muluzi, not of Mutharika, in the conflict.[8] My perception was that discourse in Malawi that had interrogated the inherent inequities of women's roles as political dancers had largely been swept under the carpet as mostly male political heavyweights battled over the most powerful political positions.

Notes

1. The SADC declaration followed the fifth meeting of the commonwealth ministers responsible for women's affairs, in November 1996, which recommended that commonwealth member countries achieve not less than 30 percent of women in decision-making positions in political, public, and private sectors by the year 2005. The recommendation

included specific strategies targeted at leaders of political and civic organizations (Hatchard 1998).

2. Southern African Development Community, Declaration on Gender and Development, http://www.sadc.int/key_documents/declarations/gender.php (accessed June 23, 2007).

3. A number of politicians and human rights activists interviewed and politicians quoted in newspaper articles falsely equate the 30 percent goal with achieving gender equality. This goal is obviously only a step toward achieving real equity.

4. The embrace of maternal ideologies of reproduction as a strategy for women to gain access to roles usually restricted to or associated primarily with males is widespread throughout the world. For example, Elaine Lawless (1993) described how Pentecostal women preachers in the United States gain access to the pulpit within discourse about fulfilling their roles as mothers and nurturers of their communities.

5. Similar patterns have been identified across the continent; see Creevy 2004: 68–69; Tripp et al. 2006; Goetz and Hassim 2003.

6. Miriam M. Johnson used the term *maternal agency* in a way similar to my use of *maternalism*. She defined maternal agency as "the actions not only of literal mothers but of any and all people who are guided by maternal attitudes of caring for others as people, not as objects to be used" (1995: 152).

7. The success of the NGOs will necessarily also depend on their access to resources to fund their projects and to the future commitment of high-ranking party leaders, who have to promote women in leadership positions in order for there to be a widespread increase in both female representation and female influence. NGOs depend largely on donor agencies to fund their projects. Prior to the 2004 elections, much of the international aid to support election campaigns was funneled through state and church structures rather than NGOs. According to the leaders of participating NGOs whom I interviewed, what support they did receive came too late to allow them to do much long-term planning because the donors were specifically providing resources for the campaign rather than for enduring efforts. The future looks no brighter, as the NGOs continue to struggle with inadequate resources. In an e-mail message to me in March 2005, Malawi Watch director Billy Banda begged me for any assistance I could give, complaining that "the organization is slowly dying due to donor fatigue."

8. This type of violence has not been limited to women dancers. *The Nation*, for example, reported on December 8, 2004, that "suspected members of the UDF Young Democrats (YDS) . . . are alleged to have been beaten by their colleagues for carrying President Bingu wa Mutharika's portraits during the opening of the First Merchant Bank's Livingstone Towers in Blantyre" (Sonani 2004).

8

Gender at the Intersection of Politics, Democratization, and Tradition

The positioning of women's singing and dancing within the political arena is complicated and demands a nuanced analysis that recognizes its important value at the same time that it considers the practice in relationship to the gender, political, and economic inequities operating in Malawi. At the heart of the phenomenon of political dancing in Malawi—whether one's gaze is directed toward situated performances, the emergence of the practice and evolution of the form, the stages of production, or the discourse that surrounds it—is the idea of tradition. The practice exists because people in the region have long used their performativity in social, political, and economic realms. Many of the details of the phenomenon have their roots in or at least are legitimized as being part and parcel of local cultural practices. The discourse of traditionality cloaking political dancing draws people into participation, makes it enjoyable and meaningful, and at times disguises aspects of its exploitative dimensions. It also ensures its perpetuation. The ongoing and ever-emergent use of dance within the political sphere also necessarily impacts and causes those very cultural forms so celebrated as "the traditional"—often linked symbolically to ideals of stasis—to transform, shaping the process through which these emergent forms continue to emerge.

Dance, Tradition, and the Gendering of Political Culture

The integration of dancing into the political arena is a vibrant feature of Malawi's political life and according to many interviewees should not and probably could not be abolished. Women's singing, dancing, drumming, clapping, and ululating add to the colorful multivalence of rallies. Women contribute their performative bodies to the political culture as expressions of agency, cultural identity, creativity, pride, and political dedication. Performing in the political arena provides poor women with avenues for making valuable contributions to their parties, enacting their political commitment, and expressing their gratitude to their leaders. Through their participation, women construct and participate in meaningful social networks, enjoy breaks from their daily routines, and gain greater access to political and material resources. In addition, participation in the political arena provides women with leadership, material, and travel opportunities.

The integration of what are valued as "traditional dances" localizes and hybridizes the postcolonial political culture, making it more relevant and accessible at least symbolically to Malawians than might a more direct replica of British political institutions. When British bureaucratic structures—such as Parliament, constitutions, party organizations, and voting—are intertwined with local singing and dancing practices, the political culture becomes Malawian. Although similar processes of hybridization occur in countries across the continent, the dance forms in Malawi serve as national identity markers, distinguishing the political culture in Malawi from that of other African countries, even those nearby such as Zambia, Zimbabwe, or Tanzania, with whose populations Malawians share some similar dance and musical practices, related histories of colonialism, and postindependence political structures modeled on the British system. The specifics of the types and combinations of dancing along with the intertextual references to the dancing in different historical periods of the country affirm the political culture as uniquely Malawian.[1]

Concurrent to these positive dimensions of the practice, women's political singing and dancing also emerges from and perpetuates social inequities. Despite the pervasive discourse generated by politicians about the importance of improving gender parity within political bodies as part of the democratization process, the practice of women's political dancing continues to legitimate and contribute to a small minority of mostly men having access to the lion's share of political and economic resources, while the majority of the population suffers from political marginalization and, in a very real way, poverty. Inasmuch as the practice exists to celebrate local cultures and promote politicians, it simultaneously articulates, enacts, and perpetuates power differentials that inherently position the women who dance—already economically disadvantaged—in the lowest rungs of political hierarchies, from which they have few opportunities to emerge.

The more that people come to associate the political participation of women at the lowest political and economic strata as only praise performers, the more their credibility as agentic political participants is challenged. When a group of women clad in DPP fabric gathered at Polytechnic, a campus of the University of Malawi, on October 7, 2005, to welcome President Mutharika on the day of a scheduled visit, Polytechnic students barred the women from attending on the grounds that "the college was an educational not political activity." An article in *The Nation* quoted students shouting, "Go away. Sorry this is Poly, a place for intellectuals and not women that dance for politicians." This quote encapsulates the degree to which some Malawians discredit the women who dance and consider them to be the disempowered puppet-like cheerleaders of politicians rather than political agents (Muwamba 2005).

In my interviews with dancers, politicians, and human rights activists, I have often asked why people thought dance featured so prominently in their political events. The most frequent responses had to do with the traditionality of the practice. Barbara Momba, MCP regional secretary for the south, explained simply that "dancing is our culture" (personal communication, May 23, 2000). Similarly, politicians from the AFORD and MCP parties during the 1999 campaign explained, "Traditional dancing is part and parcel of everyday life. The UDF tried to alienate the current era from Kamuzu's [Banda's]. They said dancing had been used as a propaganda tool. With time, they've seen that it made political nonsense to leave women out" (anonymous male AFORD candidate, personal communication, May 6, 2000). MCP candidate Mike Mvula explained, "Since our late founder of this nation, Dr. Kamuzu Banda, came to Malawi, he made the point that traditional dances should never be forgotten. He brought up traditional dances to match with political meetings and so on. So, in Malawi Congress Party, we still carry that on from the way that Kamuzu brought us up" (Group Interview with MCP Officials, March 29, 1999).

Tradition is also frequently the explanation for why dance continues into the post-Banda era despite opposition to the practice during the period of the referendum and 1994 elections. Many interviewees explained that it was not politicians who reinstituted women's political dancing, but rather women who refused to discontinue the practice. They explained that because of a combination of having become so used to dancing for Banda and the commonality of dancing at all sorts of public events, women who attended political rallies during and shortly after the transition spontaneously danced. UDF supporter Mayi Kachoka, interviewed on April 19, 2000, explained, "They say that they are our traditional dances. That is maybe why it has not changed since the UDF rule. This means that it will go on in the same way just like it was in the past." When I asked Queen Gondwe why women continued to dance after the transition, she answered, "It is traditionally . . . what happens in villages. We dance. People dance. When there is moonlight, they will go and dance. If there is a wedding, they will dance. Whatever the function is, women dance" (personal communication, June 13, 2000).

In February 2000, when human rights activists criticized then president Muluzi and other politicians for taking advantage of poor women by using material incentives to entice them to dance, Muluzi responded by attacking Vera Chirwa for trying to "stop our culture":

Muluzi: There isn't anyone here to stop our culture, No! . . . Singing is our culture. Giving each other money is our culture. If you copy some stuff from England, that's your problem.

Anonymous Female in Audience: She [Chirwa] should turn back and go there [England]! Go back there.

Muluzi: You, you see me, when I go to my village, once the accordion plays, I join them. Because we started long ago! They should not lie to you. Some people, in the name of human rights, bringing some foreign things here. No! After all, who did they consult?

(Muluzi's speech at the RAB Processors event, February 26, 2000)

Chirwa and other human rights activists were attacked for not being Malawian enough and for buying into Western ways of thinking, or copying "some stuff from England." The rhetoric of culture here trumps the practices of power.

The development of a national culture initiated by the NAC leaders during Malawi's movement for independence and then entrenched during the Banda era through the pervasive displays and opportunities to participate, always deeply embedded within rhetoric of its traditionality, traditionalized dancing and praise singing in Malawi's political arena. Politicians during the transition and into the present are again selective about what they decide to continue and thus traditionalize from the political culture associated with the Banda regime into the current dispensation. On the one hand, they reject the glorification of an individual as a symbol of the nation, state, or party. Thus, officials from all parties are careful not to design fabric featuring the party president as a symbol for the party. They select not to continue to endow this aspect of the political culture with the value of tradition; rather, they point to it as evidence of the oppression of the Banda years. On the other hand, they choose to continue to use party women's singing and dancing within the rhetoric of its traditionality.

As explained by Hymes, by labeling a practice traditional, people often consider it to be an identifiable thing or practice and emphasize its value as something that they do and believe strongly about because it has been done in the past and is associated with culture (1975). This attribution of something as "the tradition" often implicitly refers to a concept of culture as static rather than dynamic: We must do this the way it has always been done because that is what our people do. Richard Handler referred to this process whereby something is abstracted from an ongoing social milieu and bounded as a social entity that becomes representative of a group as "cultural objectification" (1988: 13–16). Though people may feel that certain aspects of their culture are static, all cultural practices are dynamic. People therefore often choose to emphasize continuity over change when they deem something to be tradition (Handler and Linnekin 1984). This tension between what people feel is static versus the reality of change contributes to the hegemonic potential of tradition. Thus, politicians in Malawi can point to the continuation of political dancing because it is traditional despite obvious changes in the "tradition." For example, though the dancing during the Banda years was used to represent the party, nation, or state, it is now used to represent a politician or party, a significant transformation in the function of this "tradition" (Gilman 2004).

Raymond Williams explained that though the use of tradition in hegemony is "radically selective," to be effective, it has to be "successfully passed off as 'the tradition'" (1977: 115–16). It is not enough for a dominant group to say that something is tradition; the subordinate group has to come to feel strongly about the practice so that members feel committed to perpetuating it. Politicians in Malawi have been able to successfully appropriate women's performative bodies because many participants value "traditional dances" highly and feel some responsibility to participate in their culture.

Furthermore, the attribution of political dancing as traditional is powerful hegemonically because it can be used to silence anyone who questions it by labeling them antitraditional and thus anti-African. In the following quote, President Muluzi explained why he gives monetary gifts: "Some say, why does Bakili give money when some are dancing? . . . Since long ago, where I come from in Machinga, when they dance—say they dance *lupanda*—if they dance well, throwing a leg well, we give money" (RAB Processors event, February 26, 2000). While critics assert that in so doing, politicians are trying to "buy votes," politicians assert that they are following a local practice; thus, their rhetoric of its traditionality masks their political agendas (Gilman 2001a).

The labeling of political dancing as traditional is especially problematic because it does not differentiate between those women who are politically motivated to attend rallies, and then dance as a way to express their support and disseminate messages, from those women who are strategically organized to dance by political leaders, though clearly some fall into both categories. It is the latter that is controversial because of the gross power and economic differentials between politicians and dancers. When political activists sang and danced at rallies during the independence movement, they did so out of their own motivation and political initiative. During Banda's rule, the government knew that most women would have little political motivation to dance, wear MCP fabric, and sing songs extolling Banda. The government therefore required women to do so to meet its objectives of controlling the population, spreading messages, and projecting the illusion of legitimacy and the appearance that they enjoyed widespread support. Since the transition to multipartyism, some women who attend and dance at rallies are politically motivated and enjoy participating through singing and dancing. Yet, many politicians interviewed explained that their rallies would be poorly attended and that most women would not dance without an incentive. The gifting of dancers is a generous gesture that conforms to local customs. However, given the widespread devastating poverty in which many of these women live, politicians take advantage of their economic neediness by giving them small amounts as strategies to obtain political power, while many of these same politicians neglect to attend to these women's long-term needs.

Furthermore, Muluzi's defense provides another example of the selectivity involved in traditionalizing. Muluzi presented himself as more culturally authentic than Chirwa and as the defender of local culture. Yet, during his presidency, he did little to promote local culture aside from encouraging dancing within the political arena (Gilman 2001a: 208–9). His presence at the event in which he made this speech was imbued with evidence of his embrace of European cultural idioms rather those of Yao, his ethnic group, or those more generally defined as Malawian: his arrival in a motorcade, his Western-style dress, his position behind a podium, and so on. An analysis of his public presentation suggests that his embrace of local culture was reduced largely to having swarms of women dressed in his party's fabric dance around him while singing about how great he was. It is also noteworthy that he celebrated local cultural practices by encouraging women to participate in them rather than doing so himself.

The labeling and justification of women's political dancing as traditional is also problematic because it implicitly equates women and their political activities as "African," while men and most of their political contributions are not presented as culture or tradition, but as professional or political (Henderson and Gilman 2004). To take the example of dress, women's political uniforms consist of "traditional wear," while male political leaders wear suits and ties, as do most male political figures throughout the world, and male audience members wear Western-style trousers and shirts, as shown in Figure 8.1; the former serve as the symbols and representatives of not only the party, but the "African" or "traditional," while men are at least symbolically and to a great extent actually intermediaries between the local and the global political arena.[2]

Similarly, if at a political rally, women party members wear "traditional" uniforms made out of party fabric, while men party members wear suits and ties or other items of Western wear, women become the embodied symbols of the party, while their male counterparts display symbolically through their dress their positions within and their alliance with the larger international political world (cf. Johnson-Odim and Strobel 1999: xxxv; Martin 1994: 413, 419). The association between women and the traditional or cultural is central to discussions currently taking place in Malawi about how to maintain or revitalize local cultural practices; many feel that local tradition or culture is being diminished and overtaken by foreign ones (Semu 2002). Despite discourse put forth by politicians, educators, and reporters about promoting traditional cultural practices, the dominant institutions vested with power and

Figure 8.1 Kaliyoma Phumisa (center) and other male UDF party leaders during Phumisa's campaign in the Ntcheu District in April 1999. They wear Western-style suits, the style of dress typical of most male politicians. *(From the author's collection.)*

authority in the country (political parties, government, jails, schools, churches) continue to be based on Western models. The implication of women being the conduits for traditional culture coupled with their more limited access to education is that they are subsequently undervalued and underrepresented in the Western institutions in the country, the primary centers of power (Semu 2002; Mullings 1976; Henderson and Gilman 2004).[3]

I am not suggesting that women should not dance at rallies, but rather that it should not be the primary option for poor women. If the main reason for the continuation of the practice is because it is part of "culture," then perhaps men and women across political and economic hierarchies should similarly embrace local practices, rather than associating dancing and African dress with the most disenfranchised segment of the population.

That women's political dancing has been classified locally as entertainment and as culture or tradition has worked hegemonically to veil its oppressive dimensions both during the Banda regime and in the current dispensation. Rather than being attended to (for the most part) as a manifestation of the economic and gendered differentiation extant within party and governmental structures, it is more often glossed as part of the preservation and participation in culture. As entertainment and tradition, it comes to be valued as inherently good and something that people feel a cultural obligation to continue (Gilman 2004). Labeling it *our culture* or *the tradition* makes it difficult for people to fight against it. Protesting gender oppression in political structures makes sense, but protesting tradition is problematic because many people take tradition to be something that exists a priori, that should not be challenged. Any overt suggestion to alter tradition threatens the very fabric of cultural identity, as was evident in people's virulent labeling of Vera Chirwa and other activists against the practice as forsakers of culture. The hegemonic benefit to valuing political dancing as tradition results in many participants accepting and participating in the practice relatively uncritically (Williams 1977: 115–16; Gilman 2004).

The extension of labeling the practice traditional into the economic realm, whereby politicians pay dancers and entice them to participate with monetary incentives, all within discourse about tradition, complicates the matter further. Both politicians and dancers can explain their actions within ideologies of tradition. Politicians can pay dancers with government moneys intended for other purposes with the reasoning that they have a cultural responsibility to show their appreciation to dancing supporters. Dancers can present themselves as dedicated party members who embrace local traditional culture while they gain what little they can from politicians' handouts. Though it is certainly understandable why both politicians and dancers capitalize on these performance practices, it is also important to recognize that both categories of participants also contribute to the general acceptance of corruption and politicians' lack of accountability.

Here Foucault's formulation of power as diffuse is useful again because it exposes the complexity of human relationships in which force relations traverse in multiple directions, creating webs of intertangled power relations impossible to describe in such simple binary terms as governing-governed, dominator-oppressed, or perpetrator-victim, and allowing for more nuanced analysis of lived experience even in the context of institutionalized systems of power (Foucault 1990 [1978]: 94). The women who dance are approaching the political arena from their own perspectives and navigating the multiple networks of power within which they operate, driven by their motivations and priorities, to make sense of and decide how to operate within the current system. Many are finding ways of manipulating the system to their benefit. However, it is possible, and I contend necessary, to recognize and celebrate these manifestations of power that subversively exist outside and at times in opposition to structures of authority, and at the same time to recognize and problematize institutionalized power inequities. Here I am informed by scholars such as Nancy Fraser (1992) and Mary P. Ryan (1992), who contend that it is important to examine the public sphere carefully to recognize that when women do not have access to the official public sphere, they often participate in alternate publics through which they are able to exert influence, as is certainly the case in Malawi. At the same time, the exclusion of many poor Malawian women from the official public sphere is not dictated; rather, official discourse—found in the constitution, government Web sites, party manifestos, and politicians' speeches—explicitly affirms a commitment to women's political participation and the contention that the democratic process should be open to them. Goetz and Hassim reminded readers that "[g]ender-sensitive institutional reform is required not just to get women through the door in politics, but also for policy making and implementation to respect gender equality. Women's movements around the world have found that such transformation is impossible without engaging with political institutions" (2003: 5).

Analysts of the practice of women's political dancing in Malawi would be remiss to accept the hegemonic exclusion of many women from official political bodies because women creatively manipulate power in more complicated ways that gain them access to resources despite oppression. Whether democracy is the best political system or whether or how poor women choose to participate in the political process, actors in the new political dispensation should align policy, discourse, and practice to open both the official public sphere and political hierarchies to all Malawians regardless of gender or class, and then let them decide how they want to participate from the full range of options.

The Impact on Malawian Dance Forms

The more the political arena becomes one of the main contexts for the performance of traditional dances, the more rallies become important sites for the preservation and continued emergence of these expressive forms. Inasmuch as dancing has been a vital feature of Malawi's political culture, the political realm has also been integral to Malawian dance forms. Over the course of conducting this research, I have frequently heard conflicting opinions regarding how political use has impacted Malawian performance genres. On the one hand are those who claim that dance forms have been destroyed or lost because of the ways that politicians have attempted to exploit them for their own purposes (e.g., Kerr 1998). At the heart of this interpretation is a romanticized idea of an authentic cultural practice that would not have changed or been destroyed if it had not been exploited in the political sphere. On the other hand are those who credit politicians' dedication to promoting dance forms, most notably the late Banda, with the continued vitality of Malawian traditional dances. As is common when strikingly divergent points of view exist, the reality is probably somewhere in the middle. There is no doubt that the use of dance in politics has affected dance genres. Unlike some, however, I do not think that we can blame politics and politicians for changes in dance traditions. Rather, it is more useful to recognize that these dance forms have always been an important dimension of the social and political landscape. Reed made the important argument that the appropriation of Dan *ge* performers by politicians in Côte d'Ivoire for use within the political arena should be recognized as an extension of historical patterns (2003: 55). Similarly, in Malawi, dance forms have always been used variously within the political domain. Their use by politicians during the independence movement, Banda's rule, and the contemporary scene does not diverge from local cultural practices but rather is an extension of what always happens. The political realm, however defined, has therefore long been a factor in the ways that these dance forms exist, are used, and change.

Furthermore, all expressive forms are emergent and are constantly transforming with every enactment (Bauman 1986: 4). Variations in availability of material resources, personalities of those involved, aesthetics, fashion, global trends, political contexts, and economic environments of dancers necessarily influence a dance form. Whether or not they had ever been used in politics, Malawian dance genres would nevertheless have changed; their integration into the political arena has been only one of many contributing factors. Nevertheless, it is illuminating to consider how the political sphere has influenced the emergence of dance forms, especially within the context of frequently expressed discourse by government officials lauding their roles in the promotion of local cultural practices. My concluding section therefore considers how the political use of dancing during Banda's rule and into the current multiparty system has affected and continues to impact some dance forms of the Nkhata Bay District. My treatment of this question is necessarily limited in that different dance forms across the country have been impacted in widely varying ways, and the dance forms I consider have continued to emerge since I conducted the research; my discussion thus provides only a glimpse into some possibilities.

Throughout Banda's thirty-year rule, his rhetoric about his dedication to promoting traditional culture provided official legitimation and valuing of these genres, and the frequent occasions to perform during his rule encouraged the vitality of some. National celebrations provided opportunities for established dance groups to receive exposure that they would not otherwise have had. While a malipenga dance team would previously have performed mostly in its own or nearby villages, with the politicization of dancing, some groups enjoyed national fame. In the case of chiwoda-like dances, the political context provided incentives for some women to improve their singing and dancing skills, and the best performers received national recognition. New songs, dance steps, and variations in performance styles were constantly introduced as women tried to surpass one another.

Regional and national events brought dancers from different parts of the country into contact. Dancers had many opportunities to watch those of similar or very different styles, providing them with opportunities to learn, be inspired, and adopt elements from one another. This cross-influence had a particularly strong impact with regard to chiwoda-like dances. All women were expected to dance within the locale where they lived. A woman living in an area dominated by the Chewa ethnic group danced chimtali while living there. If she later moved to Nkhata Bay, she would dance chiwoda regardless of her ethnic or geographic identity. Individual women also brought singing and dancing styles with them as they moved around the country, influencing dancers as they traveled. Similarly, girls practiced and performed at schools, led by their schoolteachers. The teachers and girls often came from many different parts of the country, creating opportunities for interinfluence. At political events, women saw one another perform and were inspired by innovations or stylistic features from other districts. As a result, similar melodies, songs, movements, complex entrances, and spiral formations performed by women said to be dancing chimtali, chiwoda, and ndolo continue into the present.

The interinfluence among established dance groups was less prevalent because most dance forms were not so closely related. Still, as Tonga men in the Nkhata Bay District performing malipenga and Tumbuka men from Mzimba District performing malipenga saw one another, they probably provided inspiration for change. Song lyrics of some dance forms could also easily inspire or be adapted by composers of others.

At the same time that their inclusion at rallies encouraged the creativity and performance of many dances, it did so in a selective way. Certain dances, for example, appeared at political functions more frequently than did others, while still others were never included. The frequency of these political events necessitated that dancers of established dance groups and chiwoda-like dances expend a great deal of effort in preparation, leaving little time for other dance activities. As political events to a large degree became the primary contexts for performing, those dances that were included were more likely to remain active than were those that were not. This is not to say that a dance form could not stay active unless it was performed at political functions. Chilimika was rarely included in political occasions during this period, yet it survived and continues into the present. Other dances did not fare so well.

Many factors affected whether or not a dance thrived. One had to do with the nature of the genre itself. In the case of chilimika, that the dancing of chiwoda was the main dance performed politically by Nkhata Bay women during Banda's time did not negatively impact chilimika because the latter serves a very specific purpose: the celebration of the New Year. However, another dance that was performed by men, women, girls, and boys in Nkhata Bay District called kamchoma is no longer performed. According to a number of elderly residents I interviewed, kamchoma was informally danced as a leisure-time activity, and it was not included at political functions. One explanation for the loss of its popularity was that people's time and resources were taken up with rehearsing and performing those dances that were featured in political occasions, leaving them little leisure time in which to enjoy kamchoma.

The frequency of political practices and performances also affected the contexts of performance for those dance forms that were included. For example, the selection of chiwoda as the dance performed by party women in the Nkhata Bay District had long-term implications for its contexts for performance along with certain of its stylistic features. As mentioned previously, before Banda's rule, chiwoda was performed at special events, such as weddings, installations of village headmen, and intervillage dance competitions (Chilivumbo 1971). During Banda's rule, it continued to be danced at these special events; however, the intervillage competitions have since largely come to an end. Because of the frequency of practices and performances for the party, little time or energy was left for chiwoda in other contexts, and it largely came to be associated as *gule wa chipani* (the dance of politics) (Kerr 1998: 40).

The requirement that all women perform a chiwoda-like dance also resulted in women from those ethnic groups that did not perform this type of dancing to adopt one from their neighbors. For example, Ngoni women from the Ntcheu District danced chimtali, the circle dance of their Chewa neighbors. In contemporary Malawi, Ngoni from this area continue to dance chimtali at political functions; it has thus become part of their repertoire.

The censorship at the time affected song content: No matter what the nature of song lyrics were prior to Banda's rule, afterward the songs had to praise Banda.[4] In the current song repertoires for both chiwoda and chilimika, regardless of whether or not they are performed in political contexts, there is a preponderance of songs of praise, be it for the dance group, the village headman, the village, or the people for whom the dancers perform. Praise singing predates Banda's rule; however, the overriding emphasis and the nature of the praise probably result from the thirty years of ubiquitous performances for Banda and his MCP.

The setting of political rallies also sometimes affected the formation in which a dance was performed. Banda and other guests of honor always sat in a specific location, and the dancers frequently directed their performances toward them. As mentioned previously, in most nonpolitical settings, chilimika and malipenga dancers rotate around a central point in formation, surrounded by the audience. In order to best entertain the honored guests at political functions, dancers altered their form so that they faced the VIP stand. To this day, at political rallies, chilimika and malipenga dancers perform in place facing guests rather than rotating in a circle formation, as is more typical (e.g. "Malipenga dance competition Dindano Village," http://purl.dlib.indiana.edu/iudl/eviada/5-E9204). David Kerr referred to this kind of transformation as evidence that during Banda's time, "dances had lost their authenticity due to politicization" (1998: 40). His position is exaggerated because in most nonpolitical contexts that I have observed, dancers continue to rotate within a circle-shaped arena. The adaptation to the new performance context is better understood as the creative manipulation of what were and continue to be flexible forms.

Political dancing during Banda's rule also impacted dance-costume styles, especially in the case of chiwoda-like dances. As already explained, the requirement for chiwoda-like dancers to wear the national uniform differs significantly from that of performers of established dance groups, who were expected to wear the appropriate costumes associated with their dance form regardless of whether or not it fit the dress code. In a 1971 article, Alefeyo Chilivumbo explained that styles of dress for chiwoda dancers outside the political arena reflected contemporary styles: Dancers creatively incorporated fashionable clothing into their dancing attire. This practice has changed as a result of the requirement during Banda's rule that dancers wear the national uniform representing the dress code. Even outside the political context, dancers of chiwoda continue to wear attire that conforms to Banda's government's dress code, most notably the obligatory zitenje, rather than incorporating fashionable clothing as do chilimika dancers.

The promotion of traditional dances during Banda's rule had long-term implications for types of dancing not classified as traditional. Some talented individuals, such as Zabweka Tembo and the School Band, developed new dance forms that were sometimes included at political functions. Tembo, who has lived most of his life in the Nkhata Bay District, explained to me during a conversation in August 1996 that he started the ensemble in 1954 and has kept it alive until the present time. His group was invited to perform for Banda on several occasions and even made it to Sanjika Palace, the presidential residence in Blantyre, where only the best dance groups were selected to perform. As a result, Tembo and his dance group are known by people throughout the country, and he is famous across the Nkhata Bay District even though he lives in the relatively isolated Nkhwali, which is removed from town and to which buses rarely travel.

Banda's continual promotion of the traditional over Western cultural forms greatly restricted the development of art and theatrical dancing. The lack of governmental support for the arts outside of political contexts restricted the creative development of dance forms not categorized as traditional. The only professional dancers in the country both during Banda's time and into the time of this writing belong to the Kwacha Cultural Troupe (now Malawi National Dance Troupe).[5] Members of the troupe are salaried civil servants, and their performances feature creative medleys of traditional dances, representing many of the country's cultural groups. The troupe's primary role is to promote Malawi's diverse cultures nationally and occasionally internationally (Chimombo and Chimombo 1996: 2–3). Dance as an art form (as distinguished from the traditional) has little presence in the country and has not been part of elementary, secondary, or university curricula from the time of Banda's rule into the present (Chimombo and Chimombo 1996: 8).

The popular dance scene was affected by the MCP's strategies to regulate the population's cultural activities and expressivity. The restricted economic environment, the emphasis on those cultural practices deemed traditional or African, and censorship (both self-imposed and enforced through the party machinery) limited opportunities for procuring musical equipment, performing, or producing and distributing recordings (Phiri 1998). The popular music and dance scene was limited and did not flourish to the degree that it did in neighboring countries (Chimombo and Chimombo 1996: 4). In my last visit to the country in 2004, still no store regularly sold musical instruments; Malawian musicians go to great lengths to procure instruments and sound systems from abroad.

The 1994 transition to a multiparty system of government has most profoundly impacted chiwoda. When I first came to Nkhata Bay District in July 1996, I was told that the only contexts in which chiwoda was performed were weddings, which normally occur in the months of October and November, and occasional installations of village leaders. When I returned to Nkhata Bay District in October 1998, I found that chiwoda was not performed even at weddings, having perhaps more to do with the ubiquitous Congolese popular musical form kwasakwasa also sometimes called rumba, soukous, and domboro than it does with politics. People at the weddings I attended were dancing to recorded Congolese popular music rather than dancing chiwoda.[6] The result is that immediately following the 1994 elections, few contexts for dancing chiwoda existed except for the occasional installation of a village leader.

The 1999 election campaigns provided an occasion for dancing chiwoda again, further solidifying the association between chiwoda and the political arena, and many have returned to calling it "the dance of politics." In a conversation I had with Mayi Phiri on January 16, 1999, she described her experience of having recently danced chiwoda at an AFORD political rally in Msani Village in Nkhata Bay District. This was the first time she had danced this genre since the Banda government lost power. She commented that the younger women and girls in Msani were surprised to watch the older women because they had not previously witnessed their chiwoda talents. Younger women joined the older dancers, an opportunity for the dance to continue that might not otherwise have presented itself. At the same time, dancing in the current political realm is not as widespread as it was during the Banda era, and women choose whether or not to dance. One result is that fewer women dance politically and the opportunities to dance are less frequent.

The relegation of chiwoda as the dance of politics therefore implies a much less active existence than it enjoyed in the past.

The all-male Tonga malipenga is known throughout the country to be well organized, active, and dynamic. A few years after the UDF took over, the government changed the scheduling of school holidays, making the longest one fall during the rainy season, when the hardest agricultural work takes place, to allow school-age children to help their families with farming. During my stay in Nkhata Bay District in 1998–1999, malipenga suffered an unusually weak season. In the months of October and November, the time considered to be the appropriate malipenga season, many would-be dancers were still in school. During the school holiday in December and January, people were busy farming. In the ten months I lived in the district (August 1998–April 1999) I knew of only two competitions. At the same time that the scheduling of holidays negatively impacted this dance, the president was making public declarations about his commitment to promoting traditional culture. Certainly the government's decision to change the school holidays had to do with vital economic concerns; it is noteworthy, however, that it also impacted a practice that corresponded with the culture that Muluzi claimed to promote.

In September 1998, four years after the first general elections, President Muluzi made a public proclamation in newspapers that one of the government's priorities would specifically be the promotion of traditional culture, especially dances. Soon after, I met with an official in the Ministry of Youth and Culture who was given this charge. His plan was to coordinate district-level festivals, and Nkhata Bay District was to be the first because of the vitality of malipenga. The ministry official's plans paralleled strategies in other African countries to promote and preserve local cultural practices. Askew, for example, described a series of dance competitions organized by cultural officers in Tanzania to promote and preserve local cultural heritage (2002: 196–223). In Malawi, these types of events outside the political arena have not been widespread, and the official's plan in 1998 never came to fruition, purportedly because the government would not provide the official with the funding needed to coordinate the festival.

A few months later, as the campaign for the second multiparty elections took off, members of the ruling UDF party no longer had difficulties identifying funds to allocate to dancing, this time for their own political agendas, as evidenced by the elaborate rally in Tukombo in honor of Aleke Banda on January 2, 1999 ("UDF political rally Tukombo," http://purl.dlib.indiana.edu/iudl/eviada/5-E4954). The winners of the malipenga competition won an estimated US$300, and those from all the dance forms combined received an estimated US$870, a sizable amount of money in Malawi at the time that would have more than covered the cost of transportation needed by the ministry official to organize the proposed festival. It is significant that the government could not find money to sponsor malipenga channeled through its ministry dedicated to promoting local culture, but somehow the monies made their way into the hands of a prominent politician striving to promote his candidacy.

Unlike chiwoda and malipenga, the enthusiasm for the mostly female chilimika and the frequency of its performance has increased since the 1994 transition. As the dance to celebrate the New Year, chilimika used to be performed only for the few days surrounding the first of January. Slowly the time period in which it is performed has expanded, so that now the competition season sometimes lasts as long as one to three months. A dormant period for chilimika occurred in the 1990s; many teams dissolved and for several years the dance was rarely performed. The year 1998 saw a resurgence; many groups reassembled, and many new ones came together for the first time. The reasons for the slump and the revitalization are complex and not fully attributable to the political sphere; many dancers, for example, blame it on the loss of principal dancers to the HIV/AIDS epidemic. Some reasons, however, are related to politics.

When I asked people in 1998 and 1999 why they had started or revived their chilimika groups, people told me over and over that their villages had become "dead," "there was no culture here," referring to among other things the lack of active dancing as a result of changes that came with the political transition. They decided to start chilimika teams in order to liven their villages so that, as many of them explained, their homes would once again have culture. Mayi Chirwa, the leader of the America State team in Msani, told me in an interview on February 8, 1999, that people in her community "want us to dance. They don't want us to stop dancing because our village becomes lively when we invite people to come and dance chilimika." In the examples I observed, it was individual women who initiated chilimika anew. The reason they gave for why chilimika was chosen instead of malipenga was because it was women who took the initiative. The reason it was chilimika and not chiwoda was because chiwoda is now associated with the political sphere and has not been performed in intervillage competitions for decades. The result is that chilimika is gaining a more central position as a cultural identifier for the Nkhata Bay District (e.g. "Chilimika dance competition Mukaka Village," http://purl.dlib.indiana.edu/iudl/eviada/5-E6115).

Though the malipenga competition season never gained momentum and chiwoda was rarely performed outside the political arena in 1998 and 1999, the inclusion of dancing in the 1999 political campaign provided many opportunities for performing, much as did political functions during Banda's time. Malipenga teams who had not performed during the typical malipenga season took their uniforms out of storage, gathered, practiced, and displayed their talents at political rallies. Women who had not danced chiwoda for the past five years donned their dance clothes, refreshed their singing and dancing skills, and performed elaborately. Though it had not been danced much at political events during Banda's time, because chilimika dancers had already been practicing and performing in nonpolitical settings, they were well prepared for and were featured in every political rally I attended in the district, further extending the duration of chilimika's performance season that year. Similarly, the 1999 campaigns provided rare opportunities for people to perform and enjoy honara ("AFORD political rally Nkhwali Village," http://purl.dlib.indiana.edu/iudl/eviada/5-E4475).

With regard to other dance practices, the transition to multipartyism opened the floodgates for the creative development of local and imported popular dance forms. With the liberalization of the market, audio- and videotapes of Congolese, South African, and American popular music and dancing are readily available. Local recording studios have proliferated, as have local performance groups, resulting in an expansion of creativity and dance styles in this arena (Fenn 2004). Art and theatrical dance have faired less well, as government funding of education remains a problem and the focus of research and education is increasingly on development, which often in contemporary Africa has not been considered to include the promotion of the arts (Phiri 1998: 151).

The long association of traditional dancing with the political sphere makes this arena an integral site for the continued vitality of some Malawian dance practices. In the spring of 2000, I was chatting with a television producer for Malawi Broadcasting Company, the official national television station, who identifies as an ethnomusicologist. One of his directives was to travel throughout the country to document dance performances for archival purposes and to broadcast a regular television program dedicated to promoting traditional culture. He had just returned from a weekend of filming traditional dances in Machinga District. When I asked about the context in which the dancing occurred, he told me that it was a political rally held by a member of Parliament. In his official capacity as television producer, he too relies on the political sphere to provide him with opportunities to fulfill his assignment to record and disseminate examples of traditional culture, a further indication of the central role that the political sphere has come to play in providing contexts for performance.

Notes

1. This statement should be qualified in that the neopatrimonialism of contemporary politics is also rooted in local leadership and kinship patterns. This aspect of contemporary Malawian politics, however, is not part of the official discourse or policies of parties or the government and is frequently denied as political leaders strive for local and international legitimacy. See Chabal and Daloz 1999 for a provocative argument about continuities in local leadership and kinship patterns in the politics of contemporary African states.

2. The association of "African" styles of clothing as symbolically distinct from the powerful realm of "modern" politics is common in some contexts in Africa. Writing about the Asante, Beverly Stoeltje, for example, contended that when Asante men and women

participate in special events adorned in traditional cloth, they are "pursuing the goals of modernity as seriously as any business person in a Western suit" (2003: 3). The same is not true in Malawi. With the exception of some (usually elite men) who occasionally don clothing made from West African fabrics, men in Malawi wear almost exclusively Western-style clothing.

3. Ofra Goldstein-Gidoni made a similar argument for modern Japan, where the kimono "has been invented as national attire and as a marked feminine costume. Women have become models of Japanese femininity, as contrasted with men, who have been given the role of models for rational action and achievement" (1999: 1).

4. See Gondola 1997 for a discussion of how the similarly repressive Mobutu regime in Zaire (now Democratic Republic of the Congo) impacted popular music lyrics.

5. Professional dance troupes whose members are paid government employees, who perform the dances of various ethnic groups, and who represent national identity are widespread across the continent. See Castaldi 2006 for a detailed discussion of the National Ballet of Senegal.

6. See Ewens 1994 for a discussion of how Congolese popular music has spread across sub-Saharan Africa.

Appendix A

Brief Timeline of Malawi's Recent Political History

1891	Britain establishes the British Central African Protectorate.
1907	The British Central African Protectorate becomes the Nyasaland Protectorate.
1944	Nationalist activists establish the Nyasaland African Congress.
1953–63	Britain imposes the Central African Federation, also called the Federation of Nyasaland and Rhodesia, which combines Nyasaland with Northern and Southern Rhodesia.
1958	Dr. Hastings Kamuzu Banda returns to lead the Nyasaland African Congress.
1963	Britain grants the territory self-government, and Banda is appointed prime minister.
1964	Nyasaland declares independence as Malawi.
1966	Banda becomes president of the Republic of Malawi.
1971	Banda declares himself president for life in a one-party state.
1993	In a referendum, the majority reject the one-party state and vote for a multiparty system of government.
1994	Presidential and parliamentary elections are held. The voters elect Bakili Muluzi, leader of the United Democratic Front (UDF), state president for a five-year term.
1997	Banda dies in South Africa.
1999	President Muluzi is reelected for a second term.
2004	Presidential and parliamentary elections are held. UDF candidate Bingu wa Mutharika is declared the winner of the presidential election.
2005	President Mutharika resigns from the UDF and forms the Democratic Progressive Party (DPP).

Appendix B

People Interviewed

- The orthography for people's names listed here is problematic, as many people I interviewed are nonliterate and either do not write their names at all or do not have a single way of doing so. Some names might be spelled differently here from how others in Malawi would spell them.
- The interviews conducted in Chichewa or Chitonga were transcribed and translated by research assistants I hired.
- Titles given are those that were appropriate at the time of the interview. Many political allegiances and titles have since changed.

INDIVIDUAL INTERVIEWS

Billy M.K. Banda. Executive director of Malawi Watch and vice chairperson of the Gender Electoral Support Network (GESN). Interviewed in English in Blantyre on May 31, 2004.

Rose Chibambo. Political activist during the independence movement. Interviewed in English in Mzuzu on February 4, 2000, and April 10, 2000.

Group Village Headman Chilelawana #4. Group village headman and village headman of Msani, Nkhata Bay District. Interviewed in Chitonga in Msani Village on February12, 1999.

Mayi Chimzimbe. UDF member and dancer. Interviewed in Chichewa in Blantyre on June 8, 2004.

Mayi Chirwa. Chilimika leader of America State Boma, Msani, Nkhata Bay District, who frequently dances at AFORD rallies. Interviewed in Chitonga in Msani Village on February 8, 1999.

Mary Chiume. Retired teacher and sister of M.W.K. Chiume. Informal discussions in English in Nkhata Bay on January 17, 1999, and February 3, 1999.

M.W. Kanyama Chiume. Leader in the independence movement and post-transition politician. Interviewed in English in Lilongwe on February 20, 1999, and in the town of Nkhata Bay on April 21, 1999.

Nicholas H. Dausi. Deputy regional chairman (south), MCP. Interviewed in English on May 30, 2000 at the MCP office in Blantyre.

Mayi Eliya. UDF member and dancer. Interviewed in Chichewa in Blantyre on June 8, 2004.

Queen Gondwe. Director of the Promotion of Women in Politics and a government minister during Banda's rule. Interviewed in English in Blantyre on June 13, 2000.

Mayi Japule. UDF member and dancer. Interviewed in Chichewa in Blantyre on June 8, 2004.

Reen Kachere. Executive director of the Association of Progressive Women. Interviewed in English at Chifunga Trading Center in Mwanza District on June 9, 2004.

Mayi Kachoka. UDF member and dancer in Blantyre. Interviewed in Chichewa in Blantyre on April 19, 2000.

Patricia Kaliati. Member of Parliament for Mulanje West constituency. Won on UDF ticket, then joined DPP. Interviewed in English in Blantyre on June 21, 2004.

Emma Kaliya. Chairperson, Gender Coordination Network; acting program coordinator, Malawian Human Rights Commission; coordinator, Network Against Gender-Based Violence. Phone interview in English on June 18, 2004.

Village Headman Kamoza. Village headman of Chihame Village in Nkhata Bay District. Nationalist activist who was exiled during Banda's administration. Interviewed in Chitonga in Chihame on April 21, 1999.

Mayi Kanyasu. Elderly woman who provided historical information about Nkhata Bay dance traditions. Interviewed in Chitonga in Majiga Village in Nkhata Bay District on February 12, 1999.

Mayi Kasambala. Elderly woman who provided information about the history of Nkhata Bay dance traditions, especially chilimika. Interviewed in Chitonga in Msani Village in Nkhata Bay District on February 9, 1999.

Ettinor Koloviko. Member of Parliament for Blantyre North. Won as an independent and then joined the UDF. Interviewed in English in Blantyre on June 17, 2004.

Mayi Kondowe. Leader in the MCP League of Malawi Women during Banda's administration. Interviewed in Chitonga in Nkhata Bay on March 26, 1999.

Mayi Ma. Longwe. Chilimika dancer in Nsanje Village in Nkhata Bay District. UDF supporter. Interviewed in English in Nkhata Bay on February 6, 1999.

Mayi Md. Longwe. Leader in MCP League of Malawi Women during Banda's administration. Interviewed in Chitonga in Nsanje Village in Nkhata Bay District on February 17, 1999.

Justin Malewezi. Former vice president of Malawi (1994–2004 under the UDF) and independent presidential candidate in the 2004 elections. Interviewed in English in Blantyre on June 1, 2004.

Bertha Masiku. UDF Member of Parliament for Blantyre City West. Interviewed in English in Blantyre on June 16, 2004.

Mafumu Matiki. Communications officer for PaceNet. Interviewed in English in Blantyre on June 1, 2004.

Mayi Mfuni. AFORD constituency chairman in Mzuzu. Interviewed in English in Mzuzu on April 9, 1999.

Mayi E. Mhone. Leader in the MCP League of Malawi Women during Banda's administration. Interviewed in Chitonga in Majiga Village in Nkhata Bay District on February 9, 1999.

Mayi O. Mhone. Leader in the MCP women's league during Banda's administration. Interviewed in Chitonga in her home village in Nkhata Bay District on March 22, 1999.

Barbara Momba. MCP regional secretary of the southern region and regional chairman of the MCP women's league. Interviewed in English in Blantyre on May 23, 2000.

Mayi Mphase. Leader in the MCP League of Malawi Women during Banda's administration. Interviewed in Chitonga in Nkhata Bay District on March 26, 1999.

Mayi Mtayamanja. AFORD member and dancer in Blantyre. Interviewed in Chichewa in Blantyre on June 1, 2004.

Mayi V. Mwale. Our host when we lived with the Ngwira family in the fall of 1998. Occasionally danced at UDF rallies. Informal conversations in Chitonga from 1998-2000.

John Nkhwazi. AFORD area chairman within the city of Mzuzu. Interviewed in English in Mzuzu on April 9, 1999.

Mayi E. Nyirenda. AFORD Mzuzu district committee member who regularly dances at AFORD functions. Interviewed in English in Mzuzu on April 9, 1999.

Simeon Nyirenda. Member of the Malawi Young Pioneers during Banda's presidency and my research assistant, 1998–1999. Interviewed in English in Majiga Village in Nkhata Bay District on February 12, 1999.

Mayi Phiri. One of the founders of the Msani Chilimika team, America State Boma; also dances chiwoda at AFORD functions. Interviewed in Chitonga in Msani Village in Nkhata Bay District on January 16, 1999.

Kaliyoma Phumisa. Minister of Labor and Vocational Training, member of the cabinet, and UDF politician. Interviewed in English in Ntcheu on April 24, 1999.

Loveness Schafer. Malawian woman living in the United States. Interviewed in English in Bloomington, Indiana, on November 14, 1996.

Pilirani Semu-Banda. Senior reporter of *The Nation* and country coordinator of *Africawoman* newspaper. Interviewed in English in Blantyre on May 27, 2004.

Horace Somanje. Editor of *Malawi News*, an MCP-friendly newspaper. Interviewed in English in Blantyre on January 5, 2000.

Mayi J. Tembo. Chilimika dancer who frequently dances at AFORD meetings. Interviewed in Chitonga in Nkhwali Village in Nkhata Bay District on January 10, 1999.

Zabweka Tembo. Founder and leader of the School Band dance group and active AFORD member. Participated in informal discussions in English in Nkhwali Village in Nkhata Bay District during the summer of 1996 and the 1998–1999 academic year.

Mayi Welosi. UDF member and dancer. Interviewed in Chichewa in Blantyre on June 8, 2004.

Mayi Wonga. UDF member and dancer. Interviewed in Chichewa in Blantyre on June 1, 2004.

GROUP INTERVIEWS

GROUP INTERVIEW WITH MCP OFFICIALS

Interviewed in English at their Northern Region Office in Mzuzu on March 29, 1999.

J.B. Kaunda. District chairman of MCP in Nkhata Bay.
Watson Kawirima Khonje. Parliamentary candidate in Mzimba, Hora Constituency.
Wyson Mkotchi. Chairman for the northern region.
Mike James Mvula. Parliamentary candidate in Chitipa, Central Constituency.
Ophten Ebell Sinkhala. Parliamentary candidate in Chitipa, North Constituency.

GROUP INTERVIEW WITH MEMBERS OF A UDF ACTION GROUP

These individuals regularly dance at party functions. Interviewed in Chichewa in Chilobwe, Blantyre, on April 25, 2000.

Mayi Banda
Mayi Kachoka
Mayi Kampila
Mayi Kondwani
Mayi Masekesa
Mayi Mphande
Mayi Simoko
Mayi Tambula
Mayi Tembo
Anonymous woman

GROUP INTERVIEW WITH MEMBERS OF A UDF ACTION GROUP

These individuals regularly dance at party functions. Interviewed in Chichewa in Chilobwe, Blantyre, on May 2, 2000.

Mayi Chapola
Mayi James
Mayi Jangiya
Mayi Mapanga
Mayi Nembo
Mayi Ngalande
Mayi Rojasi
Mayi Stambule
Mayi Tanaka

GROUP INTERVIEW WITH MCP WOMEN

These individuals frequently dance in Chilobwe, Blantyre. Interviewed in Chichewa in Chilobwe, Blantyre, on May 16, 2000.

Mayi Chimpeni
Mayi Kunthembwe
Mayi Mapemba
Mayi Mhone
Mayi M. Mwale
Mayi Theu

Appendix C

Political Functions Attended and Referenced

A selection of these rallies were transcribed and translated by research assistants I hired. A selection of this footage will be available through the Ethnomusicological Video for Instruction and Analysis Digital Archive project. See Appendix D.

1993	Kamuzu Banda campaigns for a single-party system in the northern region. Videotape purchased from vendors, probably recorded by the Ministry of Information.
July 6, 1996	National Independence Day Celebration. Chichiri Stadium, Blantyre. Videotaped by the author.
July 19, 1996	National Education Day. Civil Stadium, Lilongwe. Videotaped by the author.
November 7, 1998	Installation of Chief Mpimbi. Mazembe Village, Nkhata Bay District. Videotaped by the author.
November 22, 1998	AFORD rally in Nkhwali Village, Nkhata Bay District. Austin Mwenda meets with constituents. Videotaped by the author.
January 2, 1999	UDF rally in Tukombo Village, Nkhata Bay District. Aleke Banda meets with constituents. Videotaped by the author.
January 3, 1999	UDF rally in Sanga Village, Nkhata Bay District. Katenga Kaunda meets with constituents. Videotaped by the author.
March 30, 1999	MCP rally in Chinteche, Nkhata Bay District. Chirwa's parliamentary campaign. Also present: guest parliamentary candidates from Mzimba and Chitipa. Videotaped by the author.
April 16, 1999	UDF welcoming of President Muluzi at Mzuzu Airport. Muluzi's campaign launch in the northern region. Videotaped by the author.
April 17, 1999	UDF rally at Katoto Freedom Park, Mzuzu. President Bakili Muluzi launches campaign in the northern region. Videotaped by the author.

April 23, 1999	UDF rally in Mphepo Zinai, Ntcheu District. Kaliyoma Phumisa campaigns for parliamentary seat. Videotaped by the author.
April 25, 1999	UDF rally in Kaudza Village, Ntcheu District. Kaliyoma Phumisa campaigns for parliamentary seat. Videotaped by the author.
April 26, 1999	UDF rally in Kalumbu, Ntcheu District. Jane Phumisa, wife to incumbent parliamentary candidate Kaliyoma Phumisa, campaigns for him. Videotaped by the author.
April 26, 1999	UDF rally in Namale Village and another village of unknown name, Ntcheu District. Kaliyoma Phumisa campaigns for parliamentary seat. Videotaped by the author.
December 31, 1999	National Millennium Celebration. Chichiri Stadium, Blantyre. Videotaped by the author.
February 26, 2000	RAB Processors product launch in Blantyre. Attended by President Muluzi. Ministry of Information videotape.
May 10, 2000	MCP rally in Mileme Village, Phalombe, with Gwanda Chakwamba during period of court case regarding legitimacy of election results. Videotaped by the author.
July 1, 2000	MCP rally in Blantyre with Mrs. Chakwamba, organized by women's wing shortly after Chakwamba was suspended from parliament for one year. Videotaped by the author.

Appendix D

Associated Multimedia Websites

Two multimedia projects with the Ethnomusicological Video for Instruction and Analysis Digital Archive (EVIA) project comprise annotated video footage of performance events discussed in this book. EVIA Digital Archive is a creation of Indiana University and the University of Michigan with the mission of developing a preservation and online delivery system for ethnographic field video accompanied by peer-reviewed annotations (www.eviada.org). The permanent URLs for my collections will be active after April 2009.

1. "DANCES OF THE NKHATA BAY DISTRICT OF MALAWI"

http://purl.dlib.indiana.edu/iudl/eviada/5-C5818.

This collection includes ten hours of video documenting dance performances within and outside the political sphere that took place in the Nkhata Bay District in the summer of 1996 and during the 1998–99 academic year. In addition to field recordings of performance events, I provide explanations about the featured dance and musical forms along with contextual details. Of particular relevance to this book are the footage and annotations of three of the political rallies discussed in Chapter 4:

- "AFORD political rally in Nkhwale" with Austin Mwenda
- "UDF political rally in Tukombo" with Aleke Banda
- "UDF political rally in Sanga Village" with Katenga Kaunda

Footage and annotations of performances outside the political sphere of the three dance forms discussed in Chapter 8—chiwoda, malipenga, and chilimika—are available by following the links to these events:

- "Njaya tourist lodge dance performance"
- "Malipenga dance in Chipazi Village"
- "Dances at Nkhwale Village"
- "Installation of Village Headman Mazembe Village"
- "Malipenga dance competition Dindano Village"
- "Chilimika dance competition Mukaka Village"
- "Chilimika dance competition Malaza Village"

2. "MUSIC AND DANCE IN MALAWI'S PRESIDENTIAL ELECTIONS 1999"

http://purl.dlib.indiana.edu/iudl/eviada/5-C5833

This four-hour collection comprises footage and annotations of then President Bakili Muluzi's northern region campaign launch in the city of Mzuzu in April 1999, the subject of Chapter 5. The first event, "President Muluzi's welcome at the Mzuzu airport" on April 16, 1999, includes footage and annotations of women singing and dancing as Muluzi's plane arrives, as well as the speech by Muluzi that followed. The second event, "President Muluzi's campaign launch in the northern region" on April 17, 1999, comprises footage and annotations of the rally that launched Muluzi's campaign in the north. The event includes the pre-rally preparations, Muluzi's ceremonious arrival, prayer, speeches, and dance performances that took place during the entertainment segment.

References

Abu-Lughod, Lila. 1986. *Veiled Sentiments: Honour and Poetry in a Bedouin Society.* Berkeley: University of California Press.

———. 1990. The Romance of Resistance: Tracing Transformations of Power through Bedouin Women. *American Ethnologist* 17(1): 41–55.

Adamolekun, Ladipo. 1976. *Sékou Touré's Guinea: An Experiment in Nation Building.* London: Methuen.

Alidou, Ousseina D. 2005. *Engaging Modernity: Muslim Women and the Politics of Agency in Postcolonial Niger.* Madison: University of Wisconsin Press.

Amadiume, Ifi. 1987. *Male Daughters, Female Husbands.* London: Zed Books.

Anderson, Benedict. 1991 [1983]. *Imagined Communities: Reflections on the Origin and Spread of Nationalism.* New York: Verso.

Anthias, Floya, and Nira Yuval-Davis. 1994. Women and the Nation State. In *Nationalism*, ed. John Hutchinson and Anthony Smith, pp. 312–16. Oxford: Oxford University Press.

Argyle, John. 1991. Kalela, Beni, Asafo, Ingoma and the Rural-Urban Dichotomy. *African Studies* 50(1–2): 65–86.

Ashaz, Josh. 2008. Karonga-Chitipa Road will Delay says China. *Nyasa Times*, November 15.

Askew, Kelly. 1999. Female Circles and Male Lines: Gender Dynamics along the Swahili Coast. *Africa Today* 46(3): 67–102.

———. 2002. *Performing the Nation: Swahili Music and Cultural Politics in Tanzania.* Chicago: University of Chicago Press.

Bakhtin, M. M. 1981. *The Dialogic Imagination: Four Essays.* Austin: University of Texas Press.

———. 1986. *Speech Genres and Other Essays.* Ed. Caryl Emerson and Michael Holquist. Trans. Vern McGee. Austin: University of Texas Press.

Barber, Karin. 1989. Interpreting Oríkì as History and as Literature. In *Discourse and Its Disguises: The Interpretation of African Oral Texts*, ed. Karin Barber and P. F. de Moraes Farias, pp. 13–23. Birmingham: University of Birmingham, Centre of African Studies.

———. 1999. Quotation in the Constitution of Yorùbá Oral Texts. *Research in African Literatures* 30(2): 17-41).

———. 1991. *I Could Speak Tomorrow: Oriki, Women, and the Past in a Yoruba Town.* Washington, DC: Smithsonian Institution Press.

———. 1997. Introduction. In *Readings in African Popular Culture*, ed. Karin Barber, pp. 1–12. Bloomington: Indiana University Press.

———. 1999. Obscurity and Exegesis in African Oral Praise Poetry. In *Oral Literature and Performance in Southern Africa*, ed. Duncan Brown, pp. 27–49. Athens: Ohio University Press.

Bartky, Sandra Lee. 1995. Agency: What's the Problem? In *Provoking Agents: Gender and Agency in Theory and Practice*, ed. Judith Kegan Gardiner, pp.178–93. Urbana: University of Illinois Press.

Bastian, Misty L. 1996. Female "Alhajis" and Entrepreneurial Fashions: Flexible Identities in Southeastern Nigerian Clothing Practice. In *Clothing and Difference: Embodied Identities in Colonial and Post-Colonial Africa*, ed. Hildi Hendrickson, pp. 97–132. Durham, NC: Duke University Press.

Bauer, Gretchen, and Hannah E. Britton. 2006. Women in African Parliaments: A Continental Shift? In *Women in African Parliaments*, ed. Gretchen Bauer and Hannah E. Britton, pp 1–30. Boulder, CO: Lynne Rienner Publishers.

Bauer, Gretchen, and Scott D. Taylor. 2005. *Politics in Southern Africa: State and Society in Transition.* Boulder, CO: Lynne Rienner Publishers.

Bauman, Richard. 1977. *Verbal Art as Performance.* Prospect Heights, IL: Waveland Press.

———. 1986. *Story, Performance, and Event.* Cambridge: Cambridge University Press.

———. 1989. American Folklore Studies and Social Transformation: A Performance-Centered Perspective. *Text and Performance Quarterly* 9(3): 175–84.

———. 1991. Contextualization, Tradition, and the Dialogue of Genres: Icelandic Legends of the *Kraftaskald.* In *Rethinking Context*, ed. C. Goodwin and A. Duranti, pp. 125–45. Cambridge: Cambridge University Press.

———. 1992. Performance. *In Folklore, Cultural Performances, and Popular Entertainments: A Communications-Centered Handbook*, ed. Richard Bauman, pp. 41–49. New York: Oxford University Press.

———. 2004. *A World of Others' Words: Cross-Cultural Perspectives on Intertextuality.* Malden, MA: Blackwell Publishing.

Bayart, Jean-Francois. 1993. *The State in Africa: The Politics of the Belly.* New York: Longman.

Ben-Amos, Dan. 1976. Introduction. In *Folklore Genres*, ed. Dan Ben-Amos, pp. ix–xlv. Austin: University of Texas Press.

———. 1984. The Seven Strands of Tradition: Varieties in Its Meaning in American Folklore Studies. *Journal of Folklore Research* 21(2–3): 97–131.

Bendix, Regina. 1992. National Sentiment in the Enactment and Discourse of Swiss Political Ritual. *American Ethnologist* 19(4): 768–90.

Berger, Iris. 1999. Women in East and Southern Africa. In *Women in Sub-Saharan Africa*, ed. Iris Berger and E. Frances White, pp. 5–62. Bloomington: Indiana University Press.

Blomqvist, Lars Erik. 1987. Introduction. In *Symbols of Power: The Esthetics of Political Legitimating in the Soviet Union and Eastern Europe*, ed. Claes Arvidsson and Lars Erik Blomqvist, pp. 7–19. Sweden: Almqvist and Wiksell International Stockholm.

Bratton, Michael, and Nicolas van de Walle. 1997. *Democratic Experiments in Africa: Regime Transitions in Comparative Perspective.* Cambridge: Cambridge University Press.

Briggs, Charles, and Richard Bauman. 1992. Genre, Intertextuality, and Social Power. *Journal of Linguistic Anthropology* 2(2): 131–72.

Cashman, Ray. 2007. Genre and Ideology in Ireland. *Midwestern Folklore* 33(1).

Castaldi, Francesca. 2006. *Choreographies of African Identities: Négritude, Dance, and the National Ballet of Senegal.* Urbana: University of Illinois Press.

Chabal, Patrick, and Jean-Pascal Daloz. 1999. *Africa Works: Disorder as Political Instrument.* Bloomington: Indiana University Press.

Chanock, M. L. 1975. Ambiguities in the Malawi Political Tradition. *African Affairs* 74(296): 326–46.

Chazan, Naomi. 1989. Gender Perspectives on African States. In *Women and the State in Africa,* ed. Jane L. Parpart and Kathleen A. Staudt, pp. 185–201. Boulder, CO: Lynne Rienner Publishers.

Chilivumbo, Alefeyo. 1971. Malawi's Lively Art Form: Chiwoda Dancers Mirror Their Changing World in a Traditional Frame. *Africa Report* 16(7): 16–18.

———. 1972. Vimbuza or Mash awe: A Mythic Therapy. *African Music: Journal of the African Music Society* 5(2): 6–9.

Chimombo, Steve, and Moira Chimombo. 1996. *The Culture of Democracy: Language, Literature, the Arts and Politics in Malawi, 1992–1994.* Limbe, Malawi: WASI Publications.

Chinsinga, Blessings. 2001. The Politics of Poverty Alleviation in Malawi: A Critical Review. In *A Democracy of Chameleons: Politics and Culture in the New Malawi*, ed. Harri Englund, pp. 25-42. Blantyre: Christian Literature Association of Malawi.

Chipembere, Masauko Henry. 2002. *Hero of the Nation: Chipembere of Malawi: An Autobiography,* ed. with an introduction by Robert I. Rotberg. Kachere Book 12. Blantyre: Christian Literature Association of Malawi.

Chirambo, Reuben Makayiko. 1998. Politics in the Cartoon in Malawi: *The Democrat* Cartoons. In *Democratization in Malawi: A Stocktaking*, ed. Kings M. Phiri and Kenneth R. Ross, pp. 195–216. Blantyre: Christian Literature Association in Malawi.

———. 2001. Protesting Politics of "Death and Darkness" in Malawi. *Journal of Folklore Research* 38(3): 205–31.

Chirwa, Vera M. 2000. Political Rallies and Women Dancing for Political Leaders. *The Nation*, February 4.

Chirwa, W. C. 1994. Elections in Malawi: The Perils of Regionalism. *Southern African Report* 10(2): 17–20.

———. 1998. Democracy, Ethnicity, and Regionalism: The Malawian Experience, 1992–1996. In *Democratization in Malawi: A Stocktaking*, ed. Kings M. Phiri and Kenneth R. Ross, pp. 52–69. Blantyre: Christian Literature Association in Malawi.

———. 2001. Dancing towards Dictatorship: Political Songs and Popular Culture in Malawi. *Nordic Journal of African Studies* 10(1):1–27.

Chisenga, Phaless. 2005. Women Fight for Gondwe's Handouts. *The Nation,* October 10.

Chitauro, Moreblessings, Caleb Dube, and Liz Gunner. 1994. Song, Story and Nation: Women as Singers and Actresses in Zimbabwe. In *Politics and Performance: Theater, Poetry and Song in Southern Africa,* ed. Liz Gunner, pp. 111–38. Johannesburg: Witwatersrand University Press.

Concerned Citizens. 2000. Reaction by Concerned Citizens to the Statement by CARER on Political Rallies and Dancing by Women at Such Functions. *The Nation,* February 18.

The Constitution of the Malawi Congress Party and Rules and Regulations Governing the Discipline of Malawi Congress Party. October 27, 1965.

Cope, Trevor. 1968. *Izibongo Praise Poems.* Coll. James Stuart. Trans. Daniel Malcolm. Oxford: Clarendon Press.

Coplan, David B. 1994. *In the Time of Cannibals: The Word Music of South Africa's Basotho Migrants.* Chicago: University of Chicago Press.

Cowan, Jane K. 1990. *Dance and the Body Politic in Northern Greece.* Princeton, NJ: Princeton University Press.

Creevy, Lucy. 2004. Impacts of Changing Patterns of Women's Association Membership in Senegal. In *The Power of Women's Informal Networks: Lessons in Social Change from South Asia to West Africa,* ed. Bandana Purkayastha and Mangala Subramaniam, pp. 61–74. Lanham, MD: Lexington Books.

Crehan, Stewart. 1994. Patronage, the State and Ideology in Zambian Theater. In *Politics and Performance: Theater, Poetry and Song in Southern Africa,* ed. Liz Gunner, pp. 253–72. Johannesburg: Witwatersrand University Press.

Cullen, Trevor. 1994. *Malawi: A Turning Point.* Edinburgh: Pentland Press.

Dahlerup, Dryde. 2006. Introduction. In *Women, Quotas and Politics,* ed. Drude Dahlerup, pp. 3–31. New York: Routledge.

Danielson, Virginia. 1997. *The Voice of Egypt: Umm Kulthum, Arabic Song, and Egyptian Society in the Twentieth Century.* Chicago: University of Chicago Press.

De Aguilar, L. B. 1995. Masks, Society, and Hierarchy among the Chewa of Central Malawi. *Anthropos* 90(4–6): 407–21.

De Aguilar, Mario, and Laurel Birch de Aguilar. 1999. Women's Organizing Abilities: Two Case Studies of Kenya and Malawi. Organizing for Development: An International Institute ("Papers" section). http://www.odii.com. Accessed on December 2, 2005.

Del Negro, Giovanna P., and Harris M. Berger. 2004. *Identity and Everyday Life: Essays in the Study of Folklore, Music, and Popular Culture.* Middletown, CT: Wesleyan University Press.

Drewal, Margaret Thompson. 1992. *Yoruba Ritual: Performers, Play, Agency.* Bloomington: Indiana University Press.

Dzimbiri, Lewis B. 1998. Competitive Politics and Chameleon-like Leaders. In *Democratization in Malawi: A Stocktaking,* ed. Kings M. Phiri and Kenneth R. Ross, pp. 87–101. Blantyre: Christian Literature Association in Malawi.

Edelman, Murray. 1985 [1964]. *The Symbolic Uses of Politics.* Urbana: University of Illinois Press.

Edmondson, Laura. 2007. *Performance and Politics in Tanzania: The Nation on Stage.* Bloomington: Indiana University Press.

Elder, Charles D., and Roger W. Cobb. 1983. *The Political Uses of Symbols.* New York: Longman.

Englund, Harri. 2002a. Introduction: The Culture of Chameleon Politics. In *A Democracy of Chameleons: Politics and Culture in the New Malawi,* ed. Harri Englund, pp. 11–24. Stockholm: Elanders Gotab.

———. 2002b. Winning Elections, Losing Legitimacy: Multi-Partyism and the Neopatrimonial State in Malawi. In *Multi-Party Elections in Africa,* ed. Michael Cowen and Liisa Laakso, pp. 172–86. New York: Palgrave.

———. 2004. Towards a Critique of Rights Talk in New Democracies: The Case of Legal Aid in Malawi. *Discourse and Society* 15(5): 527–51.

———. 1996. Between God and Kamuzu : the transition to multi-party politics in central Malawi. In *Postcolonial identities in Africa,* eds. Richard Werbner and Terence Ranger, pp. 105-35. Atlantic Highlands,N.J. : Zed Books.

Ewens, Graeme. 1994. *Congo Colossus: The Life and Legacy of Franco and O.K. Jazz.* Norfolk, UK: Buku.

Fabian, Johannes. 1990. *Power and Performance: Ethnographic Explorations through Proverbial Wisdom and Theater in Shaba, Zaire.* Madison: University of Wisconsin Press.

———. 1997. Popular Culture in Africa: Findings and Conjectures. In *Readings in African Popular Culture,* ed. Karin Barber, pp. 18–28. Bloomington: Indiana University Press.

Fallon, Kathleen. 2003. Transforming Women's Citizenship Rights within an Emerging Democratic State: The Case of Ghana. *Gender and Society* 17(4): 525–43.

———. 2004. Using Informal Networks to Seek Formal Political Participation in Ghana. In *The Power of Women's Informal Networks: Lessons in Social Change from South Asia to West Africa,* ed. Bandana Purkayastha and Mangala Subramaniam, pp. 75–88. Lanham, MD: Lexington Books.

Fair, Laura. 2001. *Pastimes and Politics: Culture, Community, and Identity in Post-Abolition Urban Zanzibar, 1890–1945.*Athens: Ohio University Press.

Fegan, Brian. 1986. Tenants' Non-Violent Resistance to Landowner Claims in a Central Luzon Village. *Journal of Peasant Studies* 13(2): 87–106.

Femia, Joseph V. 1981. *Gramsci's Political Thought: Hegemony, Consciousness, and Revolutionary Process.* Oxford: Clarendon Press.

Fenn, John. 2004. Rap and Ragga Musics in Malawi: Youth Lives, Styles, and Performances. Ph.D. diss., Indiana University, 2004.

Fernandez, James W. 1986. *Persuasions and Performances: The Play of Tropes in Culture.* Bloomington: Indiana University Press.

Finnegan, Ruth. 1970. *Oral Literature in Africa.* Oxford: University of Oxford Press.

Flueckiger, Joyce Burkhalter. 1991. Genre and Community in the Folklore System of Chattisgarh. In *Gender, Genre, and Power in South Asian Expressive Traditions,* ed. Arjun Appadurai, Frank J. Korom, and Margaret Mills, pp. 181–2000. Philadelphia: University of Pennsylvania Press.

Forster, Peter G. 1989. *Cullen Young: Missionary and Anthropologist*. Hull: University of Hull.

———. 1994. Culture, Nationalism, and the Invention of Tradition in Malawi. *Journal of Modern African Studies* 32(3): 474–97.

Foucault, Michel. 1990 [1978]. *The History of Sexuality*. Vol. 1, *An Introduction*. New York: Vintage Books.

Fraser, Donald D. D. 1925. *The Autobiography of an African: Retold in Biographical Form and in the Wild African Setting of the Life of Daniel Mtusu*. Westport, CT: Negro Universities Press.

Fraser, Nancy. 1992. Rethinking the Public Sphere: A Contribution to the Critique of Actually Existing Democracy. In *Habermas and the Public Sphere*, ed. Craig Calhoun, pp. 109–42. Cambridge, MA: MIT Press.

Friedson, Steven M. 1996. *Dancing Prophets: Musical Experience in Tumbuka Healing*. Chicago: University of Chicago Press.

Gardiner, Judith Kegan. 1995. Introduction. In *Provoking Agents: Gender and Agency in Theory and Practice*, ed. Judith Kegan Gardiner, pp. 1–20. Urbana: University of Illinois Press.

Geiger, Susan. 1987. Women in Nationalist Struggle: Tanu Activists in Dar es Salaam. *International Journal of African Historical Studies* 20(1): 1–26.

———. 1997. *TANU Women: Gender and Culture in the Making of Tanganyikan Nationalism, 1955–1965*. Portsmouth, NH: Heinemann.

Geisler, Gisela. 1987. Sisters under the Skin: Women and the Women's League in Zambia. *Journal of Modern African Studies* 25(1): 43–66.

———. 1995. Troubled Sisterhood: Women and Politics in Southern Africa: Case Studies from Zambia, Zimbabwe and Botswana. *African Affairs* 94(377): 545–78.

———.2004. *Women and the Remaking of Politics in Southern Africa: Negotiating Autonomy, Incorporation and Representation*. Uppsala: Nordiska Afrikainstitutet.

Gilman, Lisa. 2000a. Cultural Change and the Case of Malipenga in Malawi. In *Mashindano! Competitive Music Performance in Tanzania and East Africa*, ed. Frank Gunderson and Gregory Barz, pp. 321–45. Dar es Salaam, Tanzania: Mkuki na Nyota Publishers.

———. 2000b. "The Rose Chibambo Story Part I, *Wasi: The Magazine for the Arts* Vol. 11(3): 17-19

———. 2000c. "The Rose Chibambo Story Part II *Wasi: The Magazine for the Arts* Vol. 12(1): 13-19

———. 2001a. "Purchasing Praise: Women, Dancing, and Patronage in Malawi Party Politicking." *Africa Today* 48(4): 43–64.

———. 2001b. "The Rose Chibambo Story Part II *Wasi: The Magazine for the Arts* Vol 12 (2): 8-9.

———. 2004. The Traditionalization of Women's Dancing, Hegemony, and Politics in Malawi. *Journal of Folklore Research* 41(1): 33–60.

Gilman, Lisa, and John Fenn. 2006. Dance, Gender, and Popular Music in Malawi: The Case of Rap and Ragga. *Popular Music* 25(3): 369–81.

Glassie, Henry. 1995. Tradition. *Journal of American Folklore* 108(430): 395–412.

Goetz, Anne Marie, and Shireen Hassim. 2003. Introduction: Women in Power in Uganda and South Africa, In *No Shortcuts to Power: African Women in Politics and*

Policy Making, ed. Anne Marie Goetz and Shireen Hassim, pp. 1–28. London: Zed Books.

Goldstein-Gidoni, Ofra. 1999. Kimono and the Construction of Gendered Cultural Identities. *Ethnology* 38(4): 351–71.

Gondola, Ch. Didier. 1997. Popular Music, Urban Society, and Changing Gender Relations in Kinshasa, Zaire (1950–1990). In *Gendered Encounters: Challenging Cultural Boundaries and Social Hierarchies in Africa*, ed. Maria Grosz-Ngaté and Omari H. Kokole, pp. 65–84. New York: Routledge.

Gunderson, Frank, and Gregory Barz. 2000. *Mashindano! Competitive Music Performance in East Africa.* Dar es Salaam, Tanzania: Mkuki na Nyota Publishers.

Gunner, Liz. 1995. Clashes of Interest: Gender, Status and Power in Zulu Praise Poetry. In *Power, Marginality and African Oral Literature,* ed. Graham Furniss and Liz Gunner, pp. 185–96. Cambridge: Cambridge University Press.

———. 1999. Remaking the Warrior? The Role of Orality in the Liberation Struggle and in Post-Apartheid South Africa. In *Oral Literature and Performance in Southern Africa,* ed. Duncan Brown, pp. 50–60. Athens: Ohio University Press.

Hale, Thomas A. 1998. *Griots and Griottes: Masters of Words and Music.* Bloomington: Indiana University Press.

Handler, Richard. 1988. *Nationalism and the Politics of Culture in Quebec.* Madison: University of Wisconsin Press.

Handler, Richard, and Jocelyn Linnekin. 1984. Tradition, Genuine or Spurious. In *Folk Groups and Folklore Genres*, ed. Elliott Oring, pp. 38–42. Logan: Utah State University Press.

Hanna, Judith Lynne. 1988. *Dance, Sex and Gender: Signs of Identity, Dominance, Defiance, and Desire.* Chicago: University of Chicago Press.

Hannerz, Ulf. 1987. The World in Creolization. *Africa* 57(4): 546–59.

Hatchard, John. 1998. Engendering Political Decision-Making. *Journal of African Law* 42(1): 141–43.

Heath, Deborah. 1994. The Politics of Appropriateness and Appropriation: Recontextualizing Women's Dance in Urban Senegal. *American Ethnologist* 2(1): 88–103.

Hebdige, Dick. 1979. *Subculture: The Meaning of Style.* London: Methuen.

Henderson, Clara. Forthcoming. *Rolling Away the Stone: The Africanisation of Christian Music by Presbyterian Mvano Women in Southern Malawi.* Zomba, Malawi: Kachere Series.

Henderson, Clara, and Lisa Gilman. 2004. Women as Religious and Political Praise Singers within African Institutions: The Case of the CCAP Blantyre Synod and Party Politics in Malawi. *Women and Music: A Journal of Gender and Culture* 8: 22–40.

Hill, Stephen. 2000. *Mchezo umelala* [The dance has slept]: Competition, Modernity, and Economics in Umatengo, Tanzania. In *Mashindano! Competitive Music Performance in East Africa*, ed. Frank Gunderson and Gregory F. Barz, pp.367–78. Dar es Salaam, Tanzania: Mkuki na Nyota Publishers.

Hobsbawm, Eric, and Terence Ranger, eds. 1983. *The Invention of Tradition.* Cambridge: Cambridge University Press.

Hoffman, Barbara. 1995. Power, Structure, and Mande *Jeliw*. In *Status and Identity in West Africa: Nyamakalaw of Mande*, ed. David C. Conrad and Barbara E. Frank, pp. 36–45. Bloomington: Indiana University Press.

Hollander, Anne. 1993. *Seeing through Clothes*. Berkeley: University of California Press.

Hove, Chenjerai. 1997. *Shebeen Tales: Messages from Harare*. Harare, Zimbabwe: Baobaob Books.

Hymes, Del. 1975. *Foundations in Sociolinguistics: An Ethnographic Approach*. Philadelphia: University of Pennsylvania Press.

Ihonvbere, Julius O. 1997. From Despotism to Democracy: The Rise of Multiparty Politics in Malawi. *Third World Quarterly* 18(2): 225–47.

Johnson, Miriam M. 1995. Maternal Agency vs. the Brotherhood of Males. In *Provoking Agents: Gender and Agency in Theory and Practice*, ed. Judith Kegan Gardiner, pp. 152–66. Urbana: University of Illinois Press.

Johnson-Odim, Cheryl, and Margaret Strobel. 1999. Series Editors' Introduction: Conceptualizing the History of Women in Africa, Asia, Latin America and the Caribbean, and the Middle East and North Africa. In *Women in Sub-Saharan Africa*, ed. Iris Berger and E. Frances White, pp. xxvii–lxi. Bloomington: Indiana University Press.

Johnston, Sir Harry H., K.C.B. 1969 [1897]. *British Central Africa: An Attempt to Give Some Account of a Portion of the Territories under British Influence North of the Zambezi*. New York: Negro University Press. Originally published by Methuen.

Jones. A. M. 1945. African Music: The "Mganda Dance." *African Studies* 4(4): 180–88.

Jourde, Cédric. 2005. "The President Is Coming to Visit!" Dramas and the Hijak of Democratization in the Islamic Republic of Mauritania. *Comparative Politics* 37(4): 421–40.

Kamlongera, Christopher. 1986. An Example of Syncretic Drama from Malawi: Malipenga. *Research in African Literatures* 17(2): 197–210.

Kamlongera, Christopher, Mike Nambote, Boston Soko, and Enoch Timpunza-Mvula. 1992. *Kubvina: Dance and Theater in Malawi*. Zomba: University of Malawi Research and Publication Committee.

Kapferer, Bruce. 1986. Performance and the Structuring of Meaning and Experience. In *The Anthropology of Experience*, ed. Victor W. Turner and Edward M. Bruner, pp. 188–203. Urbana: University of Illinois Press.

Kaplan, Martha, and John D. Kelly. 1994. Rethinking Resistance: Dialogics of "Disaffection" in Colonial Fiji. *American Ethnologist* 21(1): 123–51.

Kaspin, Deborah. 1995. The Politics of Ethnicity in Malawi's Democratic Transition. *Journal of Modern African Studies* 33(4): 595–620.

Kasule, Samuel. 1998. Popular Performance and the Construction of Social Reality in Post-Amin Uganda. *Journal of Popular Culture* 32(2): 39–58.

Kerr, David. 1987. Unmasking the Spirits: Theater in Malawi. *Drama Review* 31(2): 115–25.

———. 1998. *Dance, Media, Entertainment and Popular Theater in East Africa*. Bayreuth African Studies 43. Bayreuth, Germany: Bayreuth African Studies.

Kerr, David, and Mike Nambote. 1983. The Malipenga Mime of Likoma Island. *Critical Arts: A Journal of Cultural Studies* 3(1): 9–28.

Kertzer, David I. 1988. *Ritual, Politics, and Power*. New Haven, CT: Yale University Press.

Kirkwood, Deborah. 1993. Protestant Missionary Women: Wives and Spinsters. In *Women and Missions: Past and Present: Anthropological and Historical Perceptions*, ed. Fiona Bowie, Deborah Kirkwood, and Shirley Ardner, pp. 23–42. Oxford: Berg Publishers.

Kishindo, Pascal J. 1998. Politics of Language in Contemporary Malawi. In *Democratization in Malawi: A Stocktaking*, ed. Kings M. Phiri and Kenneth R. Ross, pp. 252–80. Blantyre: Christian Literature Association in Malawi.

Koma-Koma, W. P. 1965. *Mganda kapena malipenga*. Limbe: Malawi Publications and Literature Bureau.

Koskoff, Ellen. 1989. An Introduction to Women, Music, and Culture. In *Women and Music in Cross-Cultural Perspective*, ed. Ellen Koskoff, pp. 1–23. Urbana: University of Illinois Press.

Lambert, H. E. 1962–1963. The Beni Dance Songs. *Swahili* 33(1): 18–21.

Langa, Joseph. 2004. Sineki's Children Arrested. *The Nation*, December 7.

Lawless, Elaine J. 1993. Access to the Pulpit: Reproductive Images and Maternal Strategies of the Pentecostal Female Pastor. In *Feminist Theory and the Study of Folklore,* ed. Susan Tower Hollis, Linda Pershing, and M. Jane Young, pp. 258–76. Chicago: University of Illinois Press.

The Laws of Malawi, rev. ed. 1968. Government of Malawi.

Liebenow, J. Gus. 1986. *African Politics: Crises and Challenges*. Bloomington: Indiana University Press.

Life President Joins Mbumba in Traditional Dances: "1991 was remarkable." 1992. *Daily Times*, January 2.

Lindberg, Staffan I. 2006. *Democracy and Elections in Africa*. Baltimore: Johns Hopkins University Press.

Liwanda, Zainah. 2004. Opposition MPs Cry Foul over Pledged Maize Mills. *The Nation*, September 17.

———. 2005. Wakuda Retires from Politics. *The Nation*, September 30.

Lwanda, John Lloyd Chipembere. 1993. *Kamuzu Banda of Malawi: A Study in Promise, Power and Paralysis; Malawi under Dr. Banda (1961 to 1993)*. Glasgow, Scotland: Dudu Nsomba Publications.

———. 1996. *Promises, Power, Politics and Poverty: Democratic Transition in Malawi (1961–1999)*. Glasgow, Scotland: Dudu Nsomba Publications.

Mack, Beverly. 2004. *Muslim Women Sing: Hausa Popular Song*. Bloomington: Indiana University Press.

Mahmood, Saba. 2001. Feminist Theory, Embodiment, and the Docile Agent: Some Reflections on the Egyptian Islamic Revival. *Cultural Anthropology* 16(2): 202–36.

Makossah, Peter. 2004. Makwangwala to Be Arrested. *The Nation*, August 6.

Malawi Agents Raid Muluzi's Home. 2005. BBC News U.K. edition. October 27, 2005. http://news.bbc.co.uk/2/hi/africa/4382318.stm. Accessed on October 30, 2005.

Malawi Congress Party. 2004. Reconciliation, Reconstruction, and Development. Political manifesto.

Malawi MPs Renew Impeachment Bid. 2005. BBC News Online, October 21.

Malawi one-party state through ballot. 1992, *Daily Times*. April 9.

Mapanje, Jack. 2002. Afterward: The Orality of Dictatorship in Defense of My Country. In *A Democracy of Chameleons: Politics and Culture in the New Malawi*, ed. Harri Englund, pp.178–87. Sweden: Nordiska Africainstitutet; Blantyre, Malawi: Christian Literature Association in Malawi.

Markovitz, Irving Leonard. 1987. Introduction: Continuities in the Study of Power and Class in Africa. In *Studies in Power and Class in Africa,* ed. Irving Leonard Markovitz, pp. 3–19. Oxford: Oxford University Press.

Maroleng, Chris. 2004. Malawi General Election 2004: Democracy in the Firing Line. *African Security Review* 13(2): 77–81.

Martin, Phyllis. 1994. Contesting Clothes in Colonial Brazzaville. *Journal of African History* 35: 401–26.

———. 1995. *Leisure and Society in Colonial Brazzaville.* Cambridge: Cambridge University Press.

Matiki, Alfred J. 2001. The Social Significance of English in Malawi. *World Englishes* 20(2): 201–18.

Matiya, Chipiliro. 1996. Celebrations Positive Move. *The Nation,* July 5.

Mawaya, Anthony D. G., and Nandini Patel. 1995. Women's Political Participation in the Democratisation Process of Malawi. Paper presented at the Seminar on Women and the Democratisation Process in Malawi. Blantyre, Malawi, May 29–31.

Mba, Nina. 1982. *Nigerian Women Mobilized: Women's Political Activity in Southern Nigeria, 1900–1965.* Berkeley: University of California Press.

———. 1989. Kaba and Khaki: Women and the Militarized State in Nigeria. In *Women and the State in Africa,* ed. Jane L. Parpart and Kathleen A. Staudt, pp. 69–90. Boulder, CO: Lynne Rienner Publishers.

McCracken, John. 1968. African Politics in Twentieth-Century Malawi. In *Aspects of Central African History,* ed. T.O. Range. Evanston: Northwestern University Press.

———. 1977. *Politics and Christianity in Malawi 1875–1940: The Impact of the Livingstonia Mission in the Northern Province.* Cambridge: Cambridge University Press.

———. 2002. The Ambiguities of Nationalism: Flax Musopole and the Northern Factor in Malawian Politics, c. 1956–1966. *Journal of Southern African Studies* 28(1): 67–87.

McDonald, Chapalapata. 2004. Bingu Reshuffles Govt Top Posts. *The Nation,* August 6.

McMaster, Carolyn. 1974. *Malawi: Foreign Policy and Development.* London: Julian Friedman Publishers.

McNaughton, Patrick R. 1988. *The Mande Blacksmiths: Knowledge, Power, and Art in West Africa.* Bloomington: Indiana University Press.

Mills, Dora S. Yarnton, comp. 1911. *What We Do in Nyasaland.* London: Office of the Universities' Mission to Central Africa.

Mita, Cheu. 1996a. Youth Culture Show to Brighten Celebrations. *The Nation,* July 5.

———.1996b. July 6 Celebrations with a Difference. *The Nation,* July 9.

Mitchell, J. Clyde. 1956a. *The Kalela Dance: Aspects of Social Relationships among Urban Africans in Northern Rhodesia.* Manchester: Rhodes-Livingstone Institute Paper, xxvii.

———. 1956b. *The Yao Village: A Study in the Social Structure of a Nyasaland Tribe.* Manchester: Manchester University Press.

Mkamanga, Emily. 2000. *Suffering in Silence: Malawi Women's 30 Year Dance with Dr. Banda*. Glasgow, Scotland: Dudu Nsomba Publications.

Mlama, Penina. 1995. Oral Art and Contemporary Cultural Nationalism. In *Power, Marginality and African Oral Literature,* ed. Graham Furniss and Liz Gunner, pp. 23–46. Cambridge: Cambridge University Press.

Monga, Célestin. 1999. Eight Problems with African Politics. In *Democratization in Africa,* ed. Larry Diamond and Marc F. Plattner, pp. 48–62. Baltimore: Johns Hopkins University Press.

Moore, Sally Falk. 1977. Political Meetings and the Simulation of Unanimity: Kilimanjaro 1973. In *Secular Ritual,* ed. Sally F. Moore and Barbara G. Myerhoff, pp. 151–72. Amsterdam: Van Gorcum, Assen.

Morrow, Séan. 2006. Toxic Mushrooms? The Presidential Third-Term Debate in Malawi. In *Legacies of Power,* ed. Roger Southall and Melber Henning, pp. 151–74. Cape Town: Human Sciences Research Council Press.

Mphande, Lupenga. 1996. Dr. Hastings Kamuzu Banda and the Malawi Writers Group: The (un)Making of a Cultural Tradition. *Research in African Literature* 27(1): 80–102.

Msiska, Karen. 2004. Candidate Stuns Aford. *The Nation*, September 13.

Mullings, Leigh. 1976. Women and Economic Change in Africa. In *Women in Africa: Studies in Social and Economic Change,* ed. Nancy J. Hafkin and Edna G. Bay, pp. 239–63. Stanford, CA: Stanford University Press.

Muluzi, Bakili, Yusuf M. Juwayeyi, Mercy Makhambera, and Desmond D. Phiri. 1999. *Democracy with a Price: The History of Malawi since 1900.* Blantyre, Malawi: Heinemann.

Munachonga, Monica L. 1989. Women and the State: Zambia's Development Policies and Their Impact on Women. In *Women and the State in Africa,* ed. Jane L. Parpart and Kathleen A. Staudt, pp. 130–42. Boulder, CO: Lynne Rienner Publishers.

Muwamba, Emmanuel. 2005. Students Chase DPP Women. *The Nation,* October 7.

Mvula, Peter M., and Paul Kakhongwa. 1997. *Beyond Inequalities: Women in Malawi.* Zomba: University of Malawi Centre for Social Research.

National Democratic Alliance. 2004. Towards a Prosperous Malawi. Political Manifesto.

Ngunjiri, Jospeh. 2005. Prodigy Who Have Turned against Their Masters. *The Nation* (Nairobi), March 27.

Ntonya, George. 2004a. Mutharika Shuns the Media. *The Nation,* August 24.

———. 2004b. Who Owns Political Parties. *The Nation,* October 8.

———. 2005. Chilumpha Vague on UDF, Government. *The Nation,* February 20.

Nyirongo, Wezie. 2004. UDF Not Ready for More Women MPs. *The Chronicle*, March 8.

Nyoni, Frowin Paul. 2000. The Social Significance of Mganda-wa-Kinkachi Dance Contests among the Matengo. In *Mashindano! Competitive Music Performance in East Africa*, ed. Frank Gunderson and Gregory F. Barz, pp. 233–53. Dar es Salaam, Tanzania: Mkuki na Nyota Publishers.

Ogede, Ode. 1997. *Art, Society, and Performance: Igede Praise Poetry.* Gainesville: University of Florida Press.

Opland, Jeff. 1983. *Xhosa Oral Poetry: Aspects of a Black South African Tradition.* Cambridge: Cambridge University Press.

Ortner, Sherry B. 1995. Resistance and the Problem of Ethnographic Refusal. *Comparative Studies in Society and History* 37(1): 173–93.

Pachai, Bridglal. 1973. *Malawi: The History of the Nation*. London: Longman Group.

Parpart, Jane L., and Kathleen A. Staudt. 1986. Women and the State in Africa. In *Women and the State in Africa,* ed. Jane L. Parpart and Kathleen A. Staudt, pp.1–19. Boulder, CO: Lynne Rienner Publishers.

Perani, Judith, and Norma H. Wolff. 1999. *Cloth, Dress and Art Patronage in Africa.* Oxford: Berg.

Phiri, K. M. 1998. Dr. Banda's Cultural Legacy and Its Implications for a Democratic Malawi. In *Democratisation in Malawi: A Stocktaking,* ed. Kings M. Phiri and Kenneth R. Ross, pp. 149–67. Blantyre, Malawi: Christian Literature Association in Malawi.

———. 2000. Reflections on Party Ideologies and Programs. In *Malawi's Second Democratic Elections: Process, Problems, and Prospects,* ed. Martin Ott, Kings M. Phiri, and Nandini Patel, pp. 67–86. Blantyre, Malawi: Christian Literature Association in Malawi.

Phiri, Kings M., and Kenneth R. Ross. 1998. Introduction: From Totalitarianism to Democracy in Malawi. In *Democratisation in Malawi: A Stocktaking,* ed. Kings M. Phiri and Kenneth R. Ross, pp. 9–16. Blantyre, Malawi: Christian Literature Association in Malawi.

Piot, Charles. 1999. *Remotely Global: Village Modernity in West Africa.* Chicago: University of Chicago Press.

Radner, Joan N., ed. 1993. *Feminist Messages: Coding in Women's Folk Cultures.* Urbana: University of Illinois Press.

Radner, Joan N., and Susan S. Lanser. 1993. Strategy of Coding in Women's Cultures. In *Feminist Messages: Coding in Women's Folk Culture,* ed. Joan Newlong Radner, pp. 1–29. Urbana: University of Illinois Press.

Raheja, Gloria Goodwin, and Ann Grodzins Gold. 1994. *Listen to the Heron's Words: Reimagining Gender and Kinship in North India.* Berkeley: University of California Press.

Ranger, Terence O. 1975. *Dance and Society in Eastern Africa 1890–1970: The Beni Ngoma.* Berkeley: University of California Press.

———. 1983. The Invention of Tradition in Colonial Africa. In *The Invention of Tradition,* ed. Eric Hobsbawm and Terence Ranger, pp. 211–62. Cambridge, MA: Cambridge University Press.

———. 1993. The Invention of Tradition Revisited: The Case of Colonial Africa. *Legitimacy and the State in Twentieth-Century Africa: Essays in Honour of A.H.M. Kirk-Greene,* ed. Terence Ranger and Olufemi Vaughan, pp. 62–111. Oxford: St. Antony's College.

Reaction by Concerned Citizens to the Statement by CARER on Political Rallies and Dancing Women at Such Functions. 2000. *The Nation,* February 18.

Reed, Daniel B. 2003. *Dan Ge Performance: Masks and Music in Contemporary Côte D'Ivoire.* Bloomington: Indiana University Press.

———. 2005. "The *Ge* Is in the Church" and "Our Parents are Playing Muslim": Performance, Identity, and Resistance among the Dan in Postcolonial Côte d'Ivoire. *Ethnomusicology* 49(3): 347–67.

Robertson, Claire, and Iris Berger. 1986. Introduction: Analyzing Class and Gender: African Perspectives. In *Women and Class in Africa*, ed. Claire Robertson and Iris Berger, pp. 3–24. New York: Africana Publishing.

Ross, Andrew C. 1997. Some Reflections on the Malawi "Cabinet Crisis" 1964–65. *Religion in Malawi* 7: 3–12.

Rotberg, Robert I. 1965. *The Rise of Nationalism in Central Africa: The Making of Malawi and Zambia 1873–1964*. Cambridge, MA: Harvard University Press.

Ryan, Mary P. 1992. Gender and Public Access: Women's Politics in Nineteenth-Century America. In *Habermas and the Public Sphere*, ed. Craig Calhoun, pp. 259–88. Cambridge, MA: MIT Press.

Schapera, I. 1965. *Praise Poems of Tswana Chiefs*. Oxford: Clarendon Press.

Schoffeleers, J. Matthew. 1992. *River of Blood: The Genesis of a Martyr Cult in Southern Malawi, C.A.D. 1600*. Madison: University of Wisconsin Press.

Scott, James. 1985. *Weapons of the Weak: Everyday Forms of Peasant Resistance*. New Haven, CT: Yale University Press.

———. 1986a. Everyday Forms of Peasant Resistance. *Journal of Peasant Studies* 13(2): 5–35.

———. 1986b. Introduction. *Journal of Peasant Studies* 13(2): 1–3.

Second Integrated Household Survey 2005: An Extract of Findings by the Ministry of Economic Planning and Development, National Statistical Office and the World Bank. Government of Malawi. http://www.malawi.gov.mw/information1/publications/poverty%20report.pdf. Accessed on May 7, 2007.

Segal, Edwin S. 1995. Gender and Ethnicity in Banda's Malawi. Paper presented at the Annual Meeting of the American Anthropological Association, Washington DC, November 15.

Semu, Linda. 1993. Whose Human Rights? The Impact of Government Policy on Women's Access to Essential Resources in Malawi. In *Human Rights and Democracy in Southern Africa: Papers Presented at the Conference: Cultivating Co-operation amongst Human Rights Institutions in the UNITWIN Network in Southern Africa*. Windhoek: University of Namibia.

———. 2002. Kamuzu's Mbumba: Malawi Women's Embeddedness to Culture in the Face of International Political Pressure and Internal Legal Change. *Africa Today* 49(2): 77–99.

Semu-Banda, Piriani. 2005. Bingu to Launch Party Next Week: Woos Independents. *The Nation*, February 9.

Short, Philip. 1974. *Banda*. London: Routledge and Kegan Paul.

Shuman, Amy. 1993. Gender and Genre. In *Feminist Theory and the Study of Folklore*, ed. Susan Tower Hollis, Linda Pershing, and M. Jane Young, pp. 71–85. Chicago: University of Illinois Press.

Simon, Roger. 1982. *Gramsci's Political Thought*. London: Lawrence and Wishart.

Sindima, Harvey J. 1992. *The Legacy of Scottish Missionaries in Malawi*. Lewiston: Edwin Mellon Press.

Smith, Anthony. 1991. *National Identity*. Reno: University of Nevada Press.

Sonani, Bright. 2000. Two More Human Rights Bodies Condemn Dancing of Women. *Daily Times*, February 10.

———. 2004. Four UDF Young Democrats Arrested in Bingu's Portrait Saga. *The Nation,* December 8.

———. 2005. UDF Admits Muluzi Banked Donations. *The Nation*, October 19.

Spencer, Anne M. 1982. *In Praise of Heroes: Contemporary African Commemorative Cloth.* Newark: New Jersey: Newark Museum.

Stamp, Patricia. 1995. Mothers of Invention: Women's Agency in the Kenyan State. In *Provoking Agents: Gender and Agency in Theory and Practice*, ed. Judith Kegan Gardiner, pp. 69–92. Urbana: University of Illinois Press.

Staudt, Kathleen. 1986. Stratification: Implications for Women's Politics. In *Women and Class in Africa,* ed. Claire Robertson and Iris Berger, pp. 197–215. New York: Africana Publishing.

———.1987. Women's Politics, the State, and Capitalist Transformation in Africa. In *Studies in Power and Class in Africa,* ed. Irving Leonard Markovitz, pp. 193–208. Oxford: Oxford University Press.

Stites, Richard. 1987. The Origins of Soviet Ritual Style: Symbol and Festival in the Russian Revolution. In *Symbols of Power: The Esthetics of Political Legitimating in the Soviet Union and Eastern Europe*, ed. Claes Arvidsson and Lars Erik Blomqvist, pp. 23–42. Sweden: Almqvist and Wiksell International Stockholm.

Stoeltje, Beverly J. 1992. Festival. In *Folklore, Cultural Performances, and Popular Entertainments: A Communications Centered Handbook*, ed. Richard Bauman, pp. 261–71. New York: Oxford University Press.

———. 1993. Power and the Ritual Genres: American Rodeo. *Western Folklore* 52 (April): 135–56.

———. 1996. The Snake Charmer: Ritual, Competition, and Signification in American Festival. In *Beauty Queens on the Global State: Gender, Contests, and Power,* ed. Colleen Ballerino Cohen, Richard Wilk, and Beverly Stoeltje, pp. 13–29. New York: Routledge.

———. 2003. Asante Queenmothers: Precolonial Authority in a Postcolonial Society. *University of Ghana Research Review* 19(2): 1–19.

Stoeltje, Beverly J., and Richard Bauman. 1989. Community Festival and the Enactment of Modernity. In *The Old Traditional Way of Life: Essays in Honor of Warren E. Roberts,* ed. Robert E. Walls and George H. Schoemaker. Bloomington, IN: Trickster Press.

Stone, Ruth M. 1988. Performance in Contemporary African Arts: A Prologue. *Journal of Folklore Research* 25(1–2): 3–15.

———.1998. African Music in a Constellation of Arts. *Africa: The Garland Encyclopedia of World Music.* Vol. 1, ed. Ruth M. Stone, pp. 7–12. New York: Garland Publishing.

Strobel, Margaret. 1976. From Lelemama to Lobbying: Women's Associations in Mombassa, Kenya. In *Women in Africa: Studies in Social and Economic Change*, ed. Nancy J. Hafkin and Edna G. Bay, pp. 183–211. Stanford, CA: Stanford University Press.

———. 1979. *Muslim Women in Mombassa: 1890–1975*. New Haven, CT: Yale University Press.

Tangri, Roger K. 1968. The Rise of Nationalism in Colonial Africa: The Case of Colonial Malawi. *Comparative Studies in Society and History* 100(2): 142–61.

———. 1975. From the Politics of Union to Mass Nationalism: The Nyasaland African Congress, 1944–59. In *From Nyasaland to Malawi: Studies in Colonial History*, ed. Frederick Macdonald, pp. 254–81. Nairobi, Kenya: East African Publishing House.

There Will Be Soccer Matches. 1996. *The Nation*, July 9.

Timpunza Mvula, Enoch. 1985. Tumbuka Pounding Songs in the Management of Family Conflicts. *Cross Rhythms, Occasional Papers in African Folklore/Music* 2: 93–113.

———. 1986a. Chewa Women's Songs: A Verbal Strategy of Manipulating Social Tensions. *Women's Studies International Forum* 3: 265–72.

———. 1986b. Mngeniso Performance: The Articulation of Ngoni Identity and Unity. *Folklore Forum* 19(1): 51–69.

———.1987. *Women's Oral Poetry as a Social Strategy in Malawi*. Ph.D. diss., Indiana University, Folklore Institute.

———. 1990. The Performance of Gule Wamkulu: An Introduction. In *Oral Performance in Africa*, ed. Isidore Okpewho, pp. 80–97. Ibadan, Nigeria: Spectrum.

Tohidi, Nayereh. 1991. Gender and Islamic Fundamentalism: Feminist Politics in Iran. In *Third World Women and the Politics of Feminism*, ed. Chandra Talpade Mohanty, Ann Russo, and Lourdes Torres, pp. 251–67. Bloomington: Indiana University Press.

Tripp, Aili Mari. 1996. Urban Women's Movements and Political Liberalization in East Africa. In *Courtyards, Markets, City Streets: Urban Women in Africa*, ed. Kathleen Sheldon, pp. 285–308. Boulder, CO: Westview Press.

———. 2000. *Women and Politics in Uganda*. Madison: University of Wisconsin Press.

———. 2001. Women's Movements and Challenges to Neopatrimonial Rule: Preliminary Observations from Africa. *Development and Change* 32(1): 33–54.

Tripp, Aili, Dior Konaté, and Colleen Lowe-Morna. 2006. Sub-Saharan Africa: On the Fast Track to Women's Political Representation. In *Women, Quotas and Politics*, ed. Drude Dahlerup, pp. 112–37. New York: Routledge.

Tuohy, Sue. 2001. Nationalism in Modern China. *Ethnomusicology* 45(1): 107–31.

Turino, Thomas. 2000. *Nationalists, Cosmopolitans, and Popular Music in Zimbabwe*. Chicago: University of Chicago Press.

Turner, Victor. 1969. *The Ritual Process: Structure and Anti-Structure*. Chicago: Aldin Publishing.

———. 1988 [1987]. *The Anthropology of Performance*. New York: PAJ Publications.

The United Democratic Front. 2004. Forging Ahead with Social and Economic Transformation. Political Manifesto.

Urdang, Stephanie. 1989. *And Still They Dance: Women, War, and the Struggle for Change in Mozambique*. New York: Monthly Review Press.

Vail, Leroy, and Landeg White. 1989. Tribalism in the Political History of Malawi. In *The Creation of Tribalism in Southern Africa*, ed. Leroy Vail, pp. 151–92. London: James Currey.

———. 1991. *Power and the Praise Poem: Southern African Voices in History*. Charlottesville: University Press of Virginia.

Van Alstyne, Gregory. 1993. The Unvoiced Text: Allusion in Malawian Sung Poetry. *Journal of the Anthropological Society of Oxford* 24(1): 13–32.

Van Donge, Jan Kees. 1995. Kamuzu's Legacy: The Democratisation of Malawi or Searching for the Rules of the Game in African Politics. *African Affairs* 94: 225–57.

Van Velsen, J.1964. *The Politics of Kinship: A Study in Social Manipulation among the Lakeside Tongs of Nyasaland.* Manchester: Manchester University Press.

Vaughan, Megan. 1998. Exploitation and Neglect: Rural Producers and the State in Malawi and Zambia. In *History of Central Africa: The Contemporary Years since 1960,* ed. David Birmingham and Phyllis M. Martin, pp. 167–202. London: Longman Press.

Virmani, K. K. 1992. *Dr. Banda: In the Making of Malawi.* Delhi: Kalinga Publications.

Von Doepp, Peter. 1998. The Kingdom beyond Zasintha: Churches and Political Life in Malawi's Post-authoritarian Era. In *Democratization in Malawi: A Stocktaking,* ed. Kings M. Phiri and Kenneth Ross, pp. 102–26. Blantyre, Malawi: Christian Literature Association in Malawis.

Waterman, Christopher. 1990. *Jùjú: A Social History and Ethnography of an African Popular Music.* Chicago: University of Chicago Press.

Welensky, Sir Roy. 1964. *Welensky's 4000 Days: The Life and Death of the Federation of Rhodesia and Nyasaland.* St. James Place: Collins.

White, Landeg. 1987. *Magomero: Portrait of an African Village.* Cambridge: Cambridge University Press.

———.1989. "Poetic License": Oral Poetry and History. In *Discourses and Its Disguises: The Interpretation of African Oral Texts,* ed. Karin Barber and P. F. de Moraes Faria, pp. 34–38. Birmingham: Centre of African Studies, University of Birmingham.

Williams, Raymond. 1977. *Marxism and Literature.* Oxford: Oxford University Press.

Williams, T. David. 1978. *Malawi: The Politics of Despair.* Ithaca, NY: Cornell University Press.

Women in National Parliaments, Situation as of 31 January 2005. Inter-Parliamentary Union. http://www.ipu.org/wmn-e/arc/classif310105.htm. Accessed April 15, 2005.

Yankah, Kwesi. 1995. *Speaking for the Chief: Okyeame and the Politics of Akan Royal Oratory.* Bloomington: Indiana University Press.

Young, Crawford. 1994. The Colonial Construction of African Nations. In *Nationalism,* ed. John Hutchinson and Anthony D. Smith, pp. 225–31. New York: Oxford University Press.

Young, Crawford, and Thomas Turner. 1985. *The Rise and Decline of the Zairian State.* Madison: University of Wisconsin Press.

Zeleza, Paul Tiyambe. 1996. Banishing Words and Stories: Censorship in Banda's Malawi. *CODESRIA Bulletin* 1:10–15.

Index

Lisa Gilman is Assistant Professor in the English Department and Folklore Program at the University of Oregon.